WOMEN OF STEEL

Maria R. Lowe

Women of Steel

Female Bodybuilders and the Struggle for Self-Definition

New York University Press

New York and London

New York University Press
New York and London

Library of Congress Cataloging-in-Publication Data
Lowe, Maria R., 1964–
Women of steel : female bodybuilders and the struggle for self-definition / Maria R. Lowe.
p. cm.
Includes bibliographical references and index.
ISBN 0-8147-5094-X (pbk. : acid-free paper). — ISBN 0-8147-5093-1 (cloth : acid-free paper)
1. Bodybuilding for women—Social aspects—United States. 2. Femininity—United States. 3. Self-perception in women—United States. 4. Women bodybuilders—United States. I. Title.
GV546.6.W64L69 1998
646.7'5—dc21 97-21216
CIP

New York University Press books are printed on acid-free paper, and their binding materials are chosen for strength and durability.

Manufactured in the United States of America

10 9 8 7 6 5 4 3 2 1

I dedicate this book to my family,
who have always believed in me
and in my abilities
even when I did not.
With your emphasis on the
importance of education,
compassion, and laughter, you
have provided me with a solid
foundation in life, and I dedicate
my book to you with love and
appreciation.

CONTENTS

ACKNOWLEDGMENTS

As is the case with almost any work, the end product is a result of the assistance, guidance, and support of a number of people. Hence, I would like to acknowledge a myriad of people for their assistance at various stages of this project. First, I would like to thank the professors at the University of Texas at Austin who were integral in helping me with my doctoral dissertation, on which this manuscript is based. I want to warmly acknowledge the Chair of my dissertation committee, Harley Browning, for his unwavering guidance and patience throughout the writing of my dissertation. In addition, I would like to thank the members of my dissertation committee: Teresa Sullivan, Christine Williams, Christopher Ellison, and Terry Todd. Christine, thanks for sparking my sociological imagination with your feminist mind, your enthusiasm for the discipline of sociology, and your research on gender construction. Terry and Jan Todd deserve a special thank you because they provided me with access to their library, the Todd-McLean Collection, which provided me with valuable historical information. Their extraordinary knowledge of the history of weight resistance exercise and steroid use proved invaluable. I would also like to acknowledge the support, assistance, and insights of Lisa Holewyne during the various stages of dissertation writing. Susan Marshall, whose guidance during my master's thesis as well as the incipient stages of my doctoral research was essential, has my gratitude. Finally, I want to thank Susan Gonzalez-Baker and Audrey Singer, whose guidance, support, and friendship through the years have meant the world to me.

Next, I would like to acknowledge the numerous individuals in the bodybuilding arena, including the judges, journalists, officials, and particularly the bodybuilders who took the time to participate in the interviews and discuss their attitudes toward, experiences in, and insights about the world of female bodybuilding with me. Thanks go to Earline Beasley, Carol Ann Weber, and Steve Wennerstrom for their indispensable assistance. Thanks to Steve for the fantastic pictures of female bodybuilders he allowed me to use from his collection and for his dedication to the sport of female bodybuilding. In addition, I would like to thank Carol Ann Weber for her unfaltering commitment to fairness in bodybuilding. Her feminist voice is much needed in this muscular terrain.

Next, I would like to acknowledge my family—my mother, father, grandmother, and my sister, brother-in-law, and nephew—for their undying emotional support and love, not simply during this project but throughout my life. They have provided me with an extremely solid educational, emotional, and spiritual foundation. Also, thanks to my friends and colleagues at Southwestern University and those scattered around the world who have been continuously supportive and nurturing of me and my work. A special thanks goes to Traci Giuliano for her unwavering friendship (Go, Horns!) and her incredible knack to make me laugh out loud. Thanks to the many students at Southwestern over the past few years who have been so supportive of, and shown great interest in, my research.

I would also like to acknowledge my readers for their invaluable, insightful, and kind comments on my manuscript: T. Walter Herbert, Dan C. Hilliard, Edward L. Kain, and Julie Dowling. A special thanks goes to Dan Hilliard, who not only provided me with sagacious editorial suggestions, but who also gave me invaluable substantive comments in his area of expertise—the sociology of sport. In addition, thanks to Dan Yoxall for the pictures in the weight room, and to Rebecca Moore for her help with the notes and bibliography. I would like to acknowledge those at New York University Press who have assisted me with this project, especially my editor, Timothy Bartlett, who has been remarkably supportive, understanding, and encouraging during the revision process, and Niko Pfund, who was the first to express interest in my research. Many thanks go to Despina Papazoglou Gimbel for her wonderful editorial suggestions. Finally, I would simply like to acknowledge my nephew, Sean Benjamin Solis, whose bright eyes, gentle soul, and inquisitive mind give me hope for the future.

Introduction

Growing Pains

An Excursion into the Muscular Terrain of Female Bodybuilding

Gazing before the Gaze: The Afternoon Show

THE TIME IS early afternoon on Saturday, October 17, 1992, in cold, sunny, blustery Chicago during the midst of its first winter storm. The site of the event for which I have come is the Arie Crown Theater, located on the bottom floor of the McCormick Center. This enormous facility is right off windy Lake Michigan and within walking distance of Soldier Field, where the Chicago Bears play. The McCormick Center, only about 100 yards from the hotel where the judges, competitors, and a sizable number of fans are staying, is an immense multilevel structure with concrete floors and enough space for at least two football fields. The escalators take me to the bottom level of the Center where, in the distance, I see a crowd milling around. The size of the place is so overwhelming that these activities at first appear inconspicuous and somewhat insignificant. As I continue walking toward the bustling throng, however, I sense the burgeoning electricity and excitement in the air. I realize quickly that this gathering is no ordinary assembly of people—and by no means is this event mundane. The people are female bodybuilding enthusiasts, and the event is the twelfth annual Ms. Olympia, the superbowl of female bodybuilding.

Entering the crowd, I see people strolling around various booths where vendors sell a plethora of bodybuilding products aimed at enhancing both the bodybuilders' appearance and their performance. These booths are strategically positioned in front of the entrance to the auditorium so that everyone must walk by them, facilitating the purchase of the sundry display items. Although the main event will begin at 2 o'clock, most people arrive at the scene around 1:00 to check out the twenty-three booths. Often staffed by current or former female and male bodybuilders, these display booths carry goods ranging from 100% sturdy cotton T-shirts and sexy lycra body suits, to protein powders, vitamins, tanning liquids, workout equipment, nutritional supplements, workout shoes, weight-lifting belts, and many other such products.[1] A casual inspection of the items and their prices reveals that the clothes, many emblazoned with logos—"IFBB," "Mr. Olympia," "Ms. Olympia," "Body Under Construction," and the like—range in price from twenty to sixty dollars, while the actual bodybuilding equipment prices soar into the thousands. With ticket prices to the day's events extending past $250, the bodybuilding fan needs to have access to an impressive amount of disposable income. The salespeople for the nutritional supplements answer questions, hand out free samples of their power bars, sublingual vitamin B-12s, energy drinks, protein powders, and amino acid powders. Some are well-known bodybuilders themselves and sign autographs and pose for rolls of photographs with their adoring fans.

I notice that while on the surface these fans are poring over the latest in bodybuilding equipment and apparel, another more subtle inspection is occurring simultaneously—one focused on the physique of others in the crowd. When a "buff" bodybuilder saunters by, people unabashedly examine every nuance of his or her bulging musculature. If you don't happen to be a person whose body looks sculpted, then people's interest in your body and in you quickly wanes, and their attention turns to the people walking behind you. You do not pass their anatomy test—you know it and they know it—and the physique examination of others quickly resumes. The message is clear: skinny, nonmuscular, and generally out-of-shape body types need not apply!

Exactly what does it take to inspire envy in this crowd? "The Ideal" consists of two parts: the body and the presentation of self. For men, the body-type is a V-shaped torso, starting off at the neck with wide shoulders and tapering down to a small waist. Arms are huge, perhaps the circumference of an average person's thigh. Hair is short, crew cuts are popular. Legs are either hidden behind loose-fitting, blowzy pants or are flaunted by skin-tight jeans. Even baggy pants can reveal immensely muscular legs.

The female bodybuilders in the crowd prominently display the arms, legs, chest, and for some, the abdominals. The clothing style for these bodybuilders is revealing: the norm is a short, low-cut, tight fitting dress, or lycra pants with a snug top, accompanied by high heels, big, long bouncy hair, lots of makeup, and jewelry. This "look" serves a dual purpose: it displays both their musculature and their femininity.

The presentation of self is an important facet of the bodybuilding look, whether you are male or female. The "look," at least on the surface, exudes confidence, self-assurance, purpose, and perhaps even a contempt for those who lack such musculature and discipline.[2] The confidence of bodybuilders is most noticeable in their gait. Male and female bodybuilders in the crowd have a particularly slow, purposeful walk. It is an imperious walk with shoulders back, chest out, arms held out from the sides, and head cocked back.

Many of the female bodybuilders in the throng are not competing in this year's Ms. Olympia but are here to be seen by those "in the know" and to see their future competition. Most of these women are dressed explicitly to display their musculature to their future competitors as well as to the promoters, sponsors, and journalists in the crowd. Most also apparently have boyfriends or husbands, because the majority have a man at their side. Amazingly, given the large musculature of these women, their male companions are even bigger than they are (most appear to be former or current bodybuilders or powerlifters). The enormity of these men's muscles sometimes have the initial effect of making their girlfriends' muscles appear smaller than they really are. This reaction, however, is quickly assuaged upon closer inspection. The double peak of the women's biceps or their rippling washboard abs can draw attention away from even their larger male companions. In fact, quite a few female competitors have told me that male bodybuilders hate to date female bodybuilders because the women detract from the perceived largeness of their own muscles.

The crowd is getting restless, but eventually the ushers open the auditorium doors around 2:00 and people begin walking through the foyer to their seats in the darkened auditorium. The only lights are those that illuminate the front stage. Most of the audience is already seated and eagerly awaiting the head judge's voice over the intercom. His voice will signal the stage entrance of the twenty female bodybuilders and the commencement of the competition. We take our seats and I begin to look around me to acclimate myself to my new surroundings. A few things catch my eye immediately.

The stage is composed of a four-tiered, light-gray-carpeted platform where the contestants will eventually stand in two rows, ten bodybuilders per row. The backdrop of the stage contains a prominently displayed white triangle. In the triangle is an idealized drawing of Joe Weider, who is the co-founder of the IFBB and the owner of numerous bodybuilding and fitness magazines, as well as the words "Joe Weider's Ms. Olympia." Behind the white triangle is a dark backdrop with little splatterings of white, which I can only surmise to be a representation of the galaxy. On the white triangle there are the logos of three companies—Weider, Cybex, and ICOPRO—signifying their importance as sponsors of the Ms. Olympia event.

At the bottom tier of the stage are three more signs advertising some other major sponsors of the event: Great Earth, IFBB, and VALEO, who also have booths outside with information about their products. On both sides of the stage stand dark screens illuminated with the ubiquitous "Joe Weider's Ms. Olympia." Joe Weider's pictures are everywhere at this event, more common even than those of the bodybuilders. His image even appears on the large medals given to the winners at the end of contest.

The auditorium itself has two levels. During the preliminaries, the top floor is empty while approximately three-quarters of the bottom level is filled. There are about 1,500 observers in the audience, their average age the early thirties. Most of the people are white, about one-quarter are black. There are slightly more men than women, and most men are heavily muscled. Most people are in groups of three or more, and most of the couples are male-female.

The area closest to the stage is roped off from the remainder of the audience and contains the judges, the VIPs, and the photographers; here most of the pre-show commotion occurs. The judges, five women and six men, are seated at a long table in the front of the stage, conferring with one another. All eleven judges wear the official IFBB navy blue jacket with an official IFBB seal on the pocket. The male judges wear matching navy blue ties and light pants. The female judges wear skirts with their IFBB jackets, in compliance with IFBB regulations.

Music playing in the background includes some recent popular dance tunes such as Bobby Brown's "My Prerogative" and "Ain't Nobody Humpin' Around," Janet Jackson's "Escapade," Madonna's "Vogue," and an old song by Frankie Goes to Hollywood called "Relax, Don't Do it." The hum of the crowd is rising slowly over the music as more people enter the auditorium and show time approaches.

The entrance of the bodybuilders is inconspicuous and unannounced. The IFBB Chief of Protocol simply leads the competitors to the foot of the platform from where they ascend, only then receiving cheers and whistles from the audience. Myriad camera lights simultaneously flash. Many audience members have come to this event to see a favorite bodybuilder, and they call out the names of those they support.

The bodybuilders walk onto the stage from the right, their dark and hardened bodies glistening with oil and sweat. People in the crowd begin to crane their necks to see if their favorite is in top form. Does she look hard, cut, and ripped? How does she compare to the others, or how has she changed since her last competition? Judging from conversations around me, many of the bodybuilders are about ten to fifteen pounds smaller than they were at last year's Ms. Olympia because IFBB officials have said the female bodybuilders were just too big last year.

Even so, these women are still massively muscled compared to most women and men you would find on the streets or, for that matter, in gyms. Laura Creavalle and Lenda Murray, two of the most muscular women on stage, have the most vocal support from the crowd. In fact, Lenda Murray's family members are easily discernible in the crowd with their matching white sweatshirts emblazoned with "Lenda Murray, Ms. Olympia 1990–1991." Sharon Bruneau and Anja Schreiner, both of whom have good symmetry but are not as muscular as Lenda or Laura, are favorites among some of the men in the crowd. A sizable percentage of the crowd appreciate hard, cut, and ripped muscles on women, and these women get the most vocal support.

The bodybuilders line up in two rows facing the crowd, the panel of eleven judges, and the cameras. When they reach their places on stage, they assume the semi-relaxed stance, which means that all muscles are tense, but none of the five mandatory poses are assumed. They are wearing very small bikinis that "must conform to accepted standards of taste and decency."[3] Yet these bikinis must also "reveal the abdominal muscles as well as the lower back muscles."[4] The two pieces of the bikini are fastened together with two strings, and the fasteners as well as the bikini must not consist of metallic material or padding.[5] The Ms. Olympia competitors' bathing suits come in a variety of colors including blue, green, black, white, yellow, orange, red, and last but not least, pink.

Most of the twenty competitors are from the United States. Of the American women, four are of African descent and eight of European origin. Of the eight competitors from other countries, one is black. The countries represented in the Ms. Olympia competition are the United States, Guyana, Canada, Czechoslovakia, Hungary, Italy, and Germany.

At first look, an unsuspecting person might think that this is a beauty contest of sorts, and in a way, perhaps it is. The competitors have some physical characteristics that closely resemble the traditional norms of femininity exemplified in beauty contests around the world. For instance, an unusually high number of the Anglo female competitors are blond: out of the eight from the United States, six are blondes. Of the seven from outside the United States, four are blond. In addition, only one of all the competitors on stage has short hair; the rest have shoulder-length hair that is tied in a ponytail, a bun, or a French braid. The bodybuilders who have hair that is shoulder length or longer wear their hair this way because it is stipulated under IFBB regulation to do so. The IFBB Guidebook states that "during the prejudging for women, the hair must be worn off the shoulders so as not to hide the musculature of the shoulders and upper back. The hair must be styled for finals presentation."[6] Furthermore, the female competitors wear plenty of makeup on their faces, and many have painted nails. However, the competitors may not wear "footwear, watches, rings, bangles, pendants, earrings, wigs, distracting ornamentation or artificial aids to the figure. They must not chew gum or candy or smoke."[7]

Each contestant smiles while she waits for the competition to begin. The women seem strangely, supremely confident, especially so in the face of over one thousand people, most of them men, who are closely scrutinizing their bodies.[8] The parallels between this competition and beauty pageant contests are obvious—the smiles, the coiffed hair, the makeup and painted nails, the judges, and the ever-present gaze of the audience.

In addition to the numerous feminine elements, however, there are characteristics that make this event different from a beauty contest. We see images that our eyes have not seen before, that our minds have not thought possible . . . until now. These women are muscular, incredibly muscular when compared to the average person on the street, male or female. Yet, at the same time, they are adorned with traditionally feminine elements such as coiffed hair and makeup. This combination of the feminine and the muscular is almost surreal. It is a compelling image regardless of whether one finds the look appealing or repulsive. Today these women stand proud to display the muscles for which they have worked so hard; yet they present themselves through some of the most traditional signifiers of femininity. How can this be? How can these seeming contradictions coexist in a single body?

The women athletes look out to the crowd, anxious for the competition to begin.

A Ten-Minute Elimination: The Afternoon Prejudging Rounds

Professional bodybuilding competitions consist of four judged rounds. The first two rounds at the Ms. Olympia occur in the afternoon prejudging show and the last two rounds during the evening show. The first round is the symmetry round in which the judges "compare the competitors in groups of two or three in the semi-relaxed state from the front, back and both sides."[9] Here judges look for symmetry and balance between muscular groups and musculature proportional to bone structure. To begin, the first five contestants come down to the front of the stage, then the second five, and so on until all twenty competitors have been called. Next, the head judge calls three women at a time whom the judges want to evaluate together so that they can compare their semi-relaxed physiques more precisely. The contestants face the front in a semi-relaxed stance. When the head judge says "quarter turn to the right," the competitors turn to face the right stage so that the judges can see their side symmetry and proportion. They continue these right quarter-turns until they are facing the audience again. The head judge thanks them and they assume their place back in one of the two lines. Then the next group of three comes down and the ritual is repeated.

At this show, the same ten female athletes are called repeatedly in the course of the forty-five minute period, but in different combinations of three. These ten women will most likely be the top ten contenders at this year's Ms. Olympia. Those familiar with bodybuilding customs know that the head judge's call-outs in the first ten minutes of the first round reveal those bodybuilders who are going to finish well. Although the manifest purpose of the first and second rounds is to evaluate bodybuilders' symmetry and muscularity, the latent purpose is to inform the bodybuilders and audience whom the judges consider to be the contenders for the title. At this point in the contest, those at the competition can begin to see that there may be other, less tangible, factors that influence which bodybuilders are chosen for the call-outs. Sometimes those who are the real crowd pleasers are the ones who are most often called, yet at other times those who are perceived to have already "paid their dues to the sport" are called on to step forward. Members of the latter group have been in the sport for a while, followed the rules diligently, and not openly criticized those in the upper echelon.

For those left in the background during the round, the psychological effects can be devastating. They talk about becoming discouraged and losing their spirit within the first ten minutes of a meet because the judges have called them out only once: they have been around the sport long enough to know what this signifies. The women who are not called forward are left standing semi-relaxed in the back two lines, watching their competitors pose to the cadence of the head judge's call: "O.K., quarter turn to the right." After forty-five minutes, the first round is over and the competitors exit the stage. There is about a five-minute intermission.

Round two is the muscularity round in which the contestants do a series of five compulsory poses. The poses for professional female bodybuilders competing in the IFBB contests such as the Ms. Olympia include (1) front double biceps, (2) side chest, (3) rear double biceps, (4) side triceps, and (5) two-arm overhead abdominals and quadriceps. When the twenty contestants return to the stage, the IFBB Chief of Protocol takes their hand and guides them up the stairs to the top of the stage. With all bodybuilders on stage, three bodybuilders at a time are called out to the front and asked to do the five compulsory poses. The middle position is considered to be the best position of the three because the judges want to compare that person's physique to the two competitors on either side. It is an ominous sign for any competitor who lines up in the center of the three posers to be asked to move to one of the two peripheral positions in order to let another competitor stand in the middle.

Again, in this round, the judges continue to call the same women for the muscularity poses as they had for the first round. For instance, Lenda Murray, Laura Creavalle, Anja Schreiner, Sandy Riddell, Shelly Beattie, and Diana Dennis are continually asked to come to the front of the platform to perform the five compulsory poses. Some of the other women are called only once or twice and have to stand patiently in the rows behind the three women who are posing for the judges, all the while knowing that they probably will not place in the top ten at this contest.

It is interesting to note the posing style of the reigning Ms. Olympia.

She is by far the most melodramatic "performer" on stage. She takes elaborate measures to emphasize the importance of her every move. A friend who is witnessing this display with me terms her performance "the Princess Syndrome." When I discuss this phenomenon with others who are familiar with the sport, they say that this melodramatic display comes with the title of Ms. Olympia.

The final two competitors who are called to the center of the platform are Lenda Murray and Laura Creavalle. They are the two most muscular female bodybuilders and they have been called out numerous times throughout the course of these two rounds, but there has always been a third contestant with them. Now, the head judge simply says, "And finally, Lenda Murray and Laura Creavalle." The auditorium goes into a frenzy. There is thunderous yelling, whistling, and clapping. People yell wildly for their favorite of the two as they "go pose for pose" with one another. We all know that the outcome of this meet, if the judges' decisions are solely based on musculature and symmetry, will come down to these two competitors.

Interlude

No other sport[10] so embodies the tensions and contradictions between femininity, strength, and muscularity than female bodybuilding. Bodybuilding is organized, governed, and operated mostly by male social gatekeepers—officials, judges, and sponsors—who have the power to set and maintain the judging standards by which female bodybuilders are evaluated. Within this context, my study poses a series of questions: How is the dilemma of having such strong, powerful, and possibly radicalizing images of women within a largely male-dominated organization resolved? Is the image of female bodybuilders actually radicalizing, or has the image been reappropriated in order to fit within dominant notions of femininity? How does the issue of marketability affect the images of female bodybuilders? What are the roles of judges as social gatekeepers? What are the female bodybuilders' responses to the hegemonic definitions and images set by the predominantly male gatekeepers?

To shed light on the construction and negotiation of female bodybuilders' femininity, I incorporate a cultural-studies perspective in which I take as a starting point the notion that gender is not biologically determined but is rather socially constructed (see appendix B for a brief discussion of this theoretical perspective). Although both women and men have resources that allow them to either cooperate with or resist existing social arrangements to varying degrees, men have resources that are not available to women. This inequality of economic, social, and political resources gives men more power in the negotiation process. Because of this power disparity, men's ability to formulate and maintain gender definitions is enhanced, serving to regulate and constrain women's behavior and thus supporting gender inequality.[11] Historically, men have had the power to define and set the boundaries of appropriate and acceptable behaviors and appearances for women, a point to be discussed in greater detail throughout this study. Although women bring fewer resources into the negotiation process, they do have some power in which to negotiate and thus influence the outcomes of this process. In other words, women may partially accept the hegemonic or dominant culture, yet they may also attempt to redefine, negotiate, or resist it.[12] Hence, history illustrates women's sometimes conscious and other times unwitting attempts to resist the limited and narrow definitions placed on them.

One of the most effective ways to deal with women who attempt to resist the gender status quo by dismissing the dominant male-defined norms is to label these women deviant.[13] Most often, the deviant labels connote some query about these women's femininity and attractiveness, which may also serve to question their sexuality. For example, the terms "unattractive," "butch," "dyke," "masculine," and "aggressive" are often used to describe women who are perceived to have crossed gender boundaries. One of the arenas in which social gatekeepers have used deviant labels to keep women from crossing over gender boundaries is in the arena of sport. Yet, paradoxically, sport is also an arena in which women have attempted to resist narrow definitions of femininity and womanhood—some with more success than others.

Athletic women, especially women in sports where a show of strength, muscle, and sweat are prominent, have often been considered outside the boundaries of appropriate femininity since traditionally these displays have been associated with masculinity. Two ways these athletic women have historically been treated include (1) being labeled deviant—unfeminine, manlike, or lesbian, to name a few; or (2) being recast to fit within the dominant patriarchal views of femininity. An illustration of the latter occurred in 1943, when Chicago Cubs owner Philip K. Wrigley and his publicity director, Arthur Meyerhoff, began the All-American Girls Baseball League (AAGBL) and arrived at a strategy to deal with the dilemma of the association between baseball and masculinity. It was called "the femininity principle," and it "at once denied the masculinity of female ballplayers yet emphasized the masculinity of their athletic skill. Pastel skirted uniforms, makeup, long hair, and stringent controls on athletes' public appearance and personal lives aimed to highlight the attractive femininity of the ballplayers."[14] Because these women had crossed the boundaries into a "male domain," Meyerhoff and Wrigley took great pains to show that these ballplayers were still unquestionably "normal" feminine women who happened to play baseball. The "femininity principle," along with other strategies, has been very successful in either recasting female athletes back into the norms of appropriate femininity or further marginalizing those athletes who do not eventually conform to the dominant norms.[15]

The success of social gatekeepers in recasting potentially threatening definitions of femininity should not be surprising given, among other resources, their power to define behaviors and appearances as normal or deviant. However, their successes should not detract from the many female athletes who have attempted to forge daring new definitions of femininity by participating in sports originally thought to be outside the realm of appropriate femininity: Ivy Russell, a British weightlifter in the 1930s;[16] Abbye "Pudgy" Stockton of the 1940s and 1950s, considered to be the mother of female bodybuilding;[17] and Babe Didrickson, whom many consider to be the best female athlete of all time.[18] All defied the constricting feminine norms of their times.

Recently, scholars, particularly those in cultural studies, have argued that the institutions of sports and sportslike activities are important arenas in which to examine the construction and maintenance of—as well as the resistance to—the hegemonic gendered power relations found in the United States.[19] For instance, it was maintained that "in relatively stable liberal capitalist democracies, power is reproduced effectively through a variety of means; sport clearly is one of these means, in many of its forms and manifestations. But it can also be a means, whereby alternative values are protected, or developed and nurtured, and at times mobilized against a dominant culture."[20] Others have also examined sport and its role in the continuation and contestation of power, in particular gendered power, in patriarchal capitalist societies.[21] It was argued that although the current wave of women's athleticism expresses a sincere attempt by women for equality, control of their own bodies, and self-definition, there are "historical limits and constraints imposed by a consumption-oriented corporate capitalism and men's continued attempts to retain power and privilege over women."[22] Thus, organized sport, as a cultural sphere defined largely by patriarchal priorities, will continue to be "an important arena in which emerging images of active, fit, and muscular women are forged, interpreted, contested, and incorporated."[23]

In the late 1970s, a sport that could potentially challenge the current hegemonic notions of femininity emerged on the sporting horizon in the form of female bodybuilding.[24] Here is a sport in which images of fit and muscular women are seemingly accepted and promoted. Yet how do the patriarchal and capitalist interests and priorities of the sport shape these muscular images? Furthermore, how will women's attempts at equality, corporal control, and self-definition play out in this muscular economic-political terrain?

The Women of Steel and the Gatekeepers

My sample includes competitive bodybuilders, International Federation of Bodybuilders (IFBB) and National Physique Committee (NPC) officials and judges, and journalists who cover the sport. Throughout the book, I use pseudonyms to protect the identity of those who participated in this study. Overall, the vast majority of my sample are Americans; of the thirty-seven respondents, only one is a citizen of another country. The sample of bodybuilders is represented mostly by Anglos (70%) with African Americans and Latinas comprising the rest. Asian Americans were not represented. The fourteen bodybuilders in this study represent women along the continuum of competition levels: slightly more than 40 percent compete at the professional level, approximately 30 percent compete at the national amateur level, and almost 30 percent compete at the state amateur level. On average these women have been competing for six years. Although none of the women grew up hoping to become a bodybuilder, some showed a fascination with muscles and musculature development at an early age. Most got involved in bodybuilding unintentionally—by working out at a gym, not with purpose of becoming a competitive bodybuilder, but to get back in shape or to recover from an injury. Their ages ranged from twenty-four to forty-six, with the average age being thirty-three. Forty-three percent have received a college degree, 14 percent have a high school diploma with some college experience, and 43 percent have a high school degree with no college experience.

More demographic information about the interviewees can be found in appendix A.

Because officials are also likely to be contest judges, I combine these two categories for the demographic information. In the text, I separate these two positions depending on what role the person is assuming. Of the twenty officials/judges, 55 percent are men and 45 percent are women. Seventy-five percent of this group are Anglo, 5 percent are African American, 5 percent are Asian American, and 15 percent are Hispanic. Judges and officials are older than bodybuilders, and most had competed as bodybuilders before becoming judges and/or officials. The average age of the male judges/officials is forty-seven, with a range from thirty-eight to sixty-nine; for female officials/judges, the average age is thirty-four, with a range from thirty to forty-five. Of the female judges, eight out of nine, or approximately 90 percent, have participated or are currently participating as competitive bodybuilders. Of the male judges, six out of eleven, or 55 percent, are either currently participating or have participated as competitive bodybuilders.

In addition, I have interviewed three bodybuilding journalists—two women and one man.

Methodological Issues

In order to examine the substantive questions and to elucidate the mechanisms involved in the construction and negotiation of femininity, as well as the reproduction and contestation of gendered power in the sport of female bodybuilding, I used a combination of ethnographic observation and in-depth semi-structured interviews. From the fall of 1991 to the spring of 1993, I conducted a total of thirty-seven interviews with female bodybuilders, NPC and IFBB female and male judges and officials, and journalists. I met many at bodybuilding competitions either through others I had interviewed, through key informants, or by recognizing them from their magazine photos, and I interviewed most of them on the phone after they had returned home from a competition. The interview for the female bodybuilders consisted of numerous open-ended questions in five general areas: sports socialization, the process of getting ready for a meet and the meet experience, attitudes about judging, attitudes about the importance of attractiveness for female bodybuilders and about what look constitutes the ideal in female bodybuilding, and attitudes about their own experiences in the sport and the future of the sport. The interview for the female and male judges, which is included in appendix C, also consisted of open-ended questions in four general areas: sports socialization, judging experiences, attitudes about the importance of attractiveness of female bodybuilders, and their vision of the future of female bodybuilding. These interviews, which were taped and transcribed, lasted from thirty minutes to two hours and were filled with personal stories—some of determination and triumph, others of frustration and despair. The female bodybuilders with whom I spoke embodied many of the apparent contradictions and tensions of the sport: they appeared to be confident and took charge at some points during the interviews, while at other times they seemed more timid and meek.

For the participant observations, I took extensive notes while observing how bodybuilding meets are run and organized. In all, I observed five different bodybuilding shows: three regional shows, including the 1991 Texas Cup, the 1992 Texas Championships, and the 1992 Lackland Classic; two professional shows, including the 1992 Ms. Olympia and the 1993 Ms. International. The observations that I conducted allowed me to see what the protocol is for bodybuilding shows, what types of people go to these events, what bodybuilders look like when they are on stage, what types of poses they are asked to do, the role the audience plays, the role of vendors who sell bodybuilding products at shows. I could also see for myself what types of bodybuilders win at these different levels of competition.

In addition to observing bodybuilding contests and conducting in-depth interviews, I had the opportunity to watch individuals working out with free weights since some of my interviews were conducted in regional gyms. This aspect of the research is important because, as the participants in this study asserted, the gym environment is an integral part of a bodybuilder's life. Thus, by watching people work out and interact with one another and by looking at the gym environment, I became more cognizant of the role of the gym, its ambiance, the interaction of its members, and the role it plays in the lives of bodybuilders, especially when they are getting ready for a bodybuilding competition. Furthermore, I had access to a few bodybuilders in the local area and watched them train; I also had the chance to ask them numerous questions about the whys, whens, and hows of training for bodybuilding shows, which gave me an appreciation of what is entailed in a bodybuilder's workout routine. In fact, on a couple of occasions, I worked out with a bodybuilder to see what it was like to train for a meet. I regretted this endeavor, however, because for days afterwards I experienced more muscle soreness than I ever imagined possible. For more information about my methodological procedures, please refer to appendix B.

The Language of Bodybuilding

Also, as I spoke to people involved in bodybuilding, I realized that the sport had its own unique jargon—words that describe degrees of muscularity, water retention, workout strategies, and the like. Because these terms are included in quotations from those I interviewed, I have included a glossary of terms (see appendix D) to assist the reader in understanding this terminology.

What is fascinating about the language of bodybuilding is that much of this sport's jargon is filled with hidden meanings about gender. If these terms were used elsewhere, they would have very different connotations. For instance, the word, "ripped" among college students probably connotes a level of intoxication. However, in bodybuilding, the word means that the muscles are well-defined and prominent. The bodybuilding jargon communicates ideas about what the physique should and should not look like. In doing so, it also construes connotations about femininity and masculinity and their relationship to bodybuilding and muscles. For instance, in bodybuilding, words such as "hard," lean," "cut," "shredded," "ripped," and "striated" are terms toward which one strives. They represent the ideal "look" that bodybuilders want on the day of the meet. They indicate that there is little subcutaneous fat and water under the skin, that the muscle is as close to the skin as possible without any extraneous substances in between the two so that all muscles are prominent. This is evidence that the bodybuilder has done an effective job of working out, dieting, and dehydrating themselves for the meet.

On the other hand, the looks that a bodybuilder does not want are "soft" and "smooth." These terms connote too much water retention and improper dieting, or that the muscles have "already peaked." Some of this jargon, while communicating what is good and what is bad, may also serve to reproduce different ideas about gender, i.e., "hard" is oftentimes associated with masculinity while "soft" and "smooth" are associated with femininity.

Finally, to illustrate further the gendered language of bodybuilding, I include the term used to describe gynecomastia, a condition that men get when they take steroids that enlarge their breast tissue. According to

Weber, the most common reason that male bodybuilders have plastic surgery is to reduce gynecomastia,[25] a condition they call "bitch tits."

Appendix E lists a table of various bodybuilders mentioned in the book, described on a continuum based on degrees of size and femininity.

Back to the Finals of the 1992 Ms. Olympia Contest. The Pose-Down: The Evening Events

There are approximately two thousand people in the audience for the evening show.[26] Many of the people who were at the afternoon performance are at the evening competition as well. However, there are numerous new faces in the crowd. The people are dressed as if they were going out on the town on a Saturday night—in fact, that is exactly what they are doing. Most of the women are wearing short, tight leather dresses or skirts. The men are dressed in jeans or leather pants, ties, and leather jackets. The most common fabric for both women and men appears to be leather in many different colors and textures. No doubt this choice of fabrics is due to the nature of leather: it is extremely body-hugging and reveals every muscular ripple and nuance the wearer's body has to offer the voyeurs in the crowd.

The crowd is abuzz with excitement. The doors to the auditorium have not yet opened, so people are still milling around the booths.[27] There are a few additions to the afternoon display, the most notable being the arrival of a number of well-known professional and amateur bodybuilders who are here to promote and sell various bodybuilding products. People swarm around the booths they occupy to get a view and autographs.

As I wait for the show to start, I walk around the booth area and notice that Big Mike Matarazzo, one of the bodybuilders behind the booths, has agreed to have his picture taken with some of his fans. I observe how he talks to the hordes of people around him, and how he graciously accepts their requests to have photos taken with him. I turn to go, only to hear shrieks: Mike has taken off his shirt and is doing some poses for the impressed crowd. As Mike flexes, cameras flash, people gawk.

I walk over to a booth where a long line of people are waiting to see Cory Everson, six-time winner of Ms. Olympia. She has the biggest gathering of people of any bodybuilder at the booths. For about an hour, there is a steady line of thirty to forty people to meet Cory and get a picture and autograph from her. She is promoting a certain brand of workout clothes and signs pictures of herself for ten dollars each. In addition to the famous bodybuilders behind the various booths, there are also some in the crowd. Carla Dunlap, Bev Francis, and Sergio Oliva are in attendance—all of whom attract an impressive gathering of admirers.

A little after 8 o'clock, the ushers open the doors and people find their assigned seats. ESPN cameras have been set up to telecast the show live around the world. Ben Weider, the president of the International Federation of Bodybuilders, comes on stage to welcome the competitors and the audience members to the twelfth annual Ms. Olympia Contest. He then introduces the announcer, an Australian, who in turn presents Weider with a stuffed koala bear. The announcer, who has an almost incomprehensible accent, introduces the twenty contestants who are brought on stage by the IFBB Chief of Protocol. The contestants line up precisely where they stood during the preliminaries and, as they are introduced, the audience members, who are a bit more subdued now than during the afternoon show, applaud and cheer. In turn, the competitors smile and strike a pose. After everyone is introduced, the competitors file off stage to get ready for the third round of judging.

According to the IFBB *Guidebook*, round three is the "free posing" round.[28] Here the bodybuilders do "individual free posing to the music of each competitor's choice."[29] Each free-posing routine lasts about ninety seconds to three minutes, and it consists of a combination of dance movements and posing to display one's muscles. This part of the show is considered to be the most aesthetic and memorable aspect of the competition. In fact, many bodybuilders hire choreographers to help them organize their musical presentations in order to set themselves apart from their competitors.

For this part of the show, the bodybuilders can choose any piece of music they wish. Most pick current dance hits, although some choose less-popular personal favorites. The point of this round is to dazzle the audience and judges with creativity and style. The bodybuilders must work out "an intelligent presentation of the muscles choreographed together with music."[30] No props may be used. Certain poses are prohibited because they are considered too lewd. For instance, one forbidden pose is the hamstring pose, whereby the athlete turns her back to the audience and leans forward as if stretching her legs.

At the end of the free-posing round, there is an intermission, which allows the audience members an opportunity to stretch and get some refreshments. When the show restarts, a personal touch of community is expressed when the announcer asks the audience for a moment of silence in honor of Mohammed Benaziza, a professional male bodybuilder, who died of heart arrhythmia at the last show in the European Grand Prix series. Benaziza's death was rumored to have been caused by overdosing on diuretics.

The "pose down" is the fourth and last round of the contest. The top six candidates simultaneously go through the compulsory poses, which are called out by the head judge. These are followed by a series of free poses which they believe best highlight their musculature and symmetry, all done to music chosen by the promoter of the show. The contestants pose in front of the judges, vying for the best position. To do so, they continually step in front of one another to block the judges' vision, and sometimes the best bodybuilders will go pose for pose next to each other to compare muscles. Some bodybuilders nudge others out of their way. This part of the contest could easily lead to a shoving match between contestants, but the brawlers would be disqualified from the contest and perhaps be suspended from the IFBB.

The announcer informs us of the start of the pose down. The music begins and the women start posing to the music and inching closer to one another and the judges. Lenda Murray winds up in the middle, and Laura Creavalle scoots in next to her, and they go pose for pose. Other contestants try to get close to Lenda to compare their muscles with hers because they know that she is the one to beat. Whenever she does a particular pose, others follow suit, doing the exact same pose right next to her. Shouts and whistles reach a feverish pitch as audience members yell for their favorite contestant. Other contenders try to step in between Lenda and Laura, and eventually one does, but everyone knows between whom the real contest is. An equal number of fans are cheering for Laura and Lenda. The music stops and the six women get back in line to await the judges' decision.

The IFBB Chief of Protocol gets the official final score sheet from the judges. He takes it to the announcer who will inform the crowd of the placings, beginning with tenth place and continuing until he has announced the 1992 Ms. Olympia. Each of these athletes gets prize money and a trophy or medal.[31] Two of the sponsors of Ms. Olympia hand out the prizes for places ten through four, and Ben Weider awards the first three places. Shelley Beattie places third. Laura Creavalle is announced as second-place winner, leaving Lenda Murray as Ms. Olympia.[32] The majority of the crowd responds with deafening whistles and claps, while those who have been rooting for Laura react with the requisite boos and hisses. Laura first responds by pretending to strangle Lenda, and then the two well-respected competitors embrace. Camera lights flash. For her hard work, Lenda wins $35,000.00 and a gold medal with Joe Weider's image. Perhaps most important for her, the victory enhances her marketability.

As a sociologist, I sit in the audience looking at the activities on stage, wondering what must be running through the minds of the contestants, judges, and fans I see before me. Female bodybuilding is indeed filled with interesting paradoxes that have created considerable controversy—particularly this past season. To date, no one seems to be able to answer the question of how female bodybuilders should be judged. Should they be evaluated by the same judging standards as male bodybuilders, i.e., by their muscles and symmetry? Or is there an additional issue, that of femininity, which female bodybuilders must somehow put into the equation? I wonder what the bodybuilders on stage and the fans sitting next to me think about next year's female bodybuilding season—what type of physique the officials and judges will reward. The future is uncertain, but for now the Ms. Olympia contenders, who represent the best of female bodybuilders, are congratulating the winner, and photographers are hurriedly snapping pictures of the current three-time reigning queen.

ONE

Muscle Bound

Well, I was always a track athlete, some kind of athlete. Since I was five years old I was a gymnast and I was a competitive gymnast. . . . Then I went to college and ran track for one year and I was too skinny and too small and they wanted me to get stronger and build my body up so they put me on a weight program three days a week. I started seeing phenomenal growth. Especially in college you gain that fifteen pounds. I gained a little bit of weight and what happened after that is my muscularity grew because my body was ready for that. I quit track and I wanted to keep doing something physical so I joined a gym and just kept working out.
—Diane, a professional female body-builder[1]

I was a runner, and a gymnast, and a dancer. And at one point in my life I was just sort of an obsessive-compulsive. I guess what they now call an exercise addict.
—Ellen, a national-level amateur female body-builder

Diane and Ellen's words echo the formative athletic experiences of many women in my study. All were active in competitive sports at an early age, and many continued in their athletic endeavors throughout high school and even into college. All but one of these women had competed in multiple sports, including track and field, soccer, softball, and basketball. Whatever their sports backgrounds, these women eventually found themselves in the gym lifting weights and ultimately competing in their first sanctioned bodybuilding competitions. How did they go from participating in organized sports such as basketball and track as children and young adults to competing in the sport of bodybuilding? And, once they had discovered this new athletic passion, how did these athletes' family and friends respond to their new participation in such a nontraditional sport? I will discuss the key events in the athletic and personal backgrounds of these women that have led them to competitive bodybuilding. I will also address some of the social consequences they have experienced as a result of their participation in this sport.

In almost every interview I had with female bodybuilders, the words "I've been involved in sports all my life" were uttered. "I was very athletic, I played a lot of different sports when I was growing up," recalled one woman. The level of their athletic competition ranged from participation in city league teams, to high school and intercollegiate athletics. In fact, two current bodybuilders had, at one time, trained for the Olympics, one in synchronized swimming, the other in equestrian events. One of these athletes, Mary, a regional competitor, declared that "I've been an athlete all my life. Since I was ten years old, I've been in team sports and I trained for the Olympics in the early 1970s in equestrian events. Then when I was in Florida, I was on the rowing team."

Like most of the female bodybuilders in this study, Mary found great enjoyment in athletic involvement and avidly participated in numerous sports since childhood. A third bodybuilder, Susan, a regional amateur competitor, had participated in the Junior Olympics in track and field and eventually became a member of the track team at her university. Approximately one-third of the female bodybuilders had competed in intercollegiate varsity sports. Regardless of their level of sports involvement, the majority stated that sports had always been a major source of enjoyment for them. They also noted that when they were out of athletic competition for whatever reason, they felt a noticeable void in their lives. Many spoke of their athletic experiences with fondness because competitive sport was the arena in which they not only could compete but often also excel. Their athletic success, borne from practice, experience, and good genetic makeup, gave them the tools and confidence to try their muscles at bodybuilding.

None of these women grew up with the career goal of becoming a competitive female bodybuilder. This is highly understandable, given that bodybuilding was not a sport for women until the late 1970s and that the gender norms that existed when these women were younger did not encourage women to aspire to great physical strength. However, the seeds for their eventual entrance into the sport were planted long before they considered participating in competitive bodybuilding. These athletes, having been genetically endowed with muscular physiques, talked candidly about having received continual attention throughout their lives for their noticeable muscularity. Christy, a national-level amateur competitor told of always being more muscular than her peers—both female and male: "I was always muscular. People always asked me what I did for my physique and what I would do when I went to the gym, and I always used to say, 'I don't go to the gym.'" Similarly, Patty, a professional bodybuilder, remarked that before she even knew that female bodybuilding existed, she would incessantly "have people come up to me and say, 'Are you a bodybuilder?'" This type of attention made these women realize at a young age that their bodies were different. It also piqued their curiosity as to how their bodies would respond to working out with weights. Some had actually thought of bodybuilding early on, but the option did not exist for them at the time.

Besides having become motivated as a result of comments about their impressive physiques, many bodybuilders remembered being intrigued by other people's muscularity. Pam, a professional bodybuilder, recalled that when she was a child she was mesmerized by muscular people and wanted to look like them but did not know how to explore her interest properly:

> Okay, I was chubby, and being strong always fascinated me ever since I was a kid. I picked up a comic book and in the back you could get all the muscles in the world for ten cents. Charles Atlas, I always wanted to send for that. . . . When I was in fourth grade, I asked my dad and mom for ten cents to buy it, and they said it was a waste of money. But it always fascinated me to see muscles on people.

Ellen, a national-level amateur, also remembered being intrigued by a classmate's muscular frame during a college dance class:

> My only exposure to bodybuilding had been another woman who was in the dance department at my university when I was, and she had a very, what I thought, very peculiar, but intriguing body. And I, at one point, asked her what she did and she said "I'm a bodybuilder." And I used to stand next to her in class and think, "God, I could be a good one of those." Because I had always been really muscular and then

> with my athletic background, I had a pretty built physique and I was real lean.

Having received attention since her youth for her own athletic, muscular frame, Ellen found her classmate's more muscular physique compelling. She was unaware that a sport existed for women in which the goals were to enhance and display one's muscularity. When she discovered that such a sport existed, she realized she might excel in it. This realization came late to these women, and many had already gotten out of shape. And, unbeknownst to them, there was still a missing piece of the puzzle.

Many of the women, by the time they were in their early to mid-twenties, had reached a point at which they were no longer participating in athletic competition at any level. They had become sedentary, which left them with bodies that, in their eyes, were painfully out of shape—bodies that were now somehow foreign to them. At this juncture, many women went to the gym, as Denise remembers, "just to get back in shape." However, others found the process of getting back in shape a more formidable task and expressed feeling paralyzed by their new lethargy and ensuing physical deterioration. For instance, Christy recalled:

> Finally, when I turned twenty-five, I wasn't doing anything physical at all, I was like a total couch potato and I decided to join a gym so I joined and had no idea what I was doing, just went kind of infrequently. I ended up not doing much of anything when I went to the gym and then I went away for a year and came back really heavy for me, and I was sort of sick of not knowing how to control my body. I didn't know anything about nutrition. I knew that I had good muscle mass but just didn't know anything about it.

Christy, in her desire to get back in shape, spoke of her body as an object, as something that needed to be controlled from its insatiable gluttonous desires. As we will discover later in the chapter, Christy's sentiments about her body are not uncommon among female bodybuilders. Furthermore, as was true for others, getting back into shape was not easy for Christy: it took her a year and multiple attempts to get going on a healthy regimen.

Tracy, an official and a former competitor, candidly revealed that it was her fight with anorexia nervosa that compelled her mother to get her to work out at a local gym. She stated, "After high school I got real skinny. I was basically anorexic. My mother was working out at a health spa and she thought that working out would be a good way for me to get over the disease and get some weight on me." While her mother did not get her involved in the sport of bodybuilding, she did open the door for her by getting her in the gym and working out with weights. This eventually led Tracy to become a competitive bodybuilder. Although other bodybuilders' mothers became supportive of their daughters' involvement in bodybuilding, she is the only one whose mother gave her the impetus to work out with weights. She is also the only bodybuilder who worked out to gain weight instead of lose it.

Patty, who was also unhappy with her body but for different reasons, took a more circuitous path to the gym. After getting married and having children, Patty became displeased with her overweight and out-of-shape body. After trying other activities, she eventually sought advice about weight training from her ex-husband, who at the time was a college strength coach:

> I gained a lot of weight, got very large and just decided that I wasn't going to spend the second half of my life that way. I lost a bunch of weight, started long-distance running, started teaching aerobics, eventually got a stress fracture from doing so much. . . . So I stopped doing that but I had all this excess energy and I didn't know what to do with it. Plus I wasn't happy with the shape of my body, I wasn't happy with the way it looked. So my ex-husband had taught weight lifting in college and we just went into the gym one day and I said I want to try this . . . that was it, I never left.

Wanting to continue being physically active, she asked her ex-husband to teach her how to lift weights properly and, shortly thereafter, saw significant improvements in her physique. She eventually entered her first bodybuilding show and consequently competed as a professional bodybuilder and powerlifter for a number of years. Patty's virtual obsession with staying physically active resembles Ellen's: "I was a runner, and a gymnast, and a dancer. And at one point in my life I was just sort of an obsessive-compulsive. I guess what they now call an exercise addict." Both of these women expressed a loathing for their bodies when they were out of shape. Furthermore, they appear to have a drill sergeant's callousness about punishing their corpora when getting into poor condition. Again, their bodies are something not to be trusted and in need of continual vigilance lest they fall prey to any complacency, laziness, and eating excesses.

Recall Pam who went from being an active, chubby kid bewitched by muscles and strength to a woman who still wanted to be active, but was unhappy with how she looked. Although she was dissatisfied with her body at the time, she knew she had the potential to compete in bodybuilding. She recalled:

> I got a job teaching in my hometown, and after six months of teaching there was no place to really work out and have fun, just go to a gym and run and shoot hoops and stuff. I was teaching and facilities were really limited in my town. They opened up a gym about thirty miles away and at the time I was coaching, the weights kind of always fascinated me. Bodybuilding just started coming around like in the early '80s.

Brenda's fascination with weights turned into a resolve to try bodybuilding after seeing a magazine with pictures of women bodybuilders:

> This was the first part of 1981 and I walked into this Read More magazine place and they had a *Muscle and Fitness* issue. I looked at it and I saw girls in there like Carla Dunlap, Claudia Wilbourn, Laura Combes, and I saw them in high heels and I thought to myself, "Shoot, I could look just as good as they look." I went home and took my clothes off in front of the mirror and I started to cry. I had little cellulite lumps all the way down to my knees; cellulite is just a fancy word for stored fat basically, and I thought, "Oh God, how I look." So I started driving thirty miles to the gym. Within about twelve weeks, I entered my first show and ended up second.

Here, we learn that Pam finally found a suitable, albeit difficult outlet in which to pursue her childhood interest in being muscular. This interest, coupled with her unhappiness about the current condition of her body, motivated her to drive thirty miles several times a week to begin training to become a competitive bodybuilder. However, once in the gym, Pam faced the additional structural barriers that precluded her from working out in the way she wanted. Not only were there "women's days," but there were "his" and "her" sides of the gym. Later in the interview she disclosed the difficulties she experienced as a woman in the sex-segregated gym:

> I walked into the gym and they had a few women on the women's side. It was mostly all an aerobic area, and the machines were those chrome ones you see, and I mean there was nothing there. So I talked to the gym owner and said, "Listen, Steve, can I come over to the

> other side? Can I train over there? I'm serious. I'm not going to bug anybody." They made a special arrangement for me to go over to the men's side of the gym.

However, not everyone was pleased with this new arrangement.

> The first two weeks nobody talked to me. They just looked at me. My knowledge about how to get ready for bodybuilding shows was what I would see in *Muscle and Fitness.* I slept with it a few nights under my pillow; I mean it was like my bible. Anyway, in the gym, I kind of had an eye on everybody because they were watching me. Finally, after being in there for two weeks, one nerdish guy started talking to me, and I guess I had earned my keep a little bit. Then pretty soon some other people started talking to me too and then everybody did.

The gym's sex segregation had been due to the belief that women were incapable of, or uninterested in, using free weights. Hampered in her quest to compete in bodybuilding by the unavailability of such weight equipment, Pam approached the gym's owner who, after some prodding, allowed her to use the men's equipment. Having broken the gym's gender norms, she now had to face the gym's clients who at first treated her like a social pariah. She had encroached on their territory and they responded by socially isolating and castigating her—effective tools in keeping the gender order unaltered and untainted. Undaunted, Pam continued working out and not only accomplished her goal, but also succeeded in modifying the perception that women are frail beings interested only in "toning up, not pumping up."

Bodybuilders like Susan found themselves in the gym lifting weights in order to recuperate from injuries they had sustained while participating in other sporting events: "I walked into this local gym. I was going to try to work out and get a little bit stronger because I had been incapacitated for a bit—I tore my ACL [anterior cruciate ligament] a couple of months prior while competing in track." The gym owner convinced her that she would do well in bodybuilding, so she began lifting weights with the idea of eventually competing in a bodybuilding meet. Still other women had been physically active in other endeavors when they found themselves in the gym for less "ordinary" reasons. For instance, Stephanie, a professional bodybuilder, divulged her unconventional route to working out at the gym and competing in bodybuilding:

> I had this thing that I was going to be a dancer and all through college I thought the same thing. I remember towards the end of my last year at college, I went and tried out for a dancing position that lasted for two years. What happened was the first couple of times I made it and the lady said, "Well, you're a great dancer and you're great at entertaining the crowd, but we just want you to lose a little bit more weight because your thighs are a little bit too muscular." At the time, I always knew I had very shapely quads from being a sprinter. I decided okay, so I came back home—I had already made one of the cuts—I came back home and I would run and run and run, run three miles, four miles to get muscle off my thighs. I came back and by this time I had been through four tryouts, and I made the forty-five girls. She said, "Wow, you lost some weight!" and I had lost ten pounds. She said she wanted me to lose some more. So . . . I looked at her and I thought to myself, "Oh, well." So I got on the plane going home and they still had another cut to go, nine other girls would have been cut from the team.

It was at this point that Stephanie realized that she was asking the impossible from her body and this was confirmed by a friend of hers who was a bodybuilder and who eventually got her into the gym.

> I knew how miserable I felt at the weight I was at, and that I didn't think it was possible to maintain it. So I came home and I just decided not to go back. I decided to take up the offer that was given to me by one of the professional bodybuilders, who was, at the time, ranked in the top ten in the world; he would see me throughout this whole year . . . trying to be this skinny person, and he just laughed. He watched me for a whole year. And he just said, "Why are you doing it, because you were destined to have these muscular thighs." Some women don't have thin thighs, and so that Monday, I started weight training. And I never went back [to make the final cut] again.

Although the majority of bodybuilders did not follow this particular path toward bodybuilding, Stephanie's experiences illustrate the themes also expressed by other bodybuilders. First, Stephanie's significant musculature precluded her from pursuing dancing any further because, although dancers are healthy-looking and fit, they are supposed to be slim, not muscular. Thus, Stephanie inadvertently transgressed the boundaries of appropriate muscular displays for dancers—her muscularity was considered excessive and unsuitable. She was outside the hegemonic boundaries of femininity within dancing. As a result, she had two choices: conform or depart. She chose the latter. Second, we note the importance of having a practicing bodybuilder serve as mentor for women entering the sport. Throughout the year, Stephanie's friend nudged her in the direction of bodybuilding. After months of trying to trim down, she finally realized that she was asking her body to change beyond its ability to do so.

As we have seen, some women initially went to the gym to either stay or get back in shape, others went to recuperate from an injury. Only a handful went with the intention of getting ready to compete in bodybuilding. However, regardless of their reasons for taking that first step, once they had worked out for a while, they began to see improvements in their physiques. People also started complimenting them on how good they looked. The combination of resistance training and their predispositions toward muscularity allowed them and others to see dramatic improvements in their bodies. Motivated by these improvements, they continued working out with more confidence and drive than before. They began to *feel* their bodies again. Working out merely to stay in shape was no longer enough to satisfy them. At this point many of the women began to see a flicker of light from their past: they hungered for athletic competition. Denise remembered:

> I didn't even know women competed in bodybuilding when I walked into the gym. When I found out that women could compete in bodybuilding—I'm so competitive and I really don't like working out just to stay in shape—that I thought bodybuilding would be an outlet for me.

Denise's comments reflect many of the women's sentiments at this juncture in their lives. Now that they were physically active again, they desired an athletic outlet for all their labor. They needed a spark to ignite them—that spark, for most, was a mentor.

The timing of the mentor's entrance in the women's lives as well as the roles they played in their bodybuilding careers varied from woman to woman. For some, the mentor entered their lives even before they got to the gym. Recall that Stephanie, who had been trying to make the dance squad, had a male bodybuilder friend who told her there is a sport that's ideally suited for her. She went to the gym with the intent of competing in the sport. Others' mentors, however, came into their lives when they entered the gym, but before they started lifting. Throughout their lives, their unique musculature had attracted the attention not only of those outside the sport, but also from inside the sport. For others, mentors did not enter their lives until they had been working out for a while. Regardless, the mentor provided the final impetus for these women to get interested in and excited about becoming competitive bodybuilders. The roles of the mentors also differed. Some women described them as guides and informants about the informal rules of the sport. Others characterized their mentors as father figures, brothers, friends, or coaches.

In fact, one thing the mentors had in common is that most of them were men. This pattern is consistent with previous literature on women's socialization into sport.[2] One reason why this is true in bodybuilding is that it has always been an overwhelmingly male sport. The gender ratio in gyms and in the sport of bodybuilding both at the competitor and judge levels show that mentors are more likely to be men. A second reason is that bodybuilding is a nontraditional pursuit for women. As is sometimes the case when people are involved in nontraditional activities, others may question their sexual orientation. In order to shield themselves from such claims, women may choose a male instead of a female mentor. Once the women became more involved in bodybuilding and were "hooked," perhaps they could "compensate" for their involvement in a nontraditional endeavor in other ways. Nevertheless, every bodybuilder mentioned one person in particular as having had a dramatic influence in her bodybuilding career.

Take the case of Susan. Susan's eventual mentor approached her about competing in bodybuilding as soon as she set foot in his gym:

> David, the guy who owns the gym and who is an NPC official, walked up to me when I came in the gym and started talking to me. He told me I would be good at bodybuilding because I had the genetic potential and the athletic background to do well in the sport. Well, he struck the right chord in me because I wanted to start competing again, whatever the sport. So what he said gave me something to work for.

Irrespective of their athletic backgrounds, the "hook" that pulls these women into bodybuilding, that makes them think they can do it well, is this initial encouragement by someone already involved in the sport. Susan, who sorely missed the taste of lifelong athletic competition, was intrigued by David's description of competitive female bodybuilding. He had been integrally involved in bodybuilding for decades, was knowledgeable about the sport, and thus provided the initial spark she needed. He said the right words, he awakened her competitive side, and now she had "something to work for"—the possibility of athletic competition. David became Susan's coach and later in the interview Susan described his role in her life:

> My coach, David, would probably kill me if he heard this, but he sort of came into my life like a father figure and helped me. He guided me. He was always . . . well, the best way I can describe him is he pushes me harder than I've ever been pushed in my life to the point where I'll be two weeks from a contest thinking, "Why the hell am I even doing this?" And he always somehow knows when to switch gears because then he'll come up and say, "You look the best you've ever looked in your life." And I guess that's what I've always needed, maybe. . . . Bodybuilding has given me someone to respect and someone to try and gain respect from.

A combination of father figure and drill sergeant, David became a central figure in Susan's life. She saw his role as positive because he provided her with the encouragement and discipline she felt were lacking in her life.

A number of other female bodybuilders revealed that their initial interest in bodybuilding was greatly influenced by their interactions with those already involved with the sport. For instance, Denise, a professional bodybuilder, explained: "I had a friend who was a male competitor and he said, 'Let's compete together, you look good.' So I started competing." Similarly, Patty told of the impetus that set her bodybuilding career in motion: "I joined [a gym] and I met a guy who told me that I had very good genetics and that I should think about competing, which I had always been curious to do anyway. I just started from there and I basically started training consistently at the same time I decided to get ready for the shows."

Having a similar initial experience in her gym, Mary, a national-level competitor, remarked that she had had a rather extensive athletic history but had never before even been in a gym. The only reason she had joined one was because she was invited by a female friend. Then less than a week after she had joined, her friend canceled her membership. She was left to fend for herself.

> A week later the girl that invites me to go cancels her membership and quits, never to appear again after I had paid for a year's membership. So, I'm thinking, well, now what do I do? I have a year's membership to a gym and I really don't know what I'm doing. So, I continue to work out, made up my own routines, watched other people work out, incorporated it into what I was doing, and stayed with it. . . . I still at this point am just walking around not knowing much of a structure to my workout. [The gym owner] approached me and said, "You've got terrific genetics, there's a lot of potential here for you to become a competitive bodybuilder, but you have no sense of direction. Why don't you let me help you put a combination together of diet, training. I will train you and do this contest next year."

Originally resistant to the idea, Denise eventually capitulated.

> I immediately say, "No way. I don't want to be a bodybuilder." I didn't care for the look, I didn't care for the lifestyle, I certainly didn't care for the dieting. I had heard about all the horror stories on tuna and rice cakes. I'm Cuban, I like fried bananas and black beans and rice. So I thought about it for a month or two, I thought, well, what else have I got to lose, I'm not competitively involved in anything else. So, Fourth of July, I said, "Okay, we'll do it." The reason I remember that is because I was supposed to go to a party at a lake house and thought "I can't get into a bathing suit looking like this." So I said, to [the gym owner], "My body is yours. Be kind to it."

Again, we see the importance of having someone come up to you and say, "You should try this because you would be good at it." In this case, Denise simply needed some guidance about ways to work out properly. However, the gym owner, having an eye for a bodybuilder's physique, realized that she had the "genetics" to do well in the sport and trained her for her first competition. She tried her hand at her first bodybuilding meet because she had no other competitive sporting outlets, and she felt so uncomfortable with her body that she did not want to wear a bathing suit at a Fourth of July party. She concluded her explanation by telling her trainer: "My body is yours. Be kind to it," suggesting that her preparation for her first contest occurred under a man's watchful eye. This statement, along with similar ones made by other bodybuilders, are revealing because they suggest that men guide women in their preparation for bodybuilding contests, where women are evaluated, for the most part, by other men.

Although the athletic backgrounds of the women varied, they have striking similarities. For instance, all were involved in at least one type of organized sport; most had been involved in two or more competitive organized sports, and most were involved in high school and/or college sports. Bodybuilding offered these athletes a new avenue for their athletic skills and competitive spirit. In addition, most of the women remembered getting attention for their unusual muscularity—even as children. This attention, regardless of whether it was negative or positive, made them aware that they were different from others. Many of the women entered the gym with the hope of getting back in shape; others wanted to rehabilitate an injury. Only a few began working out with the intention of entering their first bodybuilding competition.

Finally, the most important factor in getting from the workout stage to the competitive bodybuilding stage was to have someone, usually a man who was already involved in bodybuilding in some way, approach them about competing in bodybuilding. In these cases, the men often became more than bodybuilding mentors; they became lovers, surrogate fathers or brothers, coaches, or friends.

The significance of mostly men socializing women into the sport of bodybuilding is multifaceted. First, it suggests that women's initial training routines, their preparation for competition, and their entire introduction into competitive bodybuilding are likely to take place under a male's watchful eyes. This may be good preparation for the scrutiny of the judges, promoters, sponsors, and officials—the vast majority of whom are men. This process helps to ensure that women, to some extent, remain male-identified in their interactions in the sport. It also positions women to see other women as competitors, not as allies, which may help to stultify any sense of sisterhood that might develop. This separation may in turn serve as a barrier for female bodybuilders to organize together to protect their interests—economic, political, and ideological—which may be perceived as threatening to the status quo of the sport.

Reactions: Parents, Partners, and Peers

After the women received their initial words of encouragement and decided to train for their first competitive bodybuilding event, they received various responses from those around them—ranging from surprise and concern to amusement and reassurance. Many parents were initially shocked by the news that their daughters were training to become competitive bodybuilders. When they continued to train, build muscles, and compete in meets, the bodybuilders began to receive more intense responses, which ranged from complete support to absolute outrage and opposition and finally to resignation. For instance, Patty confessed, "When you talk about my immediate family, my mom and dad don't understand my lifestyle, so we don't even talk about it." Others, like Diane, discussed the unwavering support they received: "They love it. They're very supportive. They think it's great. My parents are thrilled to death." Brooke explained that her mother and grandmother were not only supportive of her participation in bodybuilding, but of her involvement in all the sports in which she has participated:[3] "My mom has always been a big supporter of sports, particularly for women. So was my grandmother. So it's kind of natural. It wasn't like, 'What are you doing?' or 'That's not for girls.' No, it was support right from the beginning."

To varying degrees, most parents eventually supported their daughters' bodybuilding endeavors, though some parents were more supportive than others. The following illustrates Denise's parents reaction:

> My mom loves it. She's my number one fan, she's never missed a show, she'll travel across the country to be there. My dad, on the other hand, is very opposed to it; he's very old fashioned. I probably should be barefoot and pregnant. He went to the first show and he's never really gotten involved or asked anything further about it. He's got pictures and when he runs into someone younger and a little more openminded and they hit upon the subject or something from a picture then he'll pull them out. But after that, "No."

Her parents' gendered reactions are typical of many of the women's parents. Mothers were more likely to support their daughters' nontraditional endeavor. Fathers were more likely than mothers to disapprove of, or support only passively, their daughters' choice of an athletic career.

Pam acknowledged that her mother had always been supportive of her athletic aspirations until she became involved in bodybuilding:

> Well . . . my mother, she's always been supportive. She's been to all of my affairs and functions, everything that I did when I was younger.

> But it was like her thing was at first, "Gosh, why do you want to be a bodybuilder?" . . . When I was in track, she never said anything, she just kind of supported me and she would go. But then she was like, "I don't know about this." And my father, he was supportive in the same way, he just really didn't go to the competition, he just kind of thought it was really different. I think the thing is that my mom and dad are old-fashioned, from the old school, and a woman with muscles is just unusual. [It] didn't seem normal or right. But they came around.

Describing her parents' support now as relatively uniform, Pam recognized that her mother's initial response was unexpected because she had never questioned Pam's motivation for participating in sports before. Both parents appeared skeptical at first because this sport, more than any other in which Pam had participated, challenged the gendered norms: "A woman with muscles is just unusual."

Two of the bodybuilders revealed that their mothers initially worried about them getting too muscular and too big. Diane confided that "initially my mom was worried about me getting too big. And my dad was kind of, you know, he didn't really think anything about it. He was just kind of complacent about it." And interestingly, although Pam's parents had a similar reaction, each parent's reasons were different. Pam's mother was worried that her daughter would become too big and unfeminine from lifting weights, whereas her father was more concerned that she would get hurt: "My mom said at first, you know, 'Don't be lifting weights, you're tiny, you're petite, stay that way, you look cute, now you can't wear your cute clothes anymore.' My dad, you know, 'Don't lift too much, you're going to get hurt.'"

These quotations illustrate parents' different levels of support of their daughters' bodybuilding endeavors. In general, fathers go to shows but are not as encouraging as mothers, such as Diane's: "My mom is one of my biggest fans." This differential gendered response reflects the pattern found in some research on early childhood socialization indicating that fathers are likely to be more strict enforcers of traditional gender roles for both daughters and sons.[4]

In addition to parents, the women had partners, friends, and other family members with whom to contend. The responses of boyfriends or husbands, much like that of parents, varied, ranging from extremely supportive to inordinately unsupportive. Three bodybuilders who were currently married to men in the bodybuilding, powerlifting, and fitness industries said that their partners were very supportive of their bodybuilding endeavors. Mary, a professional bodybuilder who will soon marry related that her fiance "thinks my participation in bodybuilding is great and he really likes muscular women. He thinks it's really good and he helps me with my diet and that stuff. We haven't been together that long, but he's really encouraging, he really encourages me a lot. He's very supportive." However, she made it clear that she had not gotten this type of enthusiastic support from her previous husband, who was also a bodybuilder:

> I was married once before, and he was a bodybuilder, but I think because I was more successful than he was, he got envious, it created jealousy with him and stuff. And I think a couple of times, mother called him by *my* last name, Mr. "Smith." It created real envy and jealousy. Most of the time I've been bodybuilding, I've usually done by myself, the training, the discipline, and stuff, and I've had a few boyfriends that were always trying to demand my time when I was getting ready for a show and that broke up one or two relationships. They wanted me to give them my time and I was trying to get ready for a show.

Mary introduced a central component of the bodybuilding training and lifestyle that makes maintaining intimate relationships challenging and difficult. Many people in the sport discussed frankly the toll that the long, arduous training and dieting prior to contests takes on relationships. While training for a bodybuilding show, one must have tunnel vision and exclude any distractions from one's life. Furthermore, bodybuilders are taking their bodies to their physical limits by drastically limiting their carbohydrate and water intake and continuing to lift weights, basically starving and dehydrating themselves. This often leads to moodiness and irritability, which may cause interpersonal conflict. Thus, many bodybuilders talked about the difficulties in maintaining committed relationships. This situation is exacerbated when two competitive bodybuilders decide to date each other. One bodybuilder revealed:

> I think most of the time when they see a big huge male bodybuilder, he's with a small petite girl, you know? I don't know why, but I don't think that two competitors can be together because I tried it. I dated competitive bodybuilders and he's getting ready for [a show] and you're not, and you're getting ready for a show and he's not. And

> you're both trying to be successful and it's a me, me, me sport. Like I said, you forget everybody, your family, your friends, it's tunnel vision, it's just you. To find somebody who can accept that and help you with it, that takes a very special person.

Add to the equation the "healthy" egos of many bodybuilders and one begins to see the enormity of the potential for problems. The foregoing bodybuilder also mentioned a phenomenon that many others had discussed as well: the issue of male bodybuilders dating petite women, which seems to conflict with the fact that most of the female bodybuilders in this study dated current or former bodybuilders or powerlifters.

Both men and women in the sport recognize the phenomenon that male bodybuilders date petite women. For instance, Mark, a regional judge, commented: "You see all of the male bodybuilders with toothpick thin, skinny stringy girls." Tod, a national judge, explained:

> And here is something else that you find, that most men bodybuilders don't like to date or go out with women bodybuilders because it kind of takes some of the prestige or some of the looks away from them. Most people who get into bodybuilding anyhow do so because of lack of self-confidence. And there are always underlying problems even after you get to be big, that you're always worried about your image and everything.

In his comments, Tod, echoed the conclusions of Alan Klein in his work on male bodybuilders.[5] Tracy, who used to be a bodybuilder and is now a judge, also talked about the small size of the women whom male bodybuilders date. She confided that male bodybuilders "appreciate women bodybuilders. They don't want to date them, or marry them, or have a relationship with them." When I asked why she thought this was the case, she responded: "Their egos. A lot of them are afraid that if they date somebody that could be better than them, could be stronger than them, that's going to be a blow to the ego. So that's all it is right there, just an ego game."

Some of those who addressed this issue thought that female and male bodybuilders don't often date or get married to each other because bodybuilding requires constant care and attention to oneself. Having two competing bodybuilding egos and schedules in the same house would be difficult, especially if they were getting ready for the same show, such as the Arnold Schwarzenegger Classic and the Ms. International Contest.

There is also the problem of jealousy if one member of the couple does better than the other, or if the female detracts from the male's size and strength.

Shelley, a journalist, recently explained that the pattern of male bodybuilders with small, petite, young, blonde women on their arms is another example of "trophy-ism": the bodybuilders can better contrast their masculine prowess with a small blonde female "trophy" next to them. She concluded that "everything is a trophy to some of them . . . even the women they date." Denise agreed:

> I think most of your male egos, especially in bodybuilding, want something smaller, to kind of hang on them. I think that's fine, I don't have anything against the smaller women, I've got lots of girlfriends that are what I call normal. But I think a man wants to, he's probably got something wrong, that sounds awful, but I think he's trying to prove something at his stage in his life. Maybe male-wise it makes him feel big and strong to be so big and have a little girl he can protect.

Denise implies a distinction here: men like athletic women, but they get turned off by large women. In her eyes, when women cross a certain line, it will turn men off. She also made it clear that she had not crossed that line.

Thus, while male bodybuilders try to exaggerate the difference in physical size between them and the women they date, female bodybuilders are more like their partners. Perhaps male bodybuilders need to increase their sense of control, both physically and psychologically, in their relationships with women. For women, the pattern of dating men who are physically larger than they are is not so entrenched in psychological needs, although it still exists. Perhaps this more accommodating pattern is due to the fact that femininity, unlike masculinity, is not so directly tied to one's physical size, and female bodybuilders, unlike their male counterparts, have already transgressed gender norms by building their musculature and competing. Many male bodybuilders, with their massive musculature and their interest in petite women, seem to be taking some of the norms associated with masculinity to the extreme.

What kind of support do female bodybuilders get from their friends? Almost all the women claimed that for the most part, their friends were supportive; at worst, they were only curious. Their comments: "Most of them support it," and "Most of my friends love it." None acknowledged having experienced negative reactions from friends in response to their bodybuilding careers. "I've never had any real negative responses from anybody that I know." Others such as Denise said that their friends are supportive because they too are involved in bodybuilding: "Since this is what I do or have in the past done quite a bit, a lot of my friends are in the same industry or same sport." According to Ellen, her home is a bodybuilding haven so most of the people think the way she looks is normal, and she gets few negative reactions. Indeed, most bodybuilders appear to surround themselves with people in the sport, thus preventing serious negative responses to their physiques, dieting, and training. But those who maintained friendships with people outside the sport said that these friends also supported their bodybuilding goals. Their most likely response was one of supportive curiosity and fascination with the body-building "look" and lifestyle. For instance, Denise discussed the reaction of her athletic friends outside of bodybuilding:

> I have a lot of outside interests that pull different people in and whether they like it or not, they're in awe of it. They are very interested in it, they don't know a lot about it, but they think they know a lot about it from the media. For instance, I went to a party last night that was basically a group of female tri-athletes and marathoners and I was the only bodybuilder there. So I was very curious in what they did, I mean I'm pretty impressed by the fact that you could actually go out and run 30 miles all in one day. And they were real impressed with the fact that I leg press 1100 pounds. It's a big difference in the weight issue, too. You're looking at someone that's the same height as them that's almost fifty pounds heavier but has less body fat.

Susan disclosed that "for most of my friends, it's always a source of amusement. It's always, 'You have to be showing me something.' One friend always wants to feel my muscles." Perhaps this kind of support is due in part to amusement or curiosity about why one might want to leg-press 1100 pounds or curl forty-five pounds or do the amount of disciplined work involved in being able to lift such heavy weights. Denise later revealed that she liked to lift such massive weights because it gave her a sense of mastery and control over her body that most other people did not have.

Bodybuilders overwhelmingly agreed that overall the gym environment was supportive because gym members knew about the pain and dedication it took to be a competitive bodybuilder. Furthermore, most patrons knew when to interact with bodybuilders getting ready for competitions and when to leave them alone. Usually the "regulars" in the gym are interested to know how well the competitive bodybuilders do in their meets. Some even go to competitions to support them. The bodybuilders are often approached by people in the gym who want advice on how best to work out their calves, for instance. In addition, some felt they may intimidate some of the people in the gym with their physiques, strength, and musculature—especially the males. For instance, one professional bodybuilder, Vicky, who uses the gym at her place of employment, said that "the guys are always asking me for advice." However, she also stated that "the guys" have told her that other men at the gym have been intimidated by her strength:

> I have heard that a few of them, they haven't ever said anything to me, but I've heard it, I've had a few guys, like if I ever train in the gym at work. I've had a few guys that leave the gym, and later on I had other guys come up and tell me that these guys said, "Man, I can't train with her in there, she makes me feel bad. Man, I was curling these forty-pound dumbbells and I was like grunted out and then she comes in and grabs the forty-five pound and just goes 1-2-3-4-5. I had to leave." Those old stories have gotten back to me . . . you would think that they'd say, "Hey, if she can do it, I can do it," but they get intimidated, and then they just kind of leave.

When bodybuilders get ready for a competition, it is extremely important to have a supportive gym environment. As competitors get closer to the date of the competition, they begin what the majority of them feel to be the most tortuous part of bodybuilding: dieting. A few weeks from the competition they are still working out, yet they are starting to weed out the carbohydrates, which makes them tired and irritable. Having sympathetic people around you during this time who know what you are going through is essential. For instance, Patty believed that, for the most part, people in the gym "are supportive, but we are in an atmosphere where everyone knows, not everyone, but people know what it's like to get ready for a contest because whether [you] compete or not, you're around the people who do. You know when to leave them alone. You know when they started dieting. You know when they're going to be in a bad mood. And it's not that anybody cares, it's just that they know that person doesn't want to be bothered."

As the meet approaches, such courtesies become increasingly more important.

> When you get down to about eights weeks away from a contest, you're not allowed to have . . . I mean all of the junk food out of your diet and you're down to egg whites and green beans, you're not in a real good mood. When you get down to four weeks or two weeks, your energy level is way down because you're dieting so hard and you're doing two hours of aerobics a day and it's all you can do to get through your workout, everybody is real supportive, but they leave you alone when they know you need to be left alone. That's why this atmosphere is so good, nobody bugs you. Nobody comes up and tries to talk, and the employees know not to put any pressures on me, not to make undue appointments for me. It's a good atmosphere.

One bodybuilder contended that it is this knowledge of what it takes to get into contest shape that makes the others in the gym supportive, even if it is from a distance. For example, Denise confirmed that the people in her gym "love it. They're standoffish [when I'm getting ready for a meet]. They know that what I have to do to get ready for a show requires quite a bit of discipline and being into myself and so they just sit back and watch in awe. They know what I'm going through, they know how I feel and they know what it's going to take so they support me 100%, even doctors and lawyers."

Noticeable in the above and in the following remarks is the healthy ego exhibited by most bodybuilders. In their discussions of others' reactions to the difficult days of training and dieting before contests, both Denise and Ellen explained that the "regulars" in the gym reacted to them with "awe." Conceivably it is this perception of gym "regulars" that allows the bodybuilders to get through this demanding period. In fact, it is the distant respect of those in the gym that the athletes appreciated the most, as is illustrated by Ellen's remarks:

> They left me alone and were very respectful. . . . Because I was the only person competing at that level, people really just stay out of my way. I'm sort of in a shell of concentration, or whatever, and I don't really notice a whole lot of what's going on around me so maybe I wasn't noticing things, but I got reactions. Over the years, I've gotten reactions like, "Oh God, she's really moody" or things like that. But that's, I think in general, that's mostly envy. And then people also

> react with . . . they are just more . . . it's more awe. That someone can get into something that deeply and concentrate on it that deeply.

Mary, in her discussion of the support she has received at her gym, described the regulars as a big family:

> They're very complimenting, maybe a little bit overboard. They tease me that I'm getting bigger than them, stronger than them. I really enjoy it. Of course, you have to realize I've been around these people for five years. This is my stomping ground, this is, I consider, my gym. We're like a big family here. That's one of the nicest things about working here . . . is everybody seems to know everybody. They all attend my contests. I had people coming up to the contests that I didn't even know were that interested. . . . I can't go anywhere in [this city] without running into somebody from the gym. And they will always, always walk up, inspect my plate, make sure I'm not eating anything I'm not supposed to, sniff my drink, make sure there's no alcohol in it. And walk up and tell me the time, you know, "Isn't it late? You should be getting some sleep, you got a heavy day of training." So I have a lot of mothers and daddies out in the gym as well as in [the city] and that's been a great incentive.

Another bodybuilder explained that the people in the gym "are very supportive. They always come and ask how's the diet going. You're like, 'How do you think it's going?' But they're really good about it. They're real supportive and they're like, 'You look great,' you know? They try and push me on."

The gym environment, therefore, seems to be quite supportive in two ways. First, the people in the gym know that the bodybuilder is getting ready for a show, so they know they should leave her alone and let her do her workouts. Second, they voice their support and concern for the bodybuilder's progress. That is not to say that all bodybuilders felt that the gym environment was always supportive. Recall Pam, who in the early 1980s entered a gym in the Southwest, wanting to compete in bodybuilding. To work out on the men's side of the gym, she had to endure two weeks of silent treatment from the other gym clients until she had "proven" herself.

When asked whether they felt that other competitive female bodybuilders are supportive of them, they were not in consensus. Some argued that competitive female bodybuilders are supportive, in fact more supportive than male bodybuilders. For instance, Brooke, a professional-level competitor, commented as follows:

> You know, the women are a little different than the men, I think. And this has been the case right from the beginning, in that there is more supportiveness and camaraderie among the women. And I don't know whether that's because it's the nature of women or if it's just because there really is a big difference between our prize packages and men's prize packages. They're worlds apart.

Others felt that female bodybuilders are too critical and self-absorbed to be supportive. Many bodybuilders claimed that due to the nature of bodybuilding, a sport that is decidedly individualistic in nature, there was no chance of sustained camaraderie among its dispersed athletes.[6] Those who believed that bodybuilders were not supportive of one another gave different opinions on the pervasiveness of the lack of support. One insisted that "no, female bodybuilders are not supportive. They are a bit catty, they're so centered on themselves. Jealousy, maybe, although I can say that I am not jealous." Denise, like others, attributed the lack of support to the competitiveness of the sport. One possible reason for friction or jealousy was best explained by Pam: "It seems like there is an uneasiness because with the judging there's really . . . one minute they're looking for this, the next minute they say they're looking for that." She continued:

> With the uneasiness and the uncertainty of the sport, I think it makes the women uneasy. When you go to a pro show, you see very few pro women hanging around together before the show. Usually you go with somebody, either a training partner or a friend that's supportive of you that you walk around with or hang around with. Pro women don't really mingle and hang around with each other because I guess the sport is so uncertain, that everybody is so uncertain about themselves that it produces an edginess.

The unpredictability and uncertainty of an already subjective and individualistic sport may contribute to the lack of cohesiveness among bodybuilders. Partially attributing the lack of camaraderie among bodybuilders to this type of erratic situation, Pam argued that maintaining bonds with one's competitors is virtually impossible. Later in the interview, she contrasted the way bodybuilders interact with one another to the way powerlifters interact:

> It is more clear in powerlifting, more cut and dried and also the uneasiness of the lifters among each other, it just isn't there. You go out to eat with the competitors, the girls you're competing against. You know you hang around with each other, because you either do the lift or you don't. Your strength is there or it's not there. The uneasiness isn't near as bad as bodybuilding.

This bodybuilder thus believed that the major reason for the edginess among bodybuilders is that the judging is subjective and the criteria on how to judge female bodybuilders are in a state of flux (I will discuss this in detail in chapter 6). Even though male bodybuilding is not as subjective as female, there is a lack of camaraderie or sense of "brotherhood" among the males. This may be because the monetary stakes are decidedly higher than in female bodybuilding.

Now that the stakes in female bodybuilding have increased dramatically over the years, many involved in the sport feel that female bodybuilders are less unified than they were when the sport first started. Addressing this phenomenon, Michelle, a national judge and former bodybuilder, recalled that

> when I first started, there was a lot more camaraderie among the competitors. When you went backstage, in the pump up room, we talked to each other, we ate each other's food, we'd help each other oil up, we generally . . . for lack of a better word there was this sisterhood. And now except at the very novice levels of female bodybuilding, you go backstage at a national event and it is deadly silent. There is so much tension in the air, you could cut it with a knife. Nobody talks to anybody. [Interviewer: What's the reason for that, do you think?] Because women have become so competitive, I think it's because the stakes have become higher. The standards as far as muscularity have become higher. Women have to get to the national level, have had to do so much to change their bodies, so much money has been put out by these women to be ready for that event. It costs a lot of money and a lot of your own personal risks to get the drugs that you need, to do the cycles, to gain the mass, to compete at the national level.

It is thus possible that the combination of the capriciousness in judging and the higher monetary stakes and standards of muscularity have magnified the tension among bodybuilders.

The Responses of Outsiders

Most bodybuilders, however, talked with great disdain about the negative reactions they had received from people outside the bodybuilding subculture. When they are surrounded by friends, family, competitors, and gym clients, the bodybuilders share a common interest—enhancing their muscularity. However, such support is not often mirrored by strangers with whom they interact in public. When walking the streets or going to museums or grocery stores, female bodybuilders, because of their unusual physiques, are subject to the scrutiny of others. Sometimes their muscular physiques may evoke a sense of awe, but most of the time strangers react with shock and disgust. Ellen, a national amateur competitor, remarked that men tended to be shocked by her build and responded by comparing their own musculature to hers. This invidious comparison often did not bode well for these men. Thus perhaps for the first time they were faced with the fact that some women can be more muscular than men. Many responded in shock, others became angered. She exclaimed, "The common male reaction is 'God, your arms are bigger than mine!' My reaction to that is 'Well, duh! I've been lifting weights for the past ten years, what did you think?'"

Most bodybuilders gave examples of strangers making unsolicited negative remarks about their physiques, some of which were imbued with threats of physical violence. In fact, every bodybuilder I interviewed has had to contend with negative reactions from strangers at one time or another during her career. For instance, Brooke, a professional who started competing in the early 1980s, declared that "in the beginning it was like the norm to get yelled at. People would say the most obscene things to you." Most of those who felt compelled to make negative comments about the women's muscular physiques were men in groups while the female bodybuilder was by herself. Such remarks are performances *by* men, *for* men, affirming conventional standards of masculinity and femininity. Some bodybuilders revealed that they were not bothered at all by the negative comments; in fact, they had come to expect and tolerate such remarks. For example, one athlete dismissed strangers' negative reactions as simply "part of being a female bodybuilder. But that's part of being noticeable in any respect." However, it is not always simply "being noticeable in any respect," as is suggested by Denise's comment: "I've heard guys say to their friends, 'It's a male thing she has.'" This remark suggests that women could not possibly want to enlarge their musculature if they were "normal" women and therefore must want to be a man. Such comments are not innocuous. Rather, they serve to warn women that they have inappropriately crossed gender boundaries—and some of these warnings are more threatening than others.

Vicky recalled a run-in with a few male strangers. They first talked about her as if she were not there; then they questioned her biological sex. Finally, they questioned her sexual orientation. She explained: "I've had a couple of guys walk up to me as if I were a mannequin or something that was just standing there. One guy was, 'Hey you guys, that girl, I think I saw her in a magazine.' One guy [said], 'Oh that's a guy, come on, let's go.' Well, am I not standing here or something? 'No, no, that's a girl, she's a bodybuilder,' and then he says, 'Leave that fag alone.'" In this interaction, the men refer to Vicky as a "girl," a "guy," and a "fag." Although scholars of gender and sexuality contend that the concepts of "gender" and "sexuality" are distinct and separate terms that do not describe the same phenomenon, they are frequently used interchangeably in everyday life. In other words, people tend to conflate these concepts as referring to the same or similar phenomena. This confusion occurred when these men saw a woman with large muscles, which they perceived to be inappropriate for a woman. They consequently referred to her as a "guy" and then as a "fag"—a derisive word usually employed to refer to perceived "effeminate" males, not alleged "masculinized" females. By their comments, they were reminding one another of their commitment to traditional definitions of masculinity and femininity. As is usually the case when hegemonic gender norms are transgressed, the self-appointed sanctioners did not inform Vicky in a pleasant or sedate way, rather they were aggressive and used pejorative terms to attempt to humiliate her and realign her within appropriate gender boundaries. Calling a woman "a man" or questioning her sexuality is an effective way to notify a woman she has crossed into unacceptable behavior and appearance. The venomous disgust as well as the threatening overtones that these men displayed are a disturbingly common experience for women bodybuilders.

The bodybuilders had their own way of making sense of these people's reactions to them. For instance, Mary surmised that those who were most likely to give them negative comments were out-of-shape men:

> The men that aren't used to exercising, they find it a little bit intimidating to talk to a woman who is so attuned to her body, to pushing outside that envelope more so than most men will even attempt. . . . I have run into an occasional one that his insecurities come out and they say, "Why do you want to look like that? What's wrong with being soft and fluffy and skinny or a little overweight? You know that's the way women are supposed to be." They have this stereotype of how women should look.

By claiming that the people who are likely to make negative comments to them are out-of-shape men, the bodybuilders couch the discourse in less gendered ways; it is not just that the bodybuilders are attempting to expand the gender boundaries, it is also about the tension between being fit and being out of shape. Regardless, the women interpret these comments as stemming from insecurities: insecurities about a woman being stronger than a man and insecurities about the men's own unfit physiques. This is not to say that the negative reactions are not related to gender. The idea that this muscular woman has supposedly intentionally disturbed the gender status quo is evident by the accusatory way in which the insecure man first questions her: "What's wrong with being soft?" and then reminds her, "That's the way women are supposed to be."

Patty disclosed that she had received negative reactions from strangers as well:

> Oh yes, "You want to look like a man," you know. Back when I was competing, I was fairly large, I mean I had a fifteen inch bicep. Since I've stopped competing, I don't care anything about being that big anymore. I just want to stay athletically in shape. Oh yeah, and it's always from overweight, out of shape people that are very negative. But that doesn't bother me. . . . I mean I laugh, they're just so ridiculous. . . . People are mean.

This bodybuilder mentioned the two major points that were continually alluded to by other bodybuilders. First, people think that women who are in nontraditional roles want to look like or be a man. Second, one way that Patty attempted to make sense of this type of reaction from others is to attribute their negative comments to their insecurities about being overweight and out of shape. Although some women explained that such comments do not bother them, it appears that, in fact, they do.

They remember the incidents with clarity and when they recall them, they do so with a lot of emotion.

In public, women were not as likely as men to harass female bodybuilders. For instance, one bodybuilder, Diane, recalled her experiences at the grocery store a week before she was to do a show:

> If I go to the grocery store after I work out I'll be in my tights, and people just look at me and they're like, oh you know, you can just tell that they're talking about you, and how do you tell whether it's good or bad? One time at the cash register, I was a week out from a show, and the lady at the cash register I was handing her my money, she saw all my veins, she goes "Gee, you look so muscular." And I thought, I said to her, "Well, thank you." She goes "Well, I've never seen women like this." I said, "Well, I'm a competitor, I don't always look like this. In the off-season you get a little softer." So that was her response, but a lot of people do like it.

This woman's response is more inquisitive than accusatory or threatening, which is qualitatively different from the examples given of the women's encounters with groups of men. Perhaps this woman's softer response is due to the location of the encounter or maybe because it was a one-on-one situation. Either way, it appears that the woman did not feel that her femininity was threatened by a more muscular woman. If she was disgusted by Diane's physique, she was sensitive enough not to say so.

Since many men appear to feel uneasy around muscular women and male bodybuilders are unlikely to date them, I asked the women if they thought that men in general found their physiques attractive. Responses to this question varied. For instance, one female bodybuilder said, "I think there's mixed emotions. I have had both for and against," and another agreed: "It really does differ. Where I live, I get all the compliments in the world. However, some guys make some really crude and shitty comments." These observations suggest that some bodybuilders feel it necessary to surround themselves with others in their sport: it is a way to shield themselves from potentially brusque encounters with those not familiar with the sport or the bodybuilding look. Other female competitors confided that they thought men did not find the physiques of female bodybuilders attractive, but they were still fascinated by their unusual bodies. For instance, Ellen felt as follows: "I think that there [is] a group of men who are sort of groupies, but beyond that I think that it's more intrigue than attractiveness. I mean, if you put a Playboy bunny and a bodybuilder next to each other, the man, most men, would be curious about the bodybuilder but really actually want to go with the Playboy bunny." Mary also felt that men are attracted to a female bodybuilder's physique yet are intimidated by it:

> Yeah, men do find our bodies sexy. A lot of them are intimidated. The first lure is this girl is really different than the rest. Let's find out more about her. So they'll approach me, they'll talk to me, how I got involved. . . . They want to know more about what it takes to be a bodybuilder. What makes a person like that tick. That's always the ice breaker and we get into talking and they find that I have a professional career as well as this being a hobby and I'm well-rounded in other areas, not just a gym rat. So guys like it and then they find out that there is every bit as much femininity involved as there is the strength and the masculine drive that it takes to lift weights and pump iron and be competitive and train in an environment where it's predominantly men.

She felt that men found such women enticing: "I was pleased to find out that the majority of men really find it interesting to have a woman that is so dedicated and disciplined to taking care of her body . . . they find it kind of sexy, and not really erotic, but in a way, yes. They find it so interesting like, 'what would it be like to be with a woman that really has that much self-esteem and confidence in herself?'" Here we get a sense of the ambivalence men feel toward female bodybuilders, as well as the ambivalence female bodybuilders feel about themselves. They realize they are different from most women; this is part of the appeal of being a bodybuilder—because they stand out in a crowd. However, they also understand that it is also what simultaneously attracts yet repels men.

Christy argued that even for men who like and appreciate muscular women, there still is a line beyond which the female bodybuilder is just too muscular for them:

> I think when a man is around female bodybuilders, he appreciates it and some of them like it, a woman who's in shape. For example, a man that I dated for awhile, he said there's a fine line for female

> bodybuilders, there's a fine line where if you cross it, you've gone too far, you're not attractive anymore. And he was telling me I'm right on that line. "You're not too big but you're getting there."

Her boyfriend's sentiment about a female bodybuilder crossing a "fine line" illustrates the external constraints these woman face about limiting their size. His comment is a warning to her not to get any bigger: he tolerates her physique for now, but she risks losing him if she gets any bigger. He is in essence attempting to limit Christy's choices about her own body image by implying that he will find her unattractive and undatable if she becomes more muscular.

Mary, who is aware of the possibility of such negative reactions from men, claims that she does not mind if men are intimidated by her. She knows that she is more confident and more independent than she used to be, and she likes and respects herself more now than when she was an out-of-shape housewife: "I think me being a business owner and being a bodybuilder . . . I don't date much, I can tell you that. Yeah I do [think men get intimidated by my physique], but I don't care because I have much more confidence than I did when I was a size sixteen housewife. I wouldn't deal with men back then. Now I can hold my own with anybody, in business or out on that [gym] floor." She knows that her physique and business sense have impeded her dating possibilities, but she is more than willing to pay that price. She likes who she is and will not change in order to date men; they will have to accept her on her own terms. After I asked if she thought it was a combination of confidence and muscles that intimidated men, she responded: "Yes, I do because most of the men who know me respect me. When I meet a man for the first time, I don't have this little wimpy finger handshake, I shake their hand like 'I know who I am,' you know? 'I'm glad you got to meet me.'" She is not afraid to exude confidence and strength even if it risks offending some men. However, as we have seen, not all female bodybuilders are willing to do this.

Clearly, there is tension between female bodybuilders and the men they meet. For many of the women it is important that men find their physiques attractive, and when they do not, they dismiss these men as insecure about their own masculinity and physiques. Others, however, are not so concerned about what men may think. They say they are happy with how they look. Some bodybuilders' defensiveness about others' reactions, however, indicates the depth of their ambivalence about their appearance.

Paying the Price: The Sacrifices Made

In any sport, athletes must make tremendous sacrifices. They must have extraordinary commitment and discipline in order to succeed. This is also true for bodybuilders. In fact, I would argue that their diets and workouts are among the most demanding and grueling of any sport. Getting ready for bodybuilding competitions pervades every aspect of the person's life. According to Christy, a national amateur competitor, "As far as female bodybuilding as a way of life, it's real hard because of the strict disciplined life that you lead for so many months, that all of a sudden when you're getting ready for a show it's really hard to maintain any kind of composure after that. Most people fall way off from that."

To win at the national amateur or professional levels, bodybuilders must have extreme tunnel vision—the sport demands it. For example, Ellen, a national competitor, talked about the consequences of being involved in such a demanding sport when one is predisposed to obsessive-compulsive behavior. She stated that her family was "concerned with my compulsiveness about bodybuilding. I was always so uptight about my diet. I had to. I couldn't go on vacations because I didn't want to miss my training. It was just sort of, what they considered, slightly antisocial behavior."

When the sport's demands are combined with such unhealthy predispositions as Ellen's, one can see how bodybuilders could be swept away by the demands and rigors of preparing for a contest. Those outside the sport who see a loved one going through such a grueling routine for months become worried. Those competing in the sport feel that such control over one's body and one's life is a sign of strength and power. This control does not come without incredible pain.

Most bodybuilders will tell you that the hardest part about getting ready for a bodybuilding meet is the dieting. Although many bodybuilders eat as often as eight times a day, it is the combination of foods they must consume and the carbohydrate intake they must reduce before a contest that is hardest. Why is dieting so important? On the one hand, the competitors are trying to lose body fat, but at the same time they are also trying to retain muscle density and size. In order to do this, they eat lots of protein (a lot of chicken, turkey, and egg whites), which facilitates muscle growth. But, they have to limit their intake of carbohydrates severely when they are getting ready for a meet, to reduce bodyfat levels. For the last two weeks before a show, they eliminate carbohydrates from the diet altogether, which makes them very light-headed. Some bodybuilders confessed that they take off from work the week before a meet because without carbohydrates in their diet, they cannot carry on conversations for more than a couple of minutes without losing their train of thought. Their diet regimen can be the difference between placing first or last in a contest—that is how important diet is to the success of competitive bodybuilders.

To add to their misery before a contest, bodybuilders will severely limit their intake of water a couple of days before the show. To expedite this process, many take diuretics. Add steroid use to this regimen and one gets a picture of how unhealthy competitive bodybuilding can be. In fact, Alan Klein has claimed that bodybuilders are closer to death than to life when they are on stage.[7]

Two recent events illustrate the poignancy of this sentiment. During the 1992 European Grand Prix Tour, one male bodybuilder died after one of the shows due to excessive use of diuretics, which caused severe dehydration and eventually heart arrhythmia. Also, at the 1993 Arnold Schwarzenegger Classic, one male bodybuilder was hospitalized in intensive care for severe dehydration (he had only consumed ten ounces of water each day for three days and he had taken diuretics). He had also severely cut his caloric intake, down to 1,400 calories per day, for a number of weeks.

Three-quarters of the bodybuilders in this study confided that the hardest part about getting ready for a competition is dieting. Pam explained that the difficulty lies not only in eliminating certain foods from one's diet, but also in the length of time one has to diet: "You start getting ready actually about three months out. The first month, I don't eat much junk food, but whatever little junk food I had in my diet completely goes. So that first month isn't too bad. But by the time you get to the second month you're down to salads and mostly vegetables and just very little chicken and fish." Mary revealed the tedious nature of having to watch one's diet for competition:

> I think I had a good foundation on how to prepare food-wise for a contest, but I was not methodical enough. I mean you really have to be so detailed and write it down for six weeks prior, everything that

> goes in your mouth. Calculate it, not only calories, but grams of fat, protein. You have to stay consistent with it, that way if it works you know what you did right, wrong, you can use it again and if you can look in the mirror three weeks out and say I'm still carrying too much fat, let's drop the calories down. Let's pick up the grams here. If I'm weak, I take up more carbohydrates. But if you don't know what you're doing, you don't know where to make the changes. It all depends on how bad you really want to win. That is one of the key issues to winning a bodybuilding contest, you've got to give it 100%. You've got to be detailed with it. you have to stick with it, you can't go a day and say "Oh well, you didn't write it down, I'll make up for it in the next day." You don't have a margin for that.

Patty agreed that dieting is the hardest part of the sport and because it is, "you absolutely have to have tunnel vision. When I start getting ready for a contest, nothing will make me cheat, nothing. Not everybody can do that. But that's me. It's the difference between being a winner and being a loser." In fact, dieting is so important in competitive bodybuilding that some bodybuilders have hired professional dietitians to assist them. For instance, Mary, an amateur female bodybuilder, revealed: "Now this year is the first time I've had a professional put my diet together. . . . So he did a really good job four months out. He put me on a strict detailed diet that I have never ever had to do anything close to it in my life. I thought I was going to die. I'd call him up two weeks in advance, I said, 'You're killing me, right? somebody told you to kill me.'" The diet regimen is arduous and seemingly masochistic. However, Mary thinks the rigorous regimen is well worth it because she believes it has made all the difference in the world in how she looks, and because of her new diet, she has consistently placed higher at subsequent meets.

Denise also confessed that dieting is, by far, the most difficult aspect of the sport, but for different reasons. She remarked that dieting is difficult because a lot of people socialize over dinner, lunch, and drinks, and since her diet is so limited, it makes going out to eat quite difficult. She exclaimed that

> the diet is bad, it's really bad!! I mean our whole social system is really around social drinking or you go for dinner or "let's do lunch," or we go out on the boat, you're obviously going to have chips and beer. You're not going to go out and want to spend good money for a dish of broccoli and a half cup of rice and a chicken breast. You're

> definitely not going to get up in the morning and go, "Oh boy, I'm going to have broccoli again today, you know I've had it for eight weeks and I just can't get enough of that stuff." So yeah, I'd say diet, that's the hardest part.

Their dieting regimen further isolates some bodybuilders from those outside the sport. To avoid awkward social moments over a meal, many choose to surround themselves with others who have similar dietary needs and workout routines.

Although the diet is important for success in meets, when people limit their carbohydrate and caloric intake so severely, there are noticeable repercussions. As Patty revealed,

> The last three days before a contest, the week before the contest is the hardest because you have to, just for example, like Sunday, Monday, Tuesday, and part of Wednesday, you eat no carbohydrates. All protein. Well, carbohydrates are your brain food and by Tuesday, I cannot carry on a conversation with anyone. I mean you can sit and talk to me and I hear you but nothing that you say registers with me. I can be training my clients and forget what body part we're working. So that's the most critical three days. Most people, if they can, save their vacation for that week because that's the hardest week, because if your job depends on you thinking a lot, you can't do it. I can't read a book because I have to read the same paragraph fifteen times, and people think, why, this is stupid, you know. But it's true unless you've got some carbohydrates, you can't think.

She confirmed how difficult the actual diet is for bodybuilders, and that having a supportive and understanding environment, in her case the gym environment, was very important especially the last few days before the show.

Dieting is not a bodybuilder's only painful experience while getting ready for a competition. In addition, they must also severely limit their intake of water a couple of days before the show. Bodybuilders want to rid their body of as much water as possible in order to achieve the "hard" look for which they strive. Therefore, many take diuretics, some do aerobics in sweat suits, and others simply limit their water intake to a very minimal level. This combination makes the week before the show the most excruciating: bodybuilders are in the last stages of their diet, they have severely limited their water intake, and they are still working out, which consists of weight work plus a couple of hours of aerobics per day. Some bodybuilders maintained that limiting their water intake was not as challenging as the diet because, as one bodybuilder explained, "Bodybuilders limit their water intake, but that's only three days. You drink very little . . . sips here and there." Thus, because of its short duration, limiting one's water intake is not so difficult for some bodybuilders.

The journey from merely lifting weights to becoming a competitive national or professional level bodybuilder is a long and arduous one. It takes most bodybuilders many years to break into the professional ranks. Even when they have successfully done so, they are by no means guaranteed success at the professional level. When they have reached this small elite circle, they have to compete at still higher levels because the competition keeps getting better. Female bodybuilders put enormous amounts of time, effort, money, and sweat into preparing for a meet, and because bodybuilding is not only a subjective sport, but a political one as well, the social gatekeepers—officials, judges, promoters, and sponsors—have enormous influence in how successful the bodybuilders are in the sport. If a bodybuilder is considered a troublemaker, is too muscular, or has too big an ego, the gatekeepers may place her down at meets or may not give her sponsorships or other types of publicity. Let us now look in greater detail at the formation of the political and economic milieus of the sport of female bodybuilding.

TWO

The Few, the Powerful, the Social Gatekeepers

BODYBUILDING IS A multimillion dollar industry. The groups that effectively package and sell the sport not only make tremendous monetary profits, but also play a prominent role in determining the ideal images of its bodybuilders on stage and in magazines. Therefore, to comprehend better the various political, economic, and ideological factors that influence which images of female bodybuilders are presented in both of these arenas, one must first understand the historical development of the sport's political and organizational structures. I will therefore begin by examining the formation of various bodybuilding federations, concentrating on the top two: the International Federation of Bodybuilders (IFBB), and the National Physique Committee (NPC). Because of their significant role in the sport, I will also discuss the roles of the three major monetary supporters of bodybuilding: athlete sponsors, promoters, and event sponsors. My aim here is to illuminate the economic and political dynamics that, in large part, determine how female bodybuilders are instructed to look. Much of my focus is on the cofounders of the IFBB, Ben and Joe Weider, because, in bodybuilding, they and the IFBB wield more influence than any other people or organizations. Finally, I will explore how bodybuilders and judges perceive the Weiders' power in terms of its influence in their lives, their physical goals, and their success in the sport.

The Rise of "The Only Game in Town"

The major bodybuilding organizations were the first organized entities to offer amateur-level bodybuilding contests in the mid-1900s. Beginning in the 1930s, there was the Amateur Athletic Union (AAU), which was the first amateur bodybuilding organization, and the World Bodybuilding Guild (WBBG). Ben and Joe Weider started the International Federation of Bodybuilders (IFBB) in Canada in 1946. In 1950, Dan Lurie's private bodybuilding organization, the National Amateur British Bodybuilding Association (NABBA), was formed in England. From this time until the 1960s, the dominant organization was the AAU, followed by NABBA. Not until the mid-1960s, when the IFBB brought bodybuilding to a professional level by offering prize money to the winners of its male bodybuilding contests, did the IFBB become a legitimate threat to the power of the then dominant amateur bodybuilding organization, the AAU. In 1991, Vince McMahon, president of the World Wrestling Federation and TitanSports Inc., started the World Bodybuilding Federation (WBF); however, this organization lasted only a few months, ending in July 1992.[1]

When Ben and Joe Weider conceived of the IFBB, its official purpose was to ensure that bodybuilding was developed as "a respected, organized sport on the amateur level" because, at the time, it was viewed by many as taking a back seat to the sport of Olympic weightlifting.[2] When bodybuilding emerged as a form of athletic competition, it was usually staged only after the weightlifting portion of the show was finished.[3] To promote bodybuilding as a sport in its own right, Joe Weider began his own publication, *Muscle Builder: The Magazine of the Champions,* which was one of the first publications to focus solely on bodybuilding and was also the first "official journal" of the IFBB.[4]

The first male bodybuilding contest with prize money was held on September 18, 1965, at the Brooklyn Academy of Music and was called the Mr. Olympia contest.[5] The first man to win the contest was Larry Scott. This contest was a watershed for the sport of bodybuilding because until that time "the sport was losing many of its top competitors, who were forced to take jobs as bouncers, bodyguards and professional wrestlers because they couldn't make a living in the sport of their choice. By increasing contest incomes, the Weiders hoped to keep both veterans and rising champions in the sport."[6] The Weiders were able to see their hopes come to fruition not only in male bodybuilding, but eventually in female bodybuilding as well. In female bodybuilding, however, the Weiders were not the first to offer prize money.

In 1977 began the actual emergence of organized female bodybuilding. It developed as an outgrowth not only of the late nineteenth-century

European vaudeville and circus strongwomen acts,[7] Bernarr Macfadden's turn of the century women's physique competitions,[8] and the weightlifting of Abbye "Pudgy" Stockton,[9] but also as an outgrowth of the men's sport. The contest formats of men's events during the 1950s, 1960s, and mid-1970s had often been supplemented with either a women's beauty contest or bikini show.[10] These bikini show "had little to do with women's bodybuilding as we know it today, but they did serve as a beginning or, perhaps more properly, as a doormat for the development of future bodybuilding shows."[11]

The IFBB sponsored the first Miss Americana contest, which wasn't much more than a beauty contest, during the intermission of the Mr. America contest, which was presided over by Bud Parker on September 14, 1963.[12] Until the late 1970s, these fitness/beauty contests were the only place in which women could participate, since there were no formally organized competitive bodybuilding meets. In these shows, the female contestants wore high heels, makeup, and jewelry, and they were judged for both beauty and fitness. The winners earned titles such as Miss Body Beautiful, Miss Physical Fitness,[13] and Miss Americana.[14] Here "the bikini contest winners dutifully performed their assignments, presenting trophies to the winners of the men's contest, smiling widely as they posed, ornament-like, with the recipients."[15] It was not until the late 1970s, after the advent of the feminist movement and female powerlifting events that women were seen as capable of competing in their own bodybuilding meets.[16]

The first official female bodybuilding contest was held in Canton, Ohio, in November 1977 and was called the Ohio Regional Women's Physique Championship. It was judged strictly as a bodybuilding contest and was the first event of its kind for women.[17] Gina LaSpina, the champion, is considered the first recognized winner of a woman's bodybuilding contest.[18] The organizer of the event, Henry McGhee, told the competitors that they would be judged "like the men," with emphasis on muscular development, symmetry, and physique presentation.[19] In 1978, McGhee organized the first National Women's Physique Championship. "These early contests set the stage for bigger things to come. It was clear that there was sufficient interest among the women bodybuilders and that they were willing to travel great distances for the chance to compete."[20] In addition to organizing these bodybuilding contests, McGhee also started the short-lived United States Women's Physique Association (USWPA), which he formed to help organize women interested in competing in bodybuilding.[21] McGhee argued that the purpose of the organization, which became defunct in 1980, "was to overcome the limited, beauty queen stereotype of what the American woman should look like."[22] The rallying sentiment of the USWPA was: "Champions style their bodies with their muscles."[23]

On August 18, 1978, promoter George Snyder organized a "female bodybuilding" contest known as The Best in the World Contest, which was the first IFBB-sanctioned event for women that awarded prize money to the top finishers, with the winner receiving $2,500.[24] This contest is considered to be the forerunner of the Miss Olympia competitions he would later develop and promote for a few years until Joe Weider took over the rights to the title.[25] "His was billed as a bodybuilding contest, but everyone knew it was a beauty contest."[26] In fact, "what was most impressive about this contest was the field that failed to place, including Kay Baxter, Deborah Diana, Lynee Pirie, and . . . Sheila Herman. All of these women were more muscular than many of the judges were willing to accept. It was sanctioned as a bodybuilding show, but the women were required to appear on-stage in high heels."[27]

In a letter to Doris Barrilleaux, George Snyder described the criteria for the show. He explained:

> With the information we have sent you so far, you should realize what type of contest we are holding on August 18th. However, it is definitely not a "physique" type contest, where women do men's muscular posing. As you can see by the enclosed information on rules and judging, the contest is based on overall appearance, figure, proportion, tone, etc. If you would like to call it a beauty contest, you could, however it is a beauty contest for women bodybuilders. In looking at the newsletter you sent, which is very nice, some of the girls that are pictured would do very well in our contest and it would be worth their time. Whereas, a couple seem to be completely into muscularity and, for them, it may not be worthwhile. However, with proper presentation and the elimination of poses that highlight muscularity, they could do very well, too.

According to Barrilleaux,

> There were only two of us who did bodybuilding poses and that was a thirty-eight year old woman and myself. The rest were models that twirled and did the modeling poses, and the hoochy-koochy bur-

> lesque types who did their shaking at the audience. . . . At that contest Frank Zane took me aside and he says, "Doris, the world's not ready for women bodybuilding." And that did it. I had to show them that it was. . . . So I went home and there was a contest the next week or so, a men's contest. I said, "Would you like a guest poser?" They said, "Oh, yeah, yeah." No one had ever seen a lady guest poser. So I did it at the Southeastern, or whatever it was, there in Tampa, and after that the girls came up to me and said, "Why can't we have something for women? Why don't we start something for women?" And so then the Superior Physique Association was formed.[28]

Barrilleaux founded the Superior Physique Association in 1978, the first women's bodybuilding organization run for women and by women.[29] She also began publishing the *SPA News,* a newsletter dedicated exclusively to female bodybuilding.[30] SPA disseminated information to women about contests and proper training and dieting. On April 29, 1979, SPA held Florida's first official women's contest in which thirteen women competed. Local television station crews and journalists for national magazines and newspapers were on hand to record the event.[31] Also in 1979, the IFBB formed the IFBB Women's Committee; Christine Zane was appointed the first chairperson to serve as head of the newly formed committee.[32] One of the significant differences between the SPA and the IFBB was that while the IFBB was organized and run by men, the SPA was run by women and for women.

The Building of the Hegemonic Elite

The IFBB and NPC in general and those who run them represent the power, the hegemonic elite in bodybuilding. To date, the success of the IFBB in both women's and men's competitions has been unparalleled by any other bodybuilding organization. The IFBB literature claims that it is one of the largest sporting federations in the world. In fact, "Although it is not the only sanctioning body in the sport, thereby avoiding direct charges of monopolizing the sport, the IFBB is far and away the most compelling. . . . Until recently it [the IFBB] was the only organization that could subsidize bodybuilders or make them champions,"[33] which is one of the main reasons why the IFBB quickly burgeoned, leaving its rivals in the dust. In many ways, from the number of contests held to the amount of prize money awarded, the IFBB is untouchable by any other bodybuilding organization.[34] "Dwarfing the competition, the IFBB sanctions a range of contests and represents the most prestigious Mr./Ms. Olympia, thereby functioning as the main path along which almost all upwardly mobile competitors move."[35] If you want to make money as a professional bodybuilder, the IFBB is the organization to join. Even when rival organizations existed, many judges and bodybuilders insisted that "the IFBB is the only game in town."

Because the IFBB is a closed federation, everyone within the organization must accept and abide by its rules and regulations or face being barred. Thus, consent to the hegemonic standards by all members is written into the bylaws of the organization. The International Congress and Executive Council are IFBB's governing bodies. The IFBB has a 160-nation congress, with a delegate from each country allowed to vote on issues at the annual IFBB International Congress Meeting. The IFBB's Executive Council, which amounts to the IFBB Board of Directors, is comprised of the president, the general secretary, numerous vice-presidents, and various heads of committees. The structure of the organization gives ultimate power to these officials to resolve altercations and issues. I refer to this group as the upper-level social gatekeepers; these members are the hegemonic powerhouses: they enact and pass bodybuilding rules and regulations, and they also vote on what to do with athletes and judges who have violated the rules. Although there is a democratically elected congress to guide the organization, it usually bows to the wishes of the Executive Council. The president also has the power to override congressional concerns. Thus, Ben Weider can wield, and at times has exercised, ultimate power in determining hegemonic norms that are to be followed by all bodybuilders within the federation. This occurred in the mid-1980s when the delegates wanted to further enforce the IFBB's drug-testing standards for female bodybuilders at international competitions and the president chose not to do so.[36]

One troubling feature of the organization is the tremendous conflict of interest on the part of some members of its Executive Council. A number of them not only hold high positions in the Executive Council, but they are also promoters and vendors of bodybuilding products. This direct personal interest in the sport's financial success may conflict with the principles presumed to guide the sport. One high-ranking IFBB official is the promoter of eleven out of the eighteen male pro shows and one out of the three female pro shows. This arrangement leaves an inordinate amount of political, ideological, and economic power in the hands of only a few men, making them seemingly omnipotent in this muscular arena.

Not only does there appear to be a conflict among business and sports interests, there also seems to be a vertical power vacuum: an interlocking group of officials who hold high-ranking positions in both the IFBB and the NPC. For instance, the NPC chairwoman is also the IFBB secretary of the Judges Committee. Some judges also sit on both the IFBB and the NPC panels. The best example, however, is Jim Manion, who is the president of the NPC and the IFBB North American vice-president. Furthermore, he is frequently an IFBB judge at the most prestigious male and female bodybuilding events.[37] In these roles, Manion plays important social gatekeeping functions for female and male bodybuilders at both the amateur and professional levels. However, his influence does not stop at this point. He is also editor of the official monthly NPC magazine, *NPC News,* which prints results from previous contests, information about future competitions, and profiles of up-and-coming bodybuilders. In addition, he informs readers about bodybuilders whom he thinks promoters should consider inviting to their competitions as guest posers. His son, J. M. Manion, is the official photographer and senior writer for the *NPC News.*

In addition to his NPC and IFBB duties, Jim Manion also owns J. M. Productions, his photography company that specializes in bodybuilding and fitness photographs, and his son owns an offshoot of that company called JMP Management. According to the JMP Management Homepage, "When the NPC and IFBB decided to make its foray into women's fitness competitions, J.M. launched the management firm to help manage and promote the NPC and IFBB most Alluring Fitness Women. As this is a personal management company, the goal is to work closely with each fitness competitor to guide and develop her career."[38] The competitors that JMP manages must agree to compete in at least two NPC or IFBB fitness competitions each year. These fitness women "are available for appearances, modeling, guest posing, poster or photo signings and product endorsements."[39]

Today, the most direct route a bodybuilder can take to get to the ranks of a professional bodybuilder in the IFBB is through its American amateur affiliate, the National Physique Committee of the U.S.A. (NPC), was created by the IFBB in 1981.[40] As Jim Manion, NPC president, recently boasted: "For amateur bodybuilding in the USA, the NPC is the big kahuna. If you want to make it as a pro and take advantage of the publicity and money making opportunities, you must come up through the NPC."[41] In fact, Manion contended that nine out of ten successful bodybuilders come from the NPC and work their way to the IFBB:

> The NPC has always had the support and recognition of the IFBB, which oversees international competition and the professional side of the sport, and this has been crucial to our success. The IFBB recognizes only one amateur physique federation per country, and in the United States, the NPC is the amateur arm of the IFBB. All bodybuilders . . . must win a qualifying NPC show before they can become IFBB professionals.[42]

According to a recent article, the IFBB "sees the NPC as the strongest amateur physique organization in the world. That's no small feat considering that more than 160 nations belong to the IFBB."[43] The NPC has approximately sixty NPC district chairpersons throughout the United States, the vast majority of whom are men. In fact, according to the NPC Worldwide Web homepage, only one of fifty-eight district chairpersons is a woman, less than 2 percent. Among the eight zone supervisors (regional supervisors that incorporate numerous districts each), there are no women. The NPC and its professional affiliate, the IFBB, are both dominated by men.

Currently, the NPC has over 20,000 members and hosts between 800 to 1000 competitions annually,[44] including a number of state, regional, and national amateur bodybuilding competitions every year. For a bodybuilder to move from the local amateur level to the national amateur level competition in the NPC, she must win a qualifying contest. At the national level, the NPC sponsors such bodybuilding contests as Junior USA, USA, USA Teen, USA Collegiate, USA Masters (over age 35 for women and over age 40 for men), Junior National Championship, National Championship, and the U.S. Championships. The Nationals are the culmination of all of the local, state, and regional competitions that occur throughout the year.[45] The overall winner of the NPC USA championships and the three weight class winners of the national championship are eligible for professional status in the IFBB.[46]

Sponsors and Promoters: Bodybuilding's Economic and Ideological "Powers That Be"

Whether at the amateur or professional level, it takes money to run the sport of bodybuilding. The big money in the sport rests with three distinct but interrelated entities: athlete sponsors, promoters, and event sponsors. With their financial clout, these groups also play prominent roles in shaping the direction of the sport, the level of success of bodybuilders' careers, and the images that are conveyed about the sport and individual bodybuilders. Promoters and sponsors are the money behind the bodybuilders, the federations, the magazines, and the products. If it were not for them, the sport of bodybuilding might very well decline. These groups are the lifeline of the sport because they are the ones who offer prize money, product endorsements, and magazine coverage to the elite athletes. Promoters put on the bodybuilding shows. People promote bodybuilding contests because they are supporters of the sport and have access to the money and connections it takes to hold a competition. Furthermore, there are financial reasons for promoting a bodybuilding show because, if done correctly, it can be a lucrative venture.

It is the promoters' job to find sponsors for a competitor's event that will help to defray the costs of putting on the shows. They are responsible for contacting the NPC or IFBB, who will then sanction the shows if the rules are followed, and finally they are also responsible for financing for drug testing. However, drug testing is not always a rational choice for a promoter, for two main reasons, both of which are related to a reduction in profits. First, it is expensive to perform the drug tests;[47] and second, if it is known by the athletes ahead of time that a particular show will be testing for drugs, some of the biggest, most muscular bodybuilders may not compete because they may test positive. Thus, it is not in the promoter's best monetary interest to test athletes if there is a chance that the best and most well-known athletes will not compete. If these athletes do not compete, it will hurt ticket sales because fans will not pay fifty to two hundred dollars for tickets to see other muscular people whom they can well see in the gym! If the number of tickets sold for an event plummets, so do the profits.

Event sponsors usually consist of an array of health food and vitamin companies, sportswear companies, gyms, workout equipment companies, and bodybuilding magazines, which can sponsor both contests and individual bodybuilders. In the former situation, in return for sponsorship of the event, the promoter will allow the sponsor to exhibit and vend its product before, during, and after the bodybuilding show (usually in an area just outside the auditorium where the competition is being held), as well as have a sign in the contest area that displays the company's name for publicity. In addition, sponsors may do the following:

> Get to use their corporate name in all advertisements [for the event]; give samples of their product to the athletes competing; distribute literature to everybody in the audience; be invited to present some of the medals and trophies therefore obtaining exposure on television and in photos; and under special conditions a sponsor may use the symbol and logo of the IFBB to advertise their products.[48]

Thus, in return for the money a sponsor spends on a bodybuilding show, it receives publicity and an opportunity to display its products.

Athlete sponsors usually include vitamin and health food companies, bodybuilding magazines, and bodybuilding sportswear companies. The difference between the two types of sponsors is shown in the role they play in bodybuilding. Sponsors of contests, as we have seen, help to defray the promoter's costs for putting on the bodybuilding show, and sponsors of athletes pay bodybuilders to endorse and represent their products. For male bodybuilders, it is the big-name, muscular, attractive, and popular athletes who are most likely to get sponsorships because they are the ones who are seen as most marketable; for female bodybuilders, the ones most likely to be sponsored are feminine, big name, somewhat muscular, attractive, and well-liked bodybuilders. As with any sponsorship of this kind, sponsors benefit financially from having big-name bodybuilders under contract.

Sponsorship is extremely important for both female and male bodybuilders because it gives them financial security. However, sponsorships are probably more important for female bodybuilders because there are significantly fewer opportunities for them to make money; there are fewer professional contests for women, and the contests that do exist give less prize money.[49] In fact, one professional female bodybuilder, Brooke, angered by this income differential, complained: "There really is a big difference between our prize packages and men's prize packages. They are worlds apart. Nobody has really taken the bull by the horns and said, 'Look, we do the same amount of work and we want the same amount of pay.'"

Financial security enables bodybuilders, both female and male, to concentrate more fully on perfecting their bodies for upcoming competitions because they are less likely to have to get a job outside the sport. For instance, Diane argued that the most difficult aspect of being a bodybuilder was finding time to work out:

> Well, I work a full-time job, so the hardest thing about getting ready for a show to me is time. The diets are not a problem, the training is not a problem, it's actually . . . I teach all day. I leave school by 4:30 or 5:00. I go to the gym at 6:00. I go home and eat a meal, go train, get home. Everything else is put on the side and that's what's hard. I put my family, my friends—for twenty weeks, you forget about these people, and that's what's sad. That's what I hate about this sport. Now, if I didn't teach, it would be much better. I would have time to train twice a day.

Diane alluded to the "tunnel vision" she must have in order to do well, which often leaves friends, lovers, and family members out in the cold until the competition is over.

If bodybuilders do not have sponsors, the expenses of competing—paying for choreographers, dietitians, hairdressers, supplements, entry fees, and transportation to and from the event—can be limiting. Therefore, it is often essential that bodybuilders meet the "right" people so they can defray such costs. Of the bodybuilders who discussed finances, approximately one-half were at least partially sponsored and the other half were not. The sponsors included gyms, magazines, and other companies involved with bodybuilding. Those not sponsored said it was very costly to stay in the sport. Often, in addition to paying for expenses, a sponsor will allow bodybuilders the time to mingle with the "right" people.

The importance of a sponsorship for a bodybuilding cannot be underestimated. In fact, many professional bodybuilders get more money from their sponsorships and endorsements than they do from their contest earnings. For instance, as Wayne Demilia, vice-president of the IFBB, stated in a recent *New York Times* article, "The real money comes with endorsements and appearances."[50] As an example, the reigning Ms. Olympia, Lenda Murray, made $35,000 by winning the 1992 Ms. Olympia, but was expected to bring home an additional $300,000 in product endorsements, personal appearances, and posing for bodybuilding magazines.[51] Although most professional female bodybuilders do not earn as much as Lenda Murray, they are still likely to earn more money from endorsements than from contest earnings.

In addition to financial benefits, sponsored bodybuilders are also likely to receive more publicity than their nonsponsored colleagues. Sponsors' influences allow them to receive more publicity through such venues as magazine advertisements and articles, particularly if the sponsor owns one of the magazines. They will also get publicity when they appear at bodybuilding competitions to guest-pose or to endorse products at their sponsor's booth. Sponsors also give their contract bodybuilders free products such as clothes, shoes, workout equipment, and nutritional supplements. Finally, because many of the sponsoring companies are continually conducting research on how to enhance the human body's performance levels, sponsored bodybuilders are likely to have access to the best trainers as well as the latest information on bodybuilding equipment, techniques, and nutritional supplements.

The material benefits that sponsors provide to their bodybuilders give the sponsors *tremendous* power in creating and maintaining hegemonic appearance standards for female bodybuilders. Because of their power, sponsors are the ideological and economic liaisons between female bodybuilding and the public. In other words, they determine the female bodybuilding "look" that is presented to the public. It is not difficult to see why they promote the most marketable image of female bodybuilding—it entices the public to buy their products and in turn increases their profits.

Finally, the image that sponsors portray, as we have seen, comes from the perspective of a male gaze because an inordinate number of sponsors are men. Of all the bodybuilder and contest sponsors, Joe Weider is by far the most powerful. His younger brother, Ben, is the president of the IFBB. Together, they are the powerhouses of bodybuilding.

The Weider Empire

Joe and Ben Weider are not only synonymous with bodybuilding, but they are the undisputed patriarchs of the sport. When the Weiders talk, the sport of bodybuilding drops its collective dumbbell and listens attentively. Representing the political and economic muscle of the sport from its incipient stages to the present, the Weiders currently wield so much power that with a simple flex of their muscles, they can make or break a bodybuilder's, promoter's, or judge's career; and, according to many of those with whom I spoke, the Weiders have done both in all three groups on many occasions. Their economic and political clout also translates into extraordinary ideological or definitional power—the Weiders have an almost monopolistic influence on the types of images presented of female bodybuilders both in magazines and at contests.

Their power in any one position would be enough to rank them as the most commanding presence in the sport. The fact that they hold multiple and mutually reinforcing positions catapults them into almost unfathomable dimensions in modern organized sport. Indeed, it would be virtually impossible to discover another sport in which a single family so completely and utterly controls and dominates the past, present, and future of the sport and its members. For instance, Ben Weider has been president of the IFBB since he and his older brother Joe founded the sport in 1946. In fact, he is "president for life" of the IFBB, and in this capacity is the highest ranking official in the IFBB and the principal social gatekeeper to the professional ranks for all bodybuilders. Joe Weider, who holds the financial reins, has tremendous power in his role as a multimillion-dollar-a-year business patriarch. He is the chair and CEO of the Board for the Weider Health and Fitness Corporation, which is the largest sponsor of bodybuilders,[52] bodybuilding products and events,[53] and the owner of many of the most popular fitness and bodybuilding magazines in circulation. Together, Joe and Ben Weider have the greatest financial and political power in the sport. Speculating on what would have to occur in the sport of baseball to see a comparable power vacuum, one journalist exclaimed that "Joe Weider and his brother Ben, president of the International Federation of Bodybuilders, the worldwide professional bodybuilding organization, almost completely control the bodybuilding game. It's as if Walter O'Malley owned not only the Dodgers, but also Chavez Ravine, NBC Sports, *Sports Illustrated*—and most of the players."[54] Using a similar analogy but applying the Weider power to the NFL, Alan Klein has argued:

> In bodybuilding the relationship between sport, politics, and business is paramount and overt. So much so that at times it's difficult to be sure whether the sport preceded its commerce or vice versa. Joe and Ben Weider, the acknowledged leaders of this sport, are, in organizational terms, comparable to NFL Commissioner Peter Rozelle *if* he were to own 80% of the franchises, along with *Sports Illustrated* and

> *Sporting News.* This institutional concentration of power includes economic, political, and ideological realism. The fusing these offices into one or a few figures recalls the paramount chieftaincies of certain pre-state societies. In contemporary society such power is divided among institutions or, if concentrated, it is within classes, not persons.[55]

A new generation of Weiders is already amassing power within the IFBB empire. Eric Weider is the general secretary of the IFBB, and in this capacity, he supervises the organization of most major international bodybuilding competitions.

Much like Joe and Ben are brothers, one can easily argue that their siblingship extends to the relationship between the IFBB (the bodybuilding organization) and Weider Health and Fitness (the Weider's own business). Relying on their brotherhood to help each other in their respective positions, Joe and Ben at times obfuscate the demarcation between the two bodybuilding entities. One need only look as far as *Flex* magazine—published by Joe, the chair of Weider Health and Fitness—the official journal of the IFBB, to see the overlap in the relationship between Ben Weider and the IFBB and Joe Weider and Weider Health and Fitness. This relationship has proven to be highly lucrative. By the late 1980s, the Weider empire was estimated to be worth $250 million.[56]

Although it has not always been the case, currently almost every bodybuilding endeavor with which the Weiders are involved has the potential of a money-making venture. During their half-century of involvement in organized bodybuilding, the Weiders have deftly amassed their fortune by hawking their products.[57] When fans want to find out who is currently hot in the sport, who has won the recent bodybuilding contests, and what the new weightlifting techniques or dieting regimens are, they buy a bodybuilding magazine. Two of the most highly circulated are owned by the Weiders: *Muscle and Fitness* and *Flex.* Not only do the Weiders profit from the sale of the magazines, but they also use them to advertise their products and to spread their own ideology of the sport:[58] "Both *Muscle and Fitness* and *Flex* are clearinghouses for Weider products, . . . over 200 Weider items are sold by mail order through his magazines; these are roughly grouped as nutritional supplements, exercise equipment, videos, books, and magazines."[59] Furthermore, Tim Hoxha reveals that, more recently, the Weider Health and Fitness Corporation, whose subsidiaries publish *Muscle and Fitness, Shape, Men's*

Fitness, and *Flex* and produce vitamins and food supplements, "creates products available in some 60 countries and grosses nearly one billion dollars a year."[60] A regional judge also recognized the relationship between the Weiders' money and their power when he concluded that "the Weider brothers are powerful because of the money that they have backing them plus the money that they have personally. It's hard to realize their power. . . . By having a magazine established and, you know, everything they do to push Weider's name, it's really caused the recognition factor to be way up."

The Weiders are the largest and most influential sponsors of bodybuilders. They endorse or sponsor many of the most successful and marketable athletes, including Bev Francis, Cory Everson, and Lenda Murray. According to Hoxha, "Joe Weider himself contracts, on average, twenty athletes who perform a variety of jobs within the company, from generating articles to endorsing products and representing the Weider name. The overall expenditure on these contracts exceeds well over one million dollars."[61] These bodybuilders are commonly referred to in bodybuilding circles as "Weider athletes," and are often premiered in the Weider magazines, both in articles and advertisements. They are paid to promote the Weider products and to guest pose at contests. An example of the ease with which a show promoter can obtain a Weider athlete to guest pose is given by the regional judge:

> The fact that Joe Weider now has his own group of bodybuilders that if you put on a bodybuilding contest all you have to do as promoter of the show to get a well-known and popular guest pose is call your NPC national office and they'll call Weider to get a guest poser for you and all you have to do is list Weider as a sponsor. . . . He's getting involved more and more all the time.

Again, we see the melding of the Weiders' different areas of influence. We also see a close connection between the NPC, the national amateur affiliate of the IFBB, and Joe Weider's Weider Health and Fitness Corporation. According to the judge, the NPC national office contacts Joe Weider when there is a promoter who wants to find a bodybuilder to guest pose at an NPC competition, which then unfairly excludes bodybuilders who do not have a contract with the Weiders.

The Weiders, as is the case with all sponsors, choose to sponsor athletes they consider to be most marketable. Many of these bodybuilders were successful before they received a Weider contract, and getting the contract only serves to catapult their bodybuilding careers even further. The best illustration of what becoming a Weider athlete can do to one's bodybuilding career is Arnold Schwarzenegger, who first came to the United States to compete in the 1968 Mr. Universe competition held in Miami Beach; his trip was paid in full by Joe Weider. After the event, Arnold stayed in the U.S. for a year, again paid for by Joe Weider.[62] Tim Hoxha recalled:

> The Weiders moved Schwarzenegger to California in 1969, where they paid him $100 a week to write about his training and diet in *Muscle Builder.* Joe also took the young bodybuilder under his wing by managing his daily training schedule and tutoring him in real estate investments, media relations and the arts. Joe even loaned Schwarzenegger his favorite three paintings to decorate a new apartment. "Five years later, I tried to give them back, but Joe said, 'Keep them; they're yours.'"[63]

Serving as trainer, mentor, and financial sponsor, Joe Weider tutored the young Schwarzenegger into being a champion both onstage and off. Schwarzenegger received plenty of perks

> in return for endorsing Weider's vitamins, equipment, and training courses, he would receive a car, a furnished Santa Monica apartment, and a weekly allowance. Arrangements would be made for him to work out at Gold's near Venice Beach, acknowledged as the world's best gym. There he would have as his training partners Dave Draper and the famous stallions of Weider's West Coast stable.[64]

Probably no other bodybuilder has achieved this type of relationship with Joe Weider, but the fact remains: having a Weider contract has a positive effect on one's bodybuilding career in terms of publicity, money, and placement at contests. Patty, a former competitor and current judge, further illustrates this point: "Joe Weider invests so much money in his athletes, he's not going to let them lose after a year or two because he [has] just too much money invested in them. They have to keep going." This statement, if in fact true, implies that Joe Weider may use his money and power to influence how "his" bodybuilders are judged at contests.

Moreover, other bodybuilders and judges contend that the Weiders also use their influence in the sport to affect how judges evaluate female bodybuilders in general. Kathryn, a journalist for a bodybuilding publication, recounts a conversation she overheard by Ben Weider. Here we begin to see how the Weiders may use their power to influence the direction of the sport at the institutional level—by informing the judges that female bodybuilders should not appear "overly muscular":

> Well, it's a monopoly . . . it's Weider's idea, he's the one that's handing down how the women should look, how they should act. And we were having lunch or dinner and he was in the cafeteria, so he doesn't know who we are, and he's complaining about the women looking like men. He's like an old man with his ideas. Well, they have a judges' meeting and they tell the judges what they are looking [for], they want, Weider would say, "Soft, no overly muscular women, no striations, no excessive musculature."

It is understandable that the president of the IFBB would want to echo the IFBB's criteria for evaluating female bodybuilders. However, because of the power they wield, the Weider brothers can more successfully enforce their vision of "the ideal female bodybuilder" in the larger bodybuilding community than anyone else. Nonetheless, their influence sometimes fails, and when it did at the 1991 Ms. Olympia contest, Joe Weider is alleged to have intervened more directly.

The 1991 Ms. Olympia Contest took place in Los Angeles. It was the first Ms. Olympia contest to be televised live. Mark, one of the regional judges who was at the contest, recalls the following:

> I was at the Ms. Olympia in Los Angeles and I don't know if you are aware of it, but Bev Francis (one of the most muscular women) was leading the contest after the first two rounds in the morning and she was ahead by seven points. They flashed it up on the screen at the night show and one of my friends was sitting behind Joe Weider and he said that when Joe Weider saw that he immediately got a scratch pad and wrote on that scratch piece of paper and called the head judge over there and the piece of paper says "under no circumstances shall Bev Francis win this contest." So, for Weider, of course to him it's all marketability and money. He doesn't feel that a muscular woman is as marketable as somebody like Cory Everson or Lenda Murray.

Lenda Murray, the winner of the 1990 Ms. Olympia and a muscular but more feminine and symmetrical bodybuilder, won the contest. Bev Francis placed second. To lose a contest after leading the first two rounds by seven points is a relatively unusual occurrence in professional bodybuilding, especially given the fact that in the latter two rounds, the two competitors were said to be closely matched. A number of people acknowledged that Francis's physique was noticeably less symmetrical than Murray's, but the symmetry round had already been judged within the first two rounds. Mark correlated Joe Weider's behavior at the 1991 contest with his financial concern about the marketability of the sport, which rests on the shoulders of marketable bodybuilders such as Lenda Murray. The Weiders' economic and political power within the sport thus provided Joe Weider with the opportunity to enforce his own ideas of what female bodybuilders should look like on stage—thus usurping the usual ideological power of the judges who had, until he allegedly intervened, determined that indeed Bev Francis had the best physique of the competitors, however questionable their decision. Perhaps at the judges' meeting before the contest, the message about which type of physique would be considered the ideal was a bit obfuscated, thus allowing for the eventual outcome after the first two rounds. Maybe the judges simply misjudged the contest and the head judge stepped in (which is within his power) and overruled the other judges.

Conceivably, the judges at the 1991 Ms. Olympia contest truly believed that Bev Francis came the closest to their own image of the ideal female bodybuilder; possibly they had honestly come to the decision that Bev Francis was the best bodybuilder on stage. However, as this situation suggests, not only does Joe Weider have inordinate power; the head judge also wields power in affecting the "objective decisions" of the judges evaluating bodybuilders.

Others have also observed the effects the Weiders' power on contest outcomes:

> Some have argued that the Weiders virtually admitted fixing the 1970 Mr. Olympia contest. Sergio Oliva, a black Cuban, had been, by popular reckoning, the largest and most muscular of the pack, yet Schwarzenegger had won. When queried about this selection of a winner, Joe Weider quipped, "I put Sergio on the cover, I sell x magazines. I put Arnold on the cover, I sell 3x magazines."[65]

Weider makes no pretense about the fact that marketability and profitability affect judges' decisions.

Ironically, bodybuilding, with its almost monopolistic power hierarchy, creates an opportunity for a new physically strong look for women, yet at the same time it is run by a handful of men who have the power to determine the "appropriate" images of women's bodies. According to the athletes and judges in this study, the Weiders, who have the most power and status in the sport, are better economically and politically poised than anyone else to promote their own ideas of bodybuilding to the general public. If they want to portray a particular image of the sport or its athletes, they can and have had it promoted at contests and in magazines by rewarding those with the "ideal" look. The Weiders' "ideal" normative image for female bodybuilders changes periodically. These fluctuations are not a matter of whim, but rather seem to reflect a type of ideological "planned obsolescence" strategy—creating and recreating different "looks" to bring in a wider audience—in order to increase profit.

For bodybuilders, the most coveted rewards are contest wins and Weider sponsorships. Thus, the Weiders' ideal images are more likely than anyone else's to become the ideal images for which all bodybuilders strive. Many fans of bodybuilding would like to see certain images become the ideal within the sport, but not everyone has the power to ensure that their wishes be followed by judges. The Weiders do.

In this chapter, I have explored the macro-level historical, political, and economic aspects of the sport. The bodybuilding establishment is a tightly organized group controlled by a few powerful people, the vast majority of whom are men. The International Federation of Bodybuilders (IFBB) and the U.S. National Physique Committee (NPC) are the two largest, most successful, and most lucrative bodybuilding organizations in the world. Within bodybuilding generally and these two organizations specifically, there is an amazing interlocking power structure that is unparalleled in any other sport. Along with economic power, the power elite in this sport are also likely to wield political and ideological power. Because of this arrangement, there are a handful of men who virtually dominate the sport and its future. Let us now turn our attention to how these macro-level power dynamics trickle down into the lives and perceptions of those in the trenches of the sport: the bodybuilders and judges themselves.

THREE

The Dialectic of Female Bodybuilding

Steroids, Femininity, and Muscularity

TODAY, athletes and coaches of organized sports are under enormous pressure to win. Over the past three decades, a growing number of athletes have resorted to using anabolic steroids and other performance-enhancing drugs to increase their competitive edge. Some sports, like football and weightlifting, test their athletes for such drugs. Steroid use is thought to be particularly widespread among athletes in bodybuilding because their main goal is to build a large and massive musculature. Helping to build muscles is one of the main reasons for taking steroids:

> The dynamics of anabolic steroids have been pretty well understood for years. Synthetic variations of the male hormone testosterone, they enter the bloodstream as chemical messengers and attach themselves to muscle cells. Once attached to these cells, they deliver their twofold message: grow [muscles] and increase endurance. Steroids accomplish the first task by increasing the synthesis of protein. In sufficient quantities, they turn the body into a kind of fusion engine, converting everything, including fat, into mass and energy.

Such a drug can have an enormous effect on a bodybuilder,

> A chemical bodybuilder can put on fifty pounds of muscle in six months because most of the 6000-10000 calories he eats a day are incorporated, not excreted. The second task—increasing endurance—is achieved by stimulating the synthesis of a molecule called creatine phosphate, or CP. CP is essentially hydraulic fluid for muscles,

> allowing them to do more than just a few seconds' work. The more CP you have in your tank, the more power you generate. Olympic weightlifters and defensive linemen have huge stockpiles of CP, some portion of which is undoubtedly genetic. The better part of it, though, probably comes out of a bottle of Anadrol, a popular oral steroid that makes you big, strong, and savage—and not necessarily in that order.[1]

Whereas the physical dynamics of consuming anabolic steroids might be fairly well understood, the social aspects remain unclear—particularly for women. This is certainly true for female bodybuilders who must negotiate the norms of a sport where building muscle is required but taking steroids is frowned upon. Where does this leave the issue of steroid use among female bodybuilders? I will begin to answer this question by exploring the history of steroid use among competitive female bodybuilders as well as the institutional policies governing drug use in the sport. We will see that steroid use among female bodybuilders is integrally related to the sport's hegemonic notions about the relationship between femininity and muscularity. Many in the sport, particularly officials and judges, consider it extremely inappropriate for women to take steroids because they become too muscular and thus less feminine, whereas in male bodybuilders muscularity and masculinity are seen as compatible. I have divided people in this study into three groups based on their views toward femininity, muscularity, and signs of steroid use.

The History of Doping

IFBB officials are aware of the stigma of steroid use associated with their sport[2] and have publicly denounced the use of any International Olympic Committee (IOC) banned substance.[3] The IFBB follows the IOC guidelines[4] with regard to doping controls. Its "official" position on doping is shown in the following passage from Dr. Bob Goldman's IFBB position paper on doping: "The IFBB is totally opposed to the unhealthy and unethical use of banned substances and techniques, but realizes the drug abuse problem in sports is not a new one. It will take a comprehensive program to control and alleviate sports drug use."[5] The same paper defines "doping" as "the use by, or distribution to an athlete of certain substances which could have the effect of improving artificially the athlete's physical, and/or mental condition, and so augmenting the athlete's performance as well as being hazardous to the athlete's health."[6] In order to combat steroid use, the IFBB has established a doping commission that has implemented a program of drug testing to be followed by the national federations affiliated with the IFBB on both amateur and professional levels.

The IFBB requires that competitors must either be randomly tested or that all competitors be tested before competitions to ensure that the athletes have abided by doping control regulations.[7] Those athletes who test positive for the first time are disqualified from the competition. Those testing positive for a second time are declared ineligible from all competitions and are suspended from the federation for a period of a year. A third positive test warrants a lifetime suspension from the IFBB. According to official IFBB publications, these controls have reduced the amount of steroid use in bodybuilding.

Although the IFBB literature claims that the organization has taken drastic measures to reduce steroid use in their sport, Rick Wayne, in his book *Muscle Wars* (1985), saw things differently:

> Not one of the musclemen participating in the 1984 IFBB Mr. Universe was tested for steroid use. Otherwise it's a safe bet there would have been no contest. In my opinion, there will be no testing at IFBB events for a long time. Steroid tests would affect not only those disqualified, but also the businessmen making fortunes from the sport of bodybuilding. No shadow will be allowed to fall over this increasingly popular pursuit lest the host of new recruits turn disillusioned to other interests.[8]

According to Wayne, neither bodybuilders nor competitors are regularly tested, because doing so would significantly hinder the ability of promoters to make substantial profits from sponsoring bodybuilding contests.

Wayne also maintained that the controversy of regulating steroid use among bodybuilders has been a problem since at least the mid-1980s. He recalled a meeting in 1984 at which IFBB president Ben Weider and national members of the IFBB were in disagreement about how to test for steroid use among IFBB athletes:[9]

> In 1984, several member nations complained that they'd had a bellyful of the blatant steroid use among bodybuilders and pressed the IFBB to take a stand against drug use among its members. The head of the Norwegian delegation reminded Ben Weider that at the Singapore congress a year earlier it had been decided that IFBB athletes would

> be tested for steroid use before subsequent international events. "Would the contenders undergo such tests before the '84 Universe?" "No," replied Ben. Tests were costly and inconclusive besides. Moreover, with all the confusion surrounding the issue, there was nothing to stop a penalized athlete from taking the IFBB to court—and maybe winning his case. "I'll be happy to sanction steroid tests," offered the IFBB president, "if those conducting it will place enough money at the IFBB's disposal to be used in the event of an athlete's taking us to court." . . . The IFBB was already doing its utmost to discourage drug abuse among its members, Ben insisted. In particular, precautions were being taken to preclude "overmuscular women" from the federation's competitions—women whose physiques, according to IFBB determination, could have been achieved only via steroid use. However, he didn't say exactly what he meant by "overmuscular." . . . One delegate asked, "Why not disqualify [male] contenders with obvious signs of gynecomastia[10] . . . directly related to steroid use?" The IFBB president let that one pass without a comment.[11]

Even in the mid-1980s, IFBB policy was to test for steroid use before international events. However, in the scenario constructed by Wayne, there was a discrepancy between policy and actual practice. Thus, not only would promoters have to pick up the drug testing tab for their athletes, but they would also be liable for funding the cost of any potential law suits that occurred as a result of drug testing—an amount that would be prohibitively high for most promoters, including those at this meeting. Furthermore, Ben Weider's gender-specific comments about the organization's attempt to limit "overmuscular" women were telling.[12] The IFBB's more stringent testing of female bodybuilders appears to serve two purposes. First, it counters the delegates' charges that the IFBB is not testing its athletes as previously stated. Second, it keeps female bodybuilders from getting too muscular or "overmuscular" in the eyes of key officials in the IFBB, which may serve to keep the gender order in this nontraditional avocation intact. Doing so also ensures that revenues will remain high. The scathing diatribes of a number of officials and judges about the dangers of steroids indicate that a stronger stance against steroid use is in order. However, one is left with the feeling that the concern is not for the health of the athletes, but rather for the ability to draw the biggest crowds. This is best achieved by getting the largest and "freakiest" male bodybuilders and the most attractive yet not overly muscular female bodybuilders.

The Current Scene

Although judges cannot definitively say that a bodybuilder is taking steroids unless he or she tests positive for steroids, some judges look for tell-tale signs of steroid use such as, for female bodybuilders, the existence of facial hair, big joints,[13] a blocky waist, body acne, and a lowered voice. If the bodybuilder has not tested positive, judges are not supposed to mark him or her down even though there may be tell-tale signs of steroid use. What judges can do, however, is to say that the bodybuilder's symmetry is thrown off by her blocky waist or that the body acne detracts from her "overall package." The overall package includes such features as muscularity, symmetry, presentation, and, in the eyes of some judges and officials, characteristics such as attractiveness and sex appeal (see appendix D for a more detailed definition).

Currently, steroid use among female bodybuilders, although estimated to be not quite as high as among males, is still prevalent. In fact, a former competitor claims that steroid use may be as high as 70 percent.[14] While male officials particularly are likely to disapprove of steroid use among females, the IFBB did not test its most prestigious 1992 female bodybuilding show in Chicago. Vicky, a female bodybuilder, revealed that although the Ms. Olympia competitors were warned that all contestants would be tested, they in fact were not.

Neither the IFBB nor the NPC actually tests its athletes. Steroid testing, if done, is the sole responsibility of the promotor of the show, who decides to have either a drug-tested or a non-drug-tested meet. The reasons for the former include a concern with the health of the athletes and a sense of fairness to all athletes involved in a contest. This option, however, is expensive. Michelle, a national judge, addressed the issue of the prohibitive cost of drug testing and why promoters do not think it is always in their best interest to drug test:

> From a business point of view . . . the public in general has a hard time dealing with the muscularity of female bodybuilders, and the "powers that be," want to keep people in the sport. They say, "Well, we've got to do something and so they tried drug-tested shows and so on," but the problem with it is, number one, what drugs are you going to test for; number two, what kind of tests are you going to have? As promoters, on a national qualifier level, it costs too much money to do the kind of stringent drug testing over the wide spec-

> trum of steroids and growth hormones and all these other things that people are taking to make it feasible for the promoters to make any money.

Besides disliking the high cost of testing, many promoters are afraid that the big-name, very muscular bodybuilders who attract the largest audiences may not want to attend a drug-testing bodybuilding competition.

Promoters thus have at least two major reasons not to drug test the bodybuilders at their competitions: (1) it saves the promoter a lot of money, and (2) the top bodybuilders are more likely to compete, which will increase the promoter's ability to enhance profits because more fans will attend the competition.

Currently, the status of drug testing is unclear. The official line on drug use is still disseminated by the organization's leaders, but in fact it is not carried out. For example, one high-ranking official, Ralph, claimed that

> steroid use had actually decreased among bodybuilders, the reason being because of our very strong controls and the suspensions and the penalties that they have to take. So it's been reduced substantially. It's still too prevalent, but has reduced substantially. In other words, we'd be happy when it's down to zero. It's not a realistic goal in life, but that's why I say I'm not happy where it is, I am happy by the amount of reduction of steroid usage.

However, as previously we have seen, some of the bodybuilders and judges participating in the 1992 Ms. Olympia said that the IFBB's "very strong controls" were practically nonexistent at that contest.

Another official, Heather, discussed the extent of drug testing on an amateur and professional level:

> Yes, we drug test every show, but not everyone is tested because of the cost. What we do is at our national level when our girls go overseas to compete for the States, they are all drug tested. When you get to the pro level they have random testing throughout the year. . . . We have almost 20,000 athletes in the NPC. We're not able to do it on the same basis as the pro level. So the thing is most of the girls at the nationals are trying for the pros or trying to go to the Universe. So for them to do either of those levels, they're going to get tested. We contract the IOC to do the testing for us.

Though the cost of testing athletes for illegal substances is prohibitively high, those who make it to the international amateur or the professional ranks will apparently eventually be tested.

Countering the official rhetoric in the official bodybuilding guidebook is Denise, who contends that steroids are used by competitive bodybuilders and that the practice is quite prevalent:

> Oh, yeah. Then you go to the national level and you have all these physiques that are phenomenal, but there's a line, you can see the line between the drug user and a non-drug user, and I'm telling you if you go to a national meet, and you're not on drugs, it's like sending Miss America to the Miss America Pageant without mascara and eye shadow. Forget it, it ain't going to happen.

This observation hardly parallels the official policies stated in the guidebooks and explained by many of the high-ranking officials. Similarly, Tod, an NPC state chairperson and national judge, in discussing a professional female bodybuilder, revealed: "She dropped some size this year, because she knew that's what they were after. But the year before, they didn't do any drug testing and she knew she had to beat 'Sue.' So you gotta go with the flow and go against your competitors." Thus, according to Tod, the IFBB did not drug test the professional female bodybuilders for at least this one contest.

The unevenness in the enforcement of drug testing for female and male bodybuilders appears to be an institutional attempt to maintain gender distinctions in the sport. Although steroid use has an earlier history and is more prevalent among male bodybuilders than among females, the IFBB began testing female bodybuilders before males and has been stricter about drug testing them.[15] Officials and judges are much more critical of women taking steroids than of men because as Denise said, "It's okay for a man to be big and masculine and freaky. For a female, you start looking like a drag queen." Thus, the "usual" gender and sexuality lines become blurred and create unease among many people. If officials were really concerned about curtailing drug abuse among their athletes, they should be tackling the problem of male drug abuse: men are the ones who are dying from, and being hospitalized for, such drugs as steroids, diuretics, thyroid medication, and amphetamines.[16]

The apparent discrepancies between policy and alleged practice are both compelling and disconcerting. Perhaps this incongruity has contributed to the confusion of many female bodybuilders about the "look" that is expected of them from judges and officials at contests. I asked judges and officials about steroid use and its physical manifestations among female bodybuilders, and many said that their evaluations of female bodybuilders were directly affected by supposed signs of steroid use. In the following section, I divide officials, judges, and contestants into three separate camps based on their opinions and interpretations of physical manifestations of steroid use.

The Positioning of the Three Major Camps

The relationship between muscularity, steroid use, and femininity has created considerable controversy within the sport. Some believe that female bodybuilders should be judged like male bodybuilders—on the size of their muscles; others contend that female bodybuilders are women first and should therefore emphasize their femininity and deemphasize "extreme" muscularity; and still others' position falls in between the two. The power to determine which "look" is appropriate is unequally distributed between these groups. Bodybuilders and midlevel judges usually fall into the first or middle groups. High-level judges and officials are more likely to be at the "conservative" end of the continuum. Regardless of their position, however, the majority of people in this study found it less acceptable for female bodybuilders to take steroids than male bodybuilders.

As discussed in the last chapter, the arrangement of power in bodybuilding gives officials, who create and maintain the laws of the governing bodies, the most control in the negotiation process of the appropriate relationship between muscularity and femininity for female bodybuilders. They are the upper-level social gatekeepers of the sport. Judges, on the other hand, because they enforce the rules and regulations set by officials, are relegated to a lower-level social gatekeeping position. However, because judges determine the winners and losers of meets, they still have more power than the bodybuilders themselves in the negotiation process. Bodybuilders must follow the rules set forth by officials and enforced by judges and therefore have the least amount of power and leverage in deciding and determining how they should be evaluated and how their sport should progress. Yet, as we will see again in chapter 6, these women are not completely powerless in this negotiation process.

Members of the most conservative group, which I label "Disrupting the Gender Order," represent the hegemonic view in female bodybuilding and assume that muscularity and femininity are antithetical constructs, and they approach the issue of steroids from this position. This group would argue that female bodybuilders have become too muscular, and that the only way women can get so muscular is through the use of steroids. They believe that female bodybuilders who take steroids interfere or tamper with the "natural" gender order[17] when they take synthetic male hormones in order to increase their musculature. The people in this camp are less critical of male bodybuilders taking steroids because men's bodies naturally produce more testosterone (approximately nine times more) and thus testosterone is "natural" to their bodies. Furthermore, those in this camp believe that male bodybuilders are not tampering with the "gender order" when they take steroids because steroids, which are synthetic testosterone, make them bigger and stronger and give them more muscle mass—which are seen as inherently masculine characteristics.

It is an altogether different story for women. The most vehemently anti-steroid group of the three camps wants female bodybuilders to maintain as much of a traditionally feminine image as possible—meaning that their musculature should not be excessive. In other words, female bodybuilders should look like healthy and athletic women who are still "traditionally" aesthetically feminine, and their muscles should, in no way, rival those of their male bodybuilding counterparts.

The middle category is comprised of judges and female bodybuilders who also believe that some female (and male) bodybuilders have become excessively muscular due to steroid use. I label this group "Developing the Pinhead Effect." This view also tends to lend support, for the most part, to the hegemonic view concerning the "appropriate" relationship between femininity and muscularity. However, this group also has different, nongendered reasons for opposing steroid use. They believe that steroids put too much muscle on bodies, detracting from their symmetry. Many people in this group are concerned about steroid use, but more so because of its effects on health,[18] fearing that bodybuilders are irreparably damaging their bodies by taking steroids. In the eyes of this group, the ideal female bodybuilder is still athletic-looking, with more musculature than other female athletes—female bodybuilders should have a distinctive look that separates them from other female athletes.

The last group, which I label "Building Muscle Is the Name of the Game," is represented mostly by bodybuilders and a few judges, and believe that the sport is body*building* and should be judged as such. This group supports the counterhegemonic view concerning the relationship between muscularity and femininity. Therefore, they want the most muscular female bodybuilders who also have good symmetry and proportion to win bodybuilding contests. They contend that a female bodybuilder cannot be too muscular if she has good symmetry. Although they are not as likely to be as strongly opposed to steroid use as members of the other two groups, they are aware that steroids and other drugs are abused and lead to health problems (and none in this group espoused pro-steroid sentiments). Their ideal female bodybuilder is one who is exceptionally muscular but whose symmetry is not compromised. To limit the muscularity of female bodybuilders would be to compromise the purpose of bodybuilding, which is to build muscle. The line that demarcates "excessive muscularity" is pushed back as long as the bodybuilders' muscles have good symmetry and do not exhibit signs of excessive steroid use. The issue of femininity is still a concern for people in this group. However, they do not believe that a muscular woman is by definition not feminine. If dramatic signs of steroid use, such as body acne or a hairy face, are evident, judges in this category will mark bodybuilders down because bodybuilding is supposed to be a healthy, or at least a healthy-looking, sport.

Issues of Muscularity and Femininity

When asked the question, "Can female bodybuilders be too muscular, given that they have good symmetry?" those involved in the sport often discussed the interrelated issues of muscularity, femininity, and steroid use. As already mentioned, there were three major groupings of responses. I begin with the first group, represented by officials and judges; no bodybuilders were included.

Group 1: Disrupting the Gender Order

Members of this group contend that current female bodybuilders are too big, muscular, and masculine-looking because of steroid use. Steroids have caused some female bodybuilders to look and act in masculine ways that are alarming to officials and sponsors, who believe this image keeps away potential consumers of bodybuilding products.

Heather, a national and professional judge, at first discussed health issues when she began talking about steroid use among female bodybuilders.

> You know, if female bodybuilders come in with 4-5% body fat, that's not what I want judges to reward. . . . Women should be healthy, and that low level of body fat is not healthy. And really you're going to have a hard time convincing me that you naturally got that way anyway. I mean there is going to be some drug use and our society is never going to get rid of it, but we're going to try to, at least in the females, keep drug use to a minimum if we can.

I then asked her if she thought it was more problematic if female rather than male bodybuilders took steroids. Her response:

> Oh, my goodness, yes, I think it is more problematic for female bodybuilders to take drugs than male bodybuilders. First of all you're taking substances that are really not natural to, I mean all women have a little testosterone but most women have minute levels. And the side effects you are going to see are going to make you more masculine. But if you are male, you don't really care if you look more masculine. But the women, you do. And the thing is the longer you take them the more side effects you get. When you do eventually come off the drugs, those side effects only subside so much.

She argued that bodybuilding should not perpetuate the negative and unnatural outcomes of competitive sport: steroid use and eating disorders, the latter of which she discussed in detail later in the interview. If her concerns were purely health related, she would consider it similarly unhealthy for male bodybuilders to take steroids, as men also suffer from the deleterious effects of steroid use—such as liver, kidney, and heart problems.

Ralph, a high-ranking official who is also opposed to steroid use among female bodybuilders, felt "they [female bodybuilders] would not get that big without the use of steroids. Women are not supposed to be men." Ralph appears to believe that women can actually "lose" their gender and become men by taking steroids. When I asked him if he thought that women could exhibit such muscularity without the use of steroids, he responded:

> No. For example, you take a look at a ballerina, she's on her toes all day long, practicing in the evening and so forth. That's a heavy

> exercise to be on your toes, and you take a look, her calves are not excessively developed, her thighs are not excessively developed, so I think through regular exercise and proper nutrition you can build muscle. You can reduce the fat but not become excessively muscular as you would if you added steroids to a program.

Yet this bodybuilding official did not specifically advocate weight training to build muscle, either. He recommended only regular exercise and proper nutrition—a peculiar stance from a leading bodybuilding official.

David, a regional judge and competitor, discussed his concern that excessive muscularity can make female bodybuilders too masculine looking:

> Yes, you can be too muscular and lose your proportions. I think that some of the women nowadays, "Joanna," has that. She's become very masculine in her appearance. She's very muscular, but it's too distracting from her feminine appearance. I mean it's proportional, I would rather use the word proportion than feminine. . . . "Joanna" obviously, from my point of view, she looked like a man. . . . If you took off her head you'd have a man's physique with a bikini top on. It is so scary that she came as close to winning as she did. She only lost by a point or two but it's incredible. There are the women who can become too muscular and lose their proportion or femininity or whatever. Yes, [it applies to men too]. I think there are some men that are way out of proportion. Mohammed Benaziza is like five foot two and weighs 200 pounds.[19] That's not proportional at all. That's grotesque. I mean that's just, for that physique . . . that is way too much muscle.

However, "excessive muscularity" in a man is not grotesque for the same reason as in a woman: overly muscular male bodybuilders neither lose their masculinity nor look "too masculine." Muscularity for men simply seems to make them look too big for their frames. Thus, the arguments for excessive muscularity for women and men are qualitatively and quantitatively different from one another. In his response, David said one female bodybuilder looked "masculine in her appearance" while another one "looked like a man." Female bodybuilders who take steroids not only lose symmetry by becoming excessively muscular, but also lose characteristics associated with femininity.

Kyle, a judge and high-level IFBB official, is vehemently opposed to having extremely muscular female bodybuilders represent the sport because they keep people away from bodybuilding contests. He explained, "Well, quite honestly there's no way a woman can get that muscular without steroids is the whole thing and when they take the steroids, that's when they get the secondary [male] characteristics." Finally, Richard, a regional judge, believed that the issue is not women being too muscular, which he could understand, but that steroids actually make women look "like men with wigs on." He explained:

> It's not so much too muscular, I can understand that and it did get involved because the steroids came into play so what happened is women got involved with that and other drugs and actually looked like men with wigs on. So you've got that fine line that you want a woman that has muscle, or do you want a person that you're not sure whether it's a man or a woman. Yes [a woman can be too muscular if she's got good symmetry] because there's a difference. As an example, somebody like Carla Dunlap who has a very muscular build but is still able to keep a very feminine look. Then the opposite end, a woman with probably the most muscle would be Bev Francis. If you haven't seen her in person, and she's a super nice person and about as dedicated to bodybuilding and giving it her all, but yet she looks a lot like a male with a wig on and a female suit.

For some members of this group, it is the excessive muscularity caused by steroid use that makes the women look masculine. For others it is not the muscularity per se, but the secondary masculinizing effects of steroids, such as excess facial hair, that they find problematic. This group argued vehemently against steroid use among female bodybuilders for these two reasons: (1) women get excessively muscular, and (2) women become too masculine-looking.

Group 2: Developing the "Pinhead Effect"

The second group is represented by male and female judges and female bodybuilders. These individuals, like those in Group 1, believe that some female bodybuilders are too big and muscular and that steroid use is the reason. However, this group is different from the first one in that they give nongendered arguments against bodybuilders taking steroids. They argue not that steroids masculinize female bodybuilders, but that they (1) allow them to build too much muscle for their frame, and (2) are deleterious to their health. This group consists of one male judge, four female judges, and three female bodybuilders.

Lynn, a regional judge, discussed her concern with bodybuilders' overmuscularity:

> Yes [female bodybuilders can be too muscular]. I think a woman should always stay within her body frame size. Like myself and a friend of mine who I've competed against. [We] are only about five feet, five feet two on a good day, maybe. And if we were to get to two hundred pounds, it would be solid muscle. It would look stupid. I think you need to stay within your body's frame. And that goes with men, because a lot of times when I'm judging men it's like you see this itty, bitty head on this huge body and they look funny. And I think you can honestly pick that out. You really can.

The difference between her comment and those expressed by members of the previous group is that she believes both female and male bodybuilders can get too muscular for their frames and this effect is not unique to one gender.

Denise, a regional judge and bodybuilder, also discussed this non-gender-specific "pinhead" look:

> They can take the drugs and more than likely if you have a good structure, small waist-to-shoulder ratio, you're going to keep that structure but you're just going to be bigger and bigger and bigger, and pretty soon those muscles are going to overpower your structure. Meaning you're going to have what I call the pinhead look. You're going to have this little bitty head on this structure that should not have the thirty pounds of extra muscle on it that it's carrying. That's kind of ugly.

This bodybuilder is most concerned that bodybuilders develop too much musculature for their structure due to steroid use. So is Tod, an NPC official and judge:

> Oh yeah, it is possible for a woman to be too muscular. Because it can be too much for her frame. A perfect example of that is "Sandra." At the show last year, she weighed at 144 pounds, I think. When she competed previously she weighed 133. When she gets up to a 144, she gets ripped to shreds, her head is way too small for her body. It's just obvious that her frame is not meant to hold that much muscle.

> Her symmetry is a little bit off, her legs were a little bit behind. The main thing was it was just too much for her frame.

Brooke, a professional bodybuilder, also argued that it is a bodybuilder's symmetry that is affected by being overly muscular: "Yes. Yes, she can. Yes. Usually the symmetry in many cases will temper the overmuscularity. But I think that you can cross that line, and that is when you begin to throw even good symmetry out of proportion by being overly muscular for your frame."

Frame, proportion, esthetics, steroids, and health concerns are key issues for members of this group. When members of Group 1 discussed female bodybuilders "crossing the line," they meant the line that differentiated between female bodybuilders who look like women (the way they are supposed to look), and those who look like men or were too masculine (not an acceptable look). Although not all members of Group 2 directly discuss steroids, most of them at least implicate steroids as contributing factors in enabling both female and male bodybuilders to cross the invisible line of having too much muscularity for their frame size.

Group 3: Building Muscle Is the Name of the Game

This group is at the other end of the spectrum from Group 1 and overlaps in some ways with Group 2. These members contend that female bodybuilders, as long as they have good symmetry, cannot be too muscular. Many argued that the federations are limiting the muscularity of female bodybuilders, which some believe is due to the officials' desire to increase their profits by appealing to fans. One of the unusual characteristics of this particular group is that it consists mostly of women—all are women except for one regional judge; this group thus consists of one male judge, two female judges, no officials, and six female bodybuilders. It is noteworthy that this group not only is the most supportive of large musculature for female bodybuilders, but it also has the most women of all three groups. It is also significant that there are a number of female bodybuilders in this group.

Female bodybuilders are more likely to view the ideal female bodybuilder as one who is well defined, with large muscles and good symmetry, while officials as well as a number of judges are likely to view a symmetrical female athlete with less muscle as the ideal. Indicative of this disparity are the views of Sam, a national judge: "I will tell you that the women will give you extreme perspectives, I can guarantee you that." To illustrate this "extreme" perspective, I include a quote from Debbie, a professional bodybuilder, who stated that she did not think a female bodybuilder can be too muscular if she has a symmetrical body:

> I don't think so. If she has perfect symmetry and muscles, like Paula Bircumshaw, I thought she was awesome. And proportionately she looked, to me she looked great. . . . We don't fight backstage because I still want a physique like that, even though I'm in the show, I'm trying to win too. All I can say to her is, "Man, you look great!" I thought she looked awesome. And I didn't feel like she was like Bev. Because Bev is too blocky in the waist. You know, she [Paula] has a lot of muscle with the symmetry. . . . But I didn't think that was too much.

Stephanie, a professional bodybuilder, also mentioned Paula Bircumshaw as an example of a female bodybuilder who has both large muscle mass and good symmetry:

> That's really a hard one to call because part of the whole reason that some don't look so good is because when they are real muscular they don't have this shape. They have thick waists and neck and thick joints. But I think usually when a woman has good symmetry, that it's okay. But it just depends on how she puts it together. You have to have a certain type of woman that can . . . have that symmetry and be very muscular because I've seen a lot of them that look great. I think Paula Bircumshaw has great symmetry. Looking at her face, she was dieted down, but her face looked just the same as Anja Schreiner's.

Pam, a professional bodybuilder, also said that she did not believe female bodybuilders who have good symmetry could also be considered too muscular, but she thought that steroid use could make a bodybuilder look unhealthy:

> In my opinion, no. If she's got the lines there, the waist, the shoulders, no. But then again, you don't want to see a five o'clock shadow on this girl and zits all over, you know what I'm saying? I mean, to me, you have got to play the game, you know? You're bodybuilding for reasons, for health reasons, and once you start taking it like that,

> I mean come on, I mean you got acne on your back the size of quarters, then something is wrong.

She does express a concern about steroids when bodybuilders abuse it to the extent of manifesting noticeably masculine characteristics. Her concern, however, does not revolve around female bodybuilders getting too muscular, rather that they will begin to develop secondary sexual characteristics, which will contribute to the sport's already tarnished image when it comes to steroid use.

Susan, a regional competitor, stated there was a discrepancy between her own beliefs and the "party line":

> No, a lot of times steroids will knock your symmetry and proportion off, but if she has good symmetry . . . she can't be too muscular. To some extent, old bodybuilding was a very heavy play on stereotypical femininity. *Pumping Iron* and that nonsense is sort of like, what are you saying? "Are you a bodybuilder or are you. . . ." Like they had to make that distinction along the way . . . either you're a bodybuilder or you're a woman. And I think that as with anything you run across, whether . . . in your workplace there is sexism, or in sport, it makes you question whether or not those are your beliefs or whether they are somebody else's.

Many of those in this group expressed sheer frustration at the direction the sport has taken in the recent past. Patty, a former national competitor, emphasized that the sport is called "bodybuilding" for a reason, and should be judged accordingly:

> It's supposed to be bodybuilding! How can, and this is where I have problems, how can somebody like . . . like Bev Francis *not* be first in muscularity rounds, I mean I've seen that happen. People who are obviously the most muscular do not come in first in the muscularity round. If it's a muscularity round they're not supposed to be judging you on symmetry, they're not supposed to be judging you on your posing, they're supposed to be judging you on how much muscle you have! But they don't.

Another female judge discussed similar situations where fellow judges marked down the most muscular female bodybuilding in the muscularity round.

Christy, a national competitor, explained that in the past, bodybuilding was represented by the conviction that "the more muscle, the better," but this is no longer the case:

> I really hardly heard anybody say, "Wow, she's too big," like too muscular, too much muscle mass. That's always been the thrust of bodybuilding at least in the past was, the more muscle, the better. I think that if you have the right body to carry the muscle, then it looks the way it's supposed to look. There are a lot of people who just don't have the whole package, then it looks awkward. You see, that's what they're doing with the judging standards right now—they're saying that people are too muscular.

She later conveyed how frustrated she gets when told that female bodybuilders can be overly muscular:

> The head judge said that about the girl who took fifth in the lightweight. I mean she was the clear-cut winner, she was incredible, but she was very, very lean, and when [she] extended her leg all the way out, she had cross striations on her quads, and when she had her leg slightly bent, she didn't. So, the head judge said, "If you just would have kept your leg bent you might have won."

"Cross-striations" occur when a bodybuilder has quality muscle and minimal fat and water retention to the extent that the ridges or "shreds" in a muscle group are easily visible. Such extraordinary muscularity with low fat and water levels is regarded as rare among women and is considered to be a sign of steroid and diuretic use. Exasperated, Christy exclaimed:

> What kind of fucking garbage is that?! Come on, this is *bodybuilding,* this is about muscles, this is about displaying the best you've got! We're being told to tone it down. This is the only sport in the world where some girls didn't even train as hard as they used to train. We go into the gym going, "Well, hmm, should we lift heavy today or is that going to . . ." In every other sport in the world, you do the best you can do, and now women are being told to tone it down and I think it's such a hard thing to do.

Some judges grade female bodybuilders down for cross-striations because they assume it is a sign of steroid use, even though, as Christy stated, bodybuilding "was about displaying the best you've got." Men are allowed to have cross-striations but women aren't because it is considered to be an indication of steroid and diuretic use and thus excessive muscularity, at least in the eyes of some judges. Therefore, female bodybuilders are told, in essence, not to display their best because it will not win contests. Finally, she discussed the confusion caused by the lack of consistency in judging: she goes into the gym and does not know whether she should have a heavy lift day or a light one.

Mark, a regional judge, argued:

> It's almost like they want you to put a standard up there on the stage and say you can't be more muscular than this person here. Well, it's difficult to do that and this is women's bodybuilding, it's not women's figure presentation, I mean it's bodybuilding. And they have to remember what that is. If it's not going to be judged on the muscularity, it needs to be called, you know, have a fitness competition instead of the bodybuilding.

His argument mirrors the belief of many in this group—that the name of the sport is bodybuilding and if bodybuilders have symmetrical physiques, then they should be allowed to display as much musculature as they can build, with no double standard.

The people in this group have argued that bodybuilding today is not what it is supposed to be because of the limits placed on women's muscularity. Some bodybuilders would settle for definite stated guidelines that judges would have to follow consistently in order to make it easier to know what is expected of them. Bodybuilders in this group believe that if a female bodybuilder has good symmetry (see appendix D for definition), she will not be too muscular. A few proclaimed that judges choose female bodybuilders with smaller muscle mass to attract more people and money into the sport.

Overall, male judges and officials were likely to be in Groups 1 and 2. They were likely to express the opinion that female bodybuilders are often so muscular and big that they can either begin to look like men or tax their frames with too much muscle. Female judges were likely to have differing opinions: some concurred with the male officials and judges, while others felt that female bodybuilders who have good symmetry cannot be too muscular. One national and professional female judge discussed the health concerns related to steroids. She believed it was a judge's duty to ensure that the current unhealthy state of bodybuilding is not perpetuated. No current female bodybuilder believed that, given good symmetry, a female bodybuilder could be so muscular that she would look like a man. In fact, no bodybuilder labeled herself, using Harry Crews's words, as "a monster to behold."

The Ideal

Another way to get people's views on the issues of femininity and muscularity is to ask them the name of their ideal female bodybuilder and their reasons for choosing her. Their ideal is likely to reflect their attitudes about the appropriate relationship between muscularity and femininity. For instance, if someone chose a muscular female bodybuilder like Paula Bircumshaw as an ideal versus a more fit and less muscular type like Rachel McLish or Anja Schreiner, that person would most likely be placed in Group 3, since Paula is one of the most muscular bodybuilders in the history of the sport. Those whose ideal is Rachel and Anja would probably agree with the argument that muscularity is too extreme among female bodybuilders today, and that the sport should return to rewarding the look of yesteryear. The female bodybuilders who were most often mentioned as an ideal by those in the study were two six-time former Ms. Olympia champions: Cory Everson and Lenda Murray. However, the reasons for choosing a particular bodybuilder depended on the person's views on the issues of muscularity and femininity. Highlighted below are some of the representative quotes from each group about their ideals. Keep in mind that the views of each group support their ideas about the appropriate relationship between muscularity and femininity. Thus, a group's views about the ideal is either likely to support or refute the hegemonic norms related to the appropriate look for female bodybuilders.

Group 1: Disrupting the Gender Order

This group was the most likely of the three to view muscularity and femininity as antithetical entities. Individuals mentioned Rachel McLish, Anja Schreiner, Lenda Murray, Cory Everson, or Carla Dunlap as the embodiment of their ideal female bodybuilder. The reasons given for their choice were often related to the fact that their ideal female bodybuilder was not only feminine and pretty, but she was also not excessively muscular. For instance, Tracy argued that Cory Everson and Sharon Bruneau came the closest to her ideal because they, unlike Lenda

Murray, were not too muscular: "Cory Everson comes the closest because Lenda Murray is a little bit too big. I would go with Sharon Bruneau too. I really like the way she looks. She's got a really nice shape." Similarly, Jan, a regional judge, mentioned Anja Schreiner because "I think she looks very feminine. She's very pretty."

Illustrating how his opinions of an ideal female bodybuilder have changed across time, Richard, a regional judge, revealed:

> I thought Rachel McLish at the beginning was ideal. She was a pretty girl who had a very feminine figure and enough muscle at that time to be very impressive. I guess you would have to say that Cory now fits ideally . . . she was very feminine yet had plenty of muscle. And Lenda Murray would fit into that category probably for a hard-core person, but for the average person, they would probably think she has way too much muscle.

He alluded to the fact that across time, he has learned to accept more muscularity on female bodybuilders.

One male official still believed that the limited muscularity of Rachel McLish was the ideal for which female bodybuilders currently should strive: "I guess Rachel McLish. Lenda Murray would be in the type of physique right now that we want, nothing bigger than that. But I think that Rachel McLish is the epitome of what we're looking for, feminine, graceful, yet still muscular and athletic looking." By arguing for a "Rachel McLish look," he would like to see professional female bodybuilding go back to the early 1980s ideal—one with little muscle mass. If female bodybuilders embraced that look, they would be less muscular than many current track athletes such as Jackie Joyner-Kersee or Gail Devers.

Group 2: Developing the "Pinhead Effect"

Members of Group 2 were more likely to mention either Cory Everson or Lenda Murray as coming the closest to embodying their ideal. In addition, they were more accepting of more muscular female bodybuilders than their colleagues in Group 1. Moreover, people in this group were more likely to give varied reasons for their choice.

Heather, a national and professional judge, argued that Cory Everson was her ideal bodybuilder not only because of her "symmetry and genetics," but also for her ability to be a good spokesperson for the sport.

Staying feminine is still an important quality for female bodybuilders, according to this judge:

> Probably the top of my mind right now, I mean the one who comes the closest would be Cory Everson. You know Rachel . . . I mean she's a real athletic girl but she doesn't have near the muscle size that Cory does. Yet Cory retained her femininity, and she has great symmetry and genetics. Again, and I always think part of it is also being a spokesperson for the sport, and Cory always was very good with the general public. Always carried herself very well. So I would have to say to this day she is probably still the ideal that most girls are trying to attain. And next to her it would have to be Lenda. She has really good genetics except maybe not quite compared to Cory's. She still has to work a little bit harder to come in as lean as she does. She doesn't get super hard like some of the girls. But Lenda also is a very good role model. She is very personable and she is a very intelligent person. She is very good with the public. So probably Cory first and Lenda right close behind her would be probably the two most ideal that most girls are striving to achieve. I think no matter who looks at them, it's like looking at Jackie Joyner. You don't ever think of them as men.

Differentiating herself from members of Group 1, Heather did not consider Rachel her ideal: although she is athletic, she does not have enough muscle.

In Group 2, increased muscularity is considered a positive attribute, as is also the case in Group 3. However, there is still a perceived tension between muscularity and femininity. Furthermore, a limit is continued to be placed on muscularity because of this perceived tension. Tod revealed this tension in his discussion of a professional female bodybuilder as his ideal: "As far as personification of it . . . in some ways Lenda Murray is, Lenda Murray has a more striking shape, but she's bordered on being too muscular and when you look at her, for example, you look at her when you see Lenda in person, she looks like a thoroughbred horse, her legs are just so big. But it all fits together beautifully." Thus, increased muscularity is acceptable to him, yet there is still some tension between muscular size and proportional esthetics. Similarly, Stan, another national judge, explained:

> I think of all the bodybuilders who have ever competed, the best combination of what we were looking for in a woman bodybuilder

> was Cory Everson at her peak. Just a few years there, and I think that was the type of look that we were after. The athletic look, the not too muscular look but at the same time having a degree of muscularity, having a degree of athleticism, being very agile, being very mobile, and entertaining.

A female bodybuilder who is athletic-looking with some musculature, but not too much, is most favored by this group.

Two members of this group mentioned that the type of bodybuilder exemplified by Anja Schreiner and Rachel McLish does not have enough muscle mass to be considered the ideal look in the sport today. Muscularity is acceptable if the female bodybuilders carry it in an esthetically pleasing way, meaning that their muscle mass does not overpower their bone structure. Finally, members of this group distinguished themselves from the first group by being likely to mention additional qualities, such as being a nice person, a good spokesperson, and an ambassador for the sport.

Group 3: Building Muscle Is the Name of the Game

There are a few noteworthy similarities between this group and Group 2. For instance, many members of Group 3 mentioned the same bodybuilders as their ideal. Moreover, many discussed the importance of both muscularity and femininity. However, what sets this group apart from the rest is that although they contend that femininity is still important, muscularity cannot be compromised because of it. Linda, a regional judge, argued that the key ingredients for an ideal female bodybuilder are muscularity and professionalism: "I think the present 1992 Ms. Olympia [Lenda Murray] represents the ideal. I think that she has the muscularity and she's very, very presentable. What I mean by that is she comes across very feminine. She's very professional. And to me she is a bodybuilder because her muscularity, everything is a total package." Both muscularity and femininity are important to Linda in her assessment of Lenda Murray as her ideal female bodybuilder. Muscularity is the first characteristic she mentioned and at no point does she imply that Lenda is too muscular.

Susan, a regional competitor, also mentioned the importance of the combination of muscularity and femininity. However, instead of mentioning a previous or current Ms. Olympia, she discussed Anja Langer, who competed in the mid- and late 1980s, because she is "one of the tallest female bodybuilders who competed. She has a lot of muscle and she is tall and that takes so much more work than a short bodybuilder. It is easy to put muscle on a small frame and look symmetrical, but it is hard to do it on a tall frame. She is feminine, she is beautiful, she is *big!* She doesn't give up anything." Thus, in the eyes of this bodybuilder, Anja Langer's muscularity and femininity coexist peacefully because she has successfully combined the two ingredients.

This group is the only one that mentioned Bev Francis as an ideal female bodybuilder. According to Patty, a former national competitor:

> I mean I'd have to say that I really admire somebody like Bev Francis because I saw *Pumping Iron II.* And I saw what she looked like in *Pumping Iron II* from being a powerlifter to completely changing. That's what bodybuilding is, it's sculpting. She has completely changed her overall shape and I don't think there's anybody in all the years, I mean there's a few new ones but I mean she has such good muscularity and I think she has done more with her body than anybody else. But then you talk about, I mean, Cory Everson has absolutely the most symmetrical body of anybody I've ever seen. Plus her marketing of herself is wonderful. The woman is not an idiot by any means.

Here, Patty admired Bev Francis because of what she could do with her body—Bev's ability to change her body from that of a powerlifter to a bodybuilder. There is no mention of femininity or excessive muscularity; rather, it is one former competitor respecting another athlete for the work and dedication it must have taken to create the physical metamorphosis that Bev Francis underwent. Patty did mention Cory Everson, not because of her attractiveness or femininity, but because of her symmetrical physique and her shrewd marketing abilities.

Those in Group 3 were the most likely of any of the three groups to mention the importance of muscularity, although many qualified their comments with a reference to femininity. Again, what makes Group 3 members unique is their belief that muscularity and femininity are not inherently conflictual; in fact, some even believed that they complemented each other. Regardless of group placement, femininity is still important.

Thus, the issues of femininity, muscularity, and steroid use are at the heart of how officials and judges evaluate female bodybuilders; these issues also play an enormous role in how these people as well as female bodybuilders themselves view the purpose of their sport and the direction it's taking. Since its incipient days, there has been little to no consensus among those involved in the sport as to the appropriate relationship between these core elements, indicating a fundamental ideological conflict about gender norms between the various players in female bodybuilding. This perennial disagreement has led to confusion in judging standards and fluctuations in what ideal physical type is supposed to be rewarded. I will turn to these topics in detail in the following chapter.

FOUR

Contested Terrain

Corporal Judgment

As we have seen, female bodybuilding has been rife with controversy surrounding the "appropriate" relationship between muscularity and femininity since its earliest contests.[1] Should female bodybuilders be judged like male bodybuilders, with the most muscular and symmetrical bodybuilder prevailing, or should issues of femininity and attractiveness be included in judging criteria? This controversy continues to play out in the evaluation of female bodybuilders. Harry Crews's 1990 novel, *Body,* accurately depicts the vascillations surrounding judging standards for female bodybuilders:

> Nobody knew or could agree on what women wanted or needed to be. Not even women themselves. With men it was easy. Men needed to be as big, as thick, and as defined—their musculature cut, each muscle standing separate and distinct from every other muscle—as could possibly be accomplished. . . . But where did that leave women bodybuilders? Again, nobody knew. Everybody thought they knew when Rachel McLish won the world. She was muscular, and also perfectly symmetrical and coordinated, but most of all she could be

Note: Michael Messner (1988: 197) first used the phrase "contested terrain" in relation to the female athlete in the traditional "male domain" of sport. He argued that "the female athlete—and her body—has become a contested ideological terrain" because athletic women pose a threat to traditional male dominance. He discussed this "contested terrain" specifically in relation to female bodybuilders when he stated, "It is obvious that the new image of women being forged by female bodybuilders is itself fraught with contradiction and ambiguity as women contestants and judges constantly discuss and argue emotionally over the meaning of femininity. Should contestants be judged simply according to how well-muscled they are (as male bodybuilders are judged), or also by a separate and traditionally feminine aesthetic?" (Messner, 1988: 203).

> put in a dress and taken home to mother. But in a short period of time following Rachel McLish's reign as world champion, if you put a world-class female bodybuilder in a dress, she could not be taken home to mother or many other places because they looked like men tricked out in women's clothing. Out of posing briefs and off the stage, they were monsters to behold. The judges and the fans that followed the sport as well as the competitors themselves could not decide what the ideal woman ought to look like. It was a dogfight. One year a woman in one of the lighter divisions would take the overall; the next year a woman bigger than most men could ever hope to be, one that only looked human as long as she was under posing lights, would take it. Up close and dressed in anything feminine, female bodybuilders started looking like something God had made suffering from a divine hangover and caught in delusional terrors beyond human imagination.[2]

Although judges and officials in this study never uttered these particular descriptive references about female bodybuilders—that they were "monsters to behold" or that they could not "be taken home to mother or many other places"—some did refer to muscular female bodybuilders as looking "like guys with bikini tops" and resembling "men with wigs on." All of these references to the distasteful look of excessive musculature could easily be directed at male bodybuilders as well. However, no judges called male bodybuilders "monsters" or said "they couldn't be taken home to mother." These are clearly gender-specific criticisms. In fact, these types of sentiments do not seem to enter into the evaluation of male bodybuilders at all. They do, nevertheless, prominently affect the way female bodybuilders are evaluated. These comments not only reflect some judges' personal attitudes, they also influence how these judges evaluate female bodybuilders at competitions. However, this view does not represent a consensus among judges. Not all of the judges in this study expressed harsh views toward extreme muscularity in female bodybuilders: some voiced quite favorable opinions. Such disparities in judges' opinions and evaluations of muscularity for female bodybuilders have led to fluctuations in, and confusion about, judging decisions.

I will now explore the much contested terrain of the judging process in female bodybuilding and how judges' opinions about the appropriate relationship between femininity and muscularity cloud this already murky and highly subjective process. I will also delve into the effects such fluctuations in opinion have on those who are trying to compete as well as those who are attempting to evaluate these bodybuilders. Because the standards are set and enforced mostly by male social gatekeepers, judging appears to be the backbone of male dominance in female bodybuilding.

Subjectivity: The Trump Card

The duty of a bodybuilding judge is to determine which competitors onstage have the best muscular and symmetrical female physiques. However, determining the winners and losers in these competitions is often a difficult and confusing task. In fact, one can easily argue that the only clear-cut components of this process are the muscles. Like other subjective sports such as figure skating or gymnastics, bodybuilding relies on a panel of judges that evaluates the contestants on a series of predetermined criteria. However, in contrast to other subjective sports, bodybuilders are not judged on how closely their athletic performance comes to the ideal; rather, they are evaluated on how closely their appearance approximates the perfect muscular physique.

Furthermore, unlike other subjective sports, there are no degrees of difficulty in bodybuilding; nor are there any truly impartial measurements as are found in objective sporting endeavors such as swimming and track events. Sam, a national judge, explained the differences between such sports and bodybuilding: "Bodybuilding is not a sport where you have a person running from point A to point B and going through a tape with an electronic stopwatch catching the time. In that situation, you know exactly where competitor 1, 2, 3 placed. Judging bodybuilders, on the other hand, is a very subjective issue." For instance, there are no specific points credited to a bodybuilder who has a single- versus double-peaked bicep, or cut versus ripped muscle groups. Moreover, a seventeen-inch bicep is not inherently better than a ten-inch bicep. Thus, the decision as to which is better is left up to each of the seven to nine judges. This high degree of subjectivity brings with it the potential for inconsistencies when evaluating bodybuilders at competitions. Add the issue of femininity to this already precarious judging situation and one can begin to see the type of subjective quagmire in which female bodybuilding resides. Let's examine the actual judging process before embarking on a further discussion of judging.

Nuts and Bolts of Judging

There are five main levels of bodybuilding judges: levels A and B state amateur judges, national and international amateur judges, and judges who evaluate professional bodybuilders. One must usually first exhibit competence at the state or local levels before being asked to judge at the higher ones. For every bodybuilding meet, a panel of seven to nine judges, the majority of whom are male, usually decides which bodybuilder has come the closest to achieving a perfectly symmetrical and muscular body. In the IFBB, each judge gives a score to the bodybuilders for each of the rounds of competition, "one" for the best competitor, "two" for the second best bodybuilder, and so on. The highest and lowest scores are thrown out for each round. After four rounds, the bodybuilder with the lowest score wins. In the NPC, there are no round-by-round scores; only a single score is given to each bodybuilder at the end of the competition.

Judging in both female and male contests is usually done under the auspices of either the International Federation of Bodybuilders (IFBB) or the National Physique Committee (NPC).[3] Judges use three main criteria to evaluate the physiques of female and male bodybuilders at both NPC and IFBB competitions: overall muscularity in a series of compulsory poses,[4] symmetry and proportion,[5] and presentation of the muscles choreographed together with music.[6] All three are alleged to be of equal importance.

There are slight variations in the way NPC amateur and IFBB professional bodybuilding competitions are organized. For amateur meets, there are four judged rounds—three in the morning (muscularity, symmetry, presentation) and one in the evening (muscularity again). There is also a nonjudged musical-presentation round in the evening. The bodybuilder in each of the three weight classes with the lowest combined score wins her weight class. The posedown, which is an additional round, takes place with the winners of each weight class competing against one another to see who is the overall champion. This round lasts about one minute and is done to music chosen by the event's promoter. The overall winner in both male and female amateur bodybuilding contests is usually, but not always, the heavyweight winner. At the professional level, however, there are no separate weight classes; everyone competes together. As in the amateur ranks, the symmetry and muscularity rounds are held in the morning. However, unlike amateur contests, the presentation round, which occurs in the evening and entails individual ninety-second choreographed presentations by each of the competitors, is judged at professional shows. The purpose of this round is to display one's muscle with music in "an intelligent way."[7] The fourth round, the "posedown," consists of the top six bodybuilders vying for position in front of the judges to show off their musculature. The bodybuilder who has the lowest score wins.

Although male and female bodybuilding meets have these characteristics in common, the similarities end here. For male bodybuilders, extreme muscularity (muscle mass and muscle definition) is highly rewarded (if they also have symmetrical and proportional muscularity). In fact, recall the quote from Harry Crews's novel on the first page of this chapter: " With men it was easy. Men needed to be as big, as thick, and as defined—their musculature cut, each muscle standing separate and distinct from every other muscle—as could possibly be accomplished." However, the same cannot be said for female bodybuilding—these women have to contend with an arbitrary "invisible line" that, when crossed, connotes excessive muscularity. And, in addition to limiting their musculature, women have to enhance their feminine features as well.

The Midlevel Gatekeepers: The Road to Judgment Day

The judging process in the United States is conducted under the auspices of either the IFBB or NPC, depending on the level of competition. In both organizations, judges "must be qualified by passing examinations and [then being] duly certified."[8] Although one judge confided that the only real criterion for becoming a judge is the desire to become one, there are actually three official steps one must take to become a judge at the state or local level. The interested applicant must contact his or her NPC district chairperson, take a judging seminar, practice judging at local shows (not as an official judge), and prove his or her competence by scoring within 85 percent of the scores of judges who are on the judging panel. According to a recent article in *Muscle and Fitness,* "For example, let's say you test judged somebody in third place when they actually came in second. This would be considered one deviation. A percentage system is then used to develop a final score."[9] To qualify to become an NPC judge, you must score 85 or better. Thus, these trainees must conform to the norms set by the other judges. This procedure may in fact work to prevent change in the interpretations of the criteria by judges, particularly if they are in the minority concerning the appropriate degree of muscularity that bodybuilders should exhibit. Once the trainees successfully complete these stages, their names are placed on a list of trained judges for the particular level of competition for which they qualified. To be asked to judge at the national amateur level, one needs a recommendation from the district chairperson within the district where she or he lives.[10]

What motivates people to become bodybuilding judges? Most judges are former competitive bodybuilders. Of the nine female judges in this study, eight are former or current competitive bodybuilders and one is a former competitive powerlifter. Comparably, six of the nine male judges in this study are former competitive bodybuilders, one is currently a noncompetitive bodybuilder, another is a former competitive powerlifter, and the last judge became involved in bodybuilding as a promoter with no experience as a competitor in the sport. In fact, part of what is compelling about judging for both women and men is that it allows those who have previously competed as bodybuilders to be actively involved in the sport still, albeit in a different capacity. As Michelle, a judge explained, "Once you get bitten by the iron bug, it's really hard to get rid of it."

Because monetary benefits are minimal, none of the judges mentioned financial gain as the reason for entering this area of bodybuilding. NPC judges receive only a nominal fifty dollars in travel money plus hotel accommodations for two nights, paid for by the promoter or organizer of the show. IFBB judges receive two hundred dollars each for judging the Ms. Olympia contest and one hundred dollars each for judging other IFBB contests, plus hotel and travel accommodations. Food expenses of thirty-five dollars a day are paid for by the organizer of the contest as well.[11]

Some women were motivated to join the ranks of the judges specifically for political reasons. A few women became judges because of the limited number of female judges throughout the various levels of competition. As Heather, one such judge, explained, "I started to compete in the early '80s and I just started judging because I competed at a lot of the local shows and there were not that many women judges on the panels." She and others felt that there were notable differences in the ways that female and male judges evaluate female bodybuilders; one of the most significant is the purported importance placed on the physical attractiveness of female bodybuilders by some male judges, which I will discuss later in the chapter. There were other political motivations for becoming a judge, as Michelle revealed:

> I became a judge because it's another way for me to use some of my artistic perspective and make a difference in the sport and hopefully point it in a direction in which I would like to see it go. A lot of people complain about why so and so won or didn't win and I always say if you got a problem with that, you want to make a change, then you should become a judge, because you have the power to direct the sport.

In her response, Michelle articulated an argument often given about the relationship between voting in public elections and having a say about political issues: if a person does not like current governmental policies or public officials, then they should vote. If they do not exercise this liberty, they also, in essence, lose their right to complain about the way the government is organized and operated. Michelle can positively influence the sport and perhaps even change its direction by being a judge because, as she said, "You have the power to direct the sport."

Other reasons for entering the field also emerged in the interviews. For instance, much like social scientists Nancy Chodorow and Lillian Rubin,[12] who examined gender differences in emotional intimacy, might have predicted, some women have enjoyed judging because it has allowed them the opportunity to maintain close connections with others involved in the sport. Heather illustrated this point: "The thing I like most about judging is still being involved in the sport and basically the friends I've made, you know, with the competitors themselves, with other administrators in our sport, the worldwide traveling I've gotten to do. But basically it's the friendships that I've made with the girls that I really enjoy." Although the ability to maintain friendships with others is not the only reason she has enjoyed judging, it is, to her, one of the most important reasons. Furthermore, she specifically singled out her friendships with "the girls" in the sport as being the most enjoyable aspect of judging because of the camaraderie. None of the male judges gave friendship, companionship, or camaraderie with others as the most enjoyable aspect of judging. So what were they likely to mention?

On average, male judges tended to voice more instrumental and emotionally detached reasons for their involvement in judging than their female counterparts. Most male judges became judges and continue to judge because they feel like they have something of value to contribute to the sport of female bodybuilding as it develops. For instance, Sam, a national and professional judge, confessed that he enjoys judging because he likes "to be able to contribute to the evolution of the activity." Many of the male judges also disclosed that they have enjoyed judging because it has given them an opportunity to help others who are just learning the ropes in the sport. Mark, a regional judge, explained that the part he enjoyed most about being a judge was being a mentor to bodybuilding novices. Judging gave him the opportunity to lend advice, support, and encouragement to young bodybuilders who were beginning their careers.

The Politics of Judging

As previously stated, the task of judges is to evaluate bodybuilders according to the guidelines set forth by the IFBB or NPC for particular competition levels. There are institutional mechanisms in place which ensure that judges follow the organizational judging guidelines. One of the most effective is the process by which judges are chosen for competitions. For instance, at the amateur level, every state has at least one NPC chairperson who is in charge of the judges, bodybuilders, and bodybuilding events in his or her state. These chairs have a list of all judges in their district and are the ones who determine which judges on the list they will ask to evaluate particular contests. At the professional level, a similar process occurs, except that the NPC chairperson is replaced by the IFBB professional committee and the pool of qualified candidates increases to include an international field. If a registered judge does not consistently follow proper judging protocol, or if there are personal conflicts between him or her and the organizational chairperson or the show promoter, he or she may not be asked by the chairperson to judge future shows. For instance, one male official explained the process as follows:

> The only problem with judging is that although we can apply the rules, it's up to the individual to implement them. It's very, very difficult to get ten or eleven judges from seven or eight different countries to think alike. That's why we scrutinize all the points to make sure that the judges are judging objectively, honestly, and correctly. When we find that there is somebody who is not objective, or somebody who is not really capable, then we remove their membership card. You'll find that in Olympic sports and gymnastics and

> diving and so forth. We have good judges, we're controlling them, and we're satisfied where we are.

Having officials check the judges' scorecards to ensure their judging ability is understandable in any subjective sport where a judge can make or break an athlete's chances of doing well at a contest. However, even given the "objective" criteria used by bodybuilding federations—muscularity in a series of poses, symmetry and proportion, and presentation of muscles to music—there are still various possible interpretations of the relative placement of bodybuilders. In fact, assessing whether judges are judging "correctly" is, in and of itself, a subjective evaluation by the head judges and other bodybuilding officials.

Furthermore, thinking that people, regardless of their training, could be "objective" or that one could get nine judges who hail from as many countries to "think alike" is an improbable and perhaps even questionable goal. In fact, this does not reflect "objectivity" but rather appears to be more indicative of "conformity to group pressures."[13] The goal in judging is ostensibly to choose the most qualified bodybuilders onstage as the top finishers. Because subjectivity plays a large part in the judging process, there is likely to be disagreement among judges as to what constitutes the best physique.

Besides not following judging protocol, there are other reasons one might not be asked to judge again. In fact, one chairperson candidly revealed that

> usually I'll talk to the promoters and see if they want certain judges. Certain promoters and certain judges have conflicts . . . such as somebody that used to work out at their gym, no longer works out at their gym and they are working at a competitor's gym and is bad mouthing the gym. You know, petty stuff, but conflict still goes on and it's real petty stuff. So, I get together with the promoter to see if there is somebody they just don't want because it is their contest.

Therefore, judges who have passed all of the requirements may not be asked to evaluate bodybuilders at a particular contest not because they are poor judges, but because the promoter of the contest or the governing-body chairperson may have a personal grievance with them. Ironically, judges are supposed to adhere to "objectivity" when evaluating bodybuilders, but when promoters and chairpersons select judges for shows, they do not hold themselves to similarly "objective" guidelines.

Yet, even when they *are* asked to evaluate a contest, judges need to be able to dodge other political landmines that potentially lurk in the nooks and crannies. For instance, in exposing the types of political cues judges must read at contests, Michelle, a judge at the national level, disclosed:

> I tell you, honestly speaking, especially when you get up to the national level, okay as a national judge, you have to work harder to make sure that you appease the right people to stay a national judge. What I'm saying is that the way the judging process works and especially when it's at the national level, you know by the way they call out the comparison about what placing people belong in, you know, top five, middle five, bottom five, top fifteen, etc. And sometimes to be quite honest, I haven't agreed with some of the callouts, thinking for instance, that maybe somebody who wound up in the middle five that should definitely have belonged in the top five.

Although she may disagree with the callouts, Michelle realizes that in order to continue judging at the national level, she must be politically astute and accurately read the head judge's tacit messages embedded in his or her callouts. Her words convey her feelings of powerlessness:

> But the judges don't have any control over that . . . the head judge basically kind of sets the tone for the way things are judged in that sense. They will bring out these groups and if you're smart and perceptive enough you can tell that if you don't at least follow that grouping, not necessarily that specific placing, but that grouping, you're not going to hit it right. And so there is a compromise there which sometimes tends to grate on me especially when I think that the call is not right. Somebody that I really wanted in the top five, I know is going to wind up in tenth place or something like that and I've got to go along with it.

I then asked, "Or perhaps you wouldn't be asked to judge on the national level anymore?" She responded, "Well, yeah, my scores would reflect that I'm just not on the ball." "Being on the ball" in this context means a judge must be able to read, accept, and reflect the head judge's opinion as to which bodybuilders onstage are to be chosen as the best at the contest. If judges can do this effectively, they will probably be asked to evaluate bodybuilders again. If judges do not conform, they probably will not be asked again. Similarly, Greg Ptacek found support for such tactics when he interviewed an IFBB judge: "Steve Wennerstrom, an assistant track coach at UCLA (in the early 1980s) and a private instructor of women's bodybuilding, recently judged his first IFBB contest after several years of trying. Judging, he says, 'can be manipulated to fit a standard the Weiders want by selecting judges who agree with the Weider philosophy of bodybuilding.'"[14] Thus, "conformity" to a particular ideological standard rather than "objectivity" appears to be a central issue in the selection process of judges.

In addition to the paradoxes involved in the selection process of judges, we also see a clash between "ideal" and "real" cultures in two of Michelle's comments. Recall that she is the same judge who declared, "If you want to make a change, then you should become a judge because you have the power to direct the sport." However, her comments about the politics of judging belie the sentiment that judges can truly effect change in this sport. In fact, it appears that the change or reform one can elicit as a judge, given the political nature of the sport, is at best minimal; if a judge is seen as a troublemaker or as not "being on the ball," then she is not likely to be asked to judge again. Therefore, judges need to be able to follow the lead set by the head judge if they want to continue judging at a particular level or be asked to judge at a higher level.

Because of the way the organization is run, the top officials are able to fill the upper echelons of judging with people who support their own vision of bodybuilding. Thus, the higher-level judges are the ones most likely to endorse the official stance on what constitutes the ideal female bodybuilder. Local or regional judges are the most likely to voice dissenting opinions. These judges may be better judges than those at the higher levels, but if they do not agree with the officials, they have a difficult time reaching the national and professional levels.

The head judge, who is usually a high-ranking male official in one of the governing bodies, is the person who calls out groups of two to five bodybuilders at a time from the line of all competitors. They will pose at center stage so that the judges can more easily compare their symmetry, proportion, and muscularity. Recall from the ethnographic account that when a head judge calls out certain bodybuilders several times and others only once, judges and bodybuilders alike can tell which bodybuilders the head judge thinks should be placed at the top of the list and which should be placed toward the bottom. If Michelle's statement is accurate, bodybuilding officials may be less concerned with judges' "objective" and accurate evaluations of bodybuilders onstage than with their ability to read the implicit and explicit messages given by the head judge.

Finally, the presumption that the head judge is the most "objective" and accurate judge on the panel, and that other judges must simply take his or her lead to "see the light," may be contradicted by their ties to sponsors and organizers.

The Rumblings of Inconsistency Begin

In the 1991 and 1992 seasons, the dual issues of judging inconsistency and perceived excessive muscularity among female bodybuilders came to a cacophonous head when at back-to-back professional female bodybuilding meets (the 1991 Ms. Olympia and the 1992 Ms. International) the judges rewarded opposite looks; at one meet, they rewarded the ripped, hard look; at the other, the smooth, soft look. The event that precipitated the IFBB's decision to limit female bodybuilders' muscularity was the 1991 Ms. Olympia contest which was held in Los Angeles and televised live on ESPN. This was the first professional female bodybuilding meet aired on live TV. Many of the female bodybuilders at this contest were big, ripped, and cut. Apparently this muscular look was not well received by ESPN viewers, because the channel and the IFBB allegedly received letters and calls from people who found the muscularity of the female bodybuilders disconcerting, or worse. In response to the negative reactions received by the station, officials apparently were prompted to set limits on female bodybuilders' muscularity. Diane, a professional bodybuilder, described the event and its aftermath:

> When the Ms. Olympia was live, it was like, those women were huge—just monstrous women and the IFBB got so many negative comments about this from the general public. The people who buy the magazines are like, "What is your sport? What are you becoming? What are these women doing? They are looking like men." So that's when the IFBB said, "Well, wait a minute, ladies. We want you smaller, we want you more feminine."

Thus, the issue of possibly alienating its commercial constituency appears to have been the impetus for the move back to smaller-muscled, more "feminine-looking" female bodybuilders.

At the next women's professional competition, the officials' desire for less muscular and more feminine bodybuilders could be seen. At the 1992 Ms. International show, the most muscular woman did not even place in the top six. One extremely muscular female bodybuilder, Laura

1. The guns of Juliette Bergmann. (Photo courtesy of *Women's Physique World Magazine.*)

2. Posing in the weight room: Tanya Herman. (Photo courtesy of *Women's Physique World Magazine.*)

3. The feminine apologetic revealed: Bernie Price. (Photo courtesy of *Women's Physique World Magazine.*)

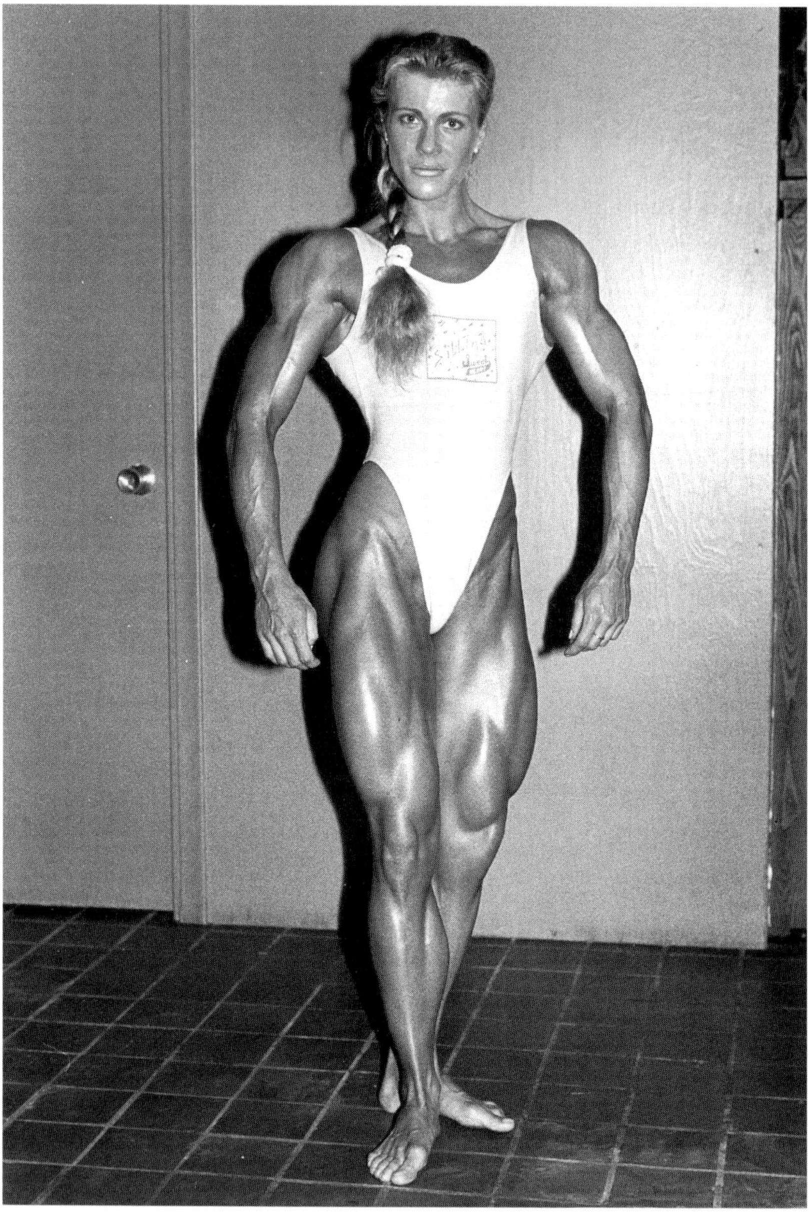

4. The elusive V shape: Anja Langer. (Photo courtesy of *Women's Physique World Magazine.*)

5. The semi-relaxed stance: Barbara Kafkora, Czech Republic. (Photo courtesy of *Women's Physique World Magazine.*)

6. Sea-side flexing: Roser Hernandez. (Photo courtesy of *Women's Physique World Magazine.*)

7. Muscular lines, in the muscularity round, side chest with bicep: Cathy LeFrançois. (Photo courtesy of *Women's Physique World Magazine.*)

8. Posing during the presentation round: Frederique Auchart, France. (Photo courtesy of *Women's Physique World Magazine.*)

9. Posing and flexing during the presentation round: Caron Hospedales, USA. (Photo courtesy of *Women's Physique World Magazine.*)

10. Back-to-back competition: Tami Imbriale (*left*) and Cathy Palyo. (Photo courtesy of *Women's Physique World Magazine.*)

11. Buff and hard: Zdenka Razymova, Czech Republic. (Photo courtesy of *Women's Physique World Magazine*.)

12. Cut and ripped during the muscularity round, side chest with bicep: Judy Moshkosky. (Photo courtesy of *Women's Physique World Magazine.*)

13. Strike a pose, presentation round: Caron Hospedales, USA. (Photo courtesy of *Women's Physique World Magazine.*)

14. Some of bodybuilding's heavyweights, in the symmetry round and the semi-relaxed stance: Lenda Murray (*left*), Sandy Riddell (*center*), and Bev Francis (*right*). (Photo courtesy of *Women Physique World Magazine.*)

15. Holding up more than half of the sky: Andrea Izard, Australia. (Photo courtesy of *Women's Physique World Magazine.*)

16. Spreading her wings: Rita Dytuco, Canada. (Photo courtesy of *Women's Physique World Magazine.*)

17. A shredded deltoid and the Horseshoe tricep: Amelia Hernandez, Spain. (Photo courtesy of *Women's Physique World Magazine.*)

18. Back in black: the muscular moguls of Paula Suzuki, USA. (Photo courtesy of *Women's Physique World Magazine.*)

19. A six-gun salute, the muscularity round: Jan Tana Pro Classic. (Photo courtesy of *Women's Physique World Magazine.*)

Creavalle, did place third. However, the winner of the contest was one of the least muscular and most "traditionally" attractive female bodybuilders (blond hair, blue eyes, and a former fitness competitor) competing on the professional circuit. Confusion reigned. Heather, a national and professional judge, reflected:

> I think when Anja Schreiner and Debbie Muggli [two softer women] were picked in the higher classes at the Ms. International, it was way out in left field. They tried to set an example that was far too harsh because there were girls there who were just as feminine on a little bit more muscular basis, but at least their muscularity fit their frames. The two they picked really are not predisposed to be great bodybuilders.

Similarly, David, a state judge, explained:

> At the Ms. Olympia, they put Bev Francis second, and then you go up to the Ms. International at Columbus and they put Debbie Muggli second and Laura Creavalle third in both contests. You know it's really confusing what they've done. And Paula Bircumshaw would have probably been up there somewhere but they changed their whole judging criteria from one extreme to the other, because Anja Schreiner who won the Ms. International, in my opinion, shouldn't have even been in the top six. She's a pretty girl and has good symmetry, but she doesn't have much muscle.

Thus, inconsistencies occurred not just between shows but within the same show as well. David shared a comment by another judge: "If they are going to be critical of women's muscularity, they need to either put Bev Francis first or last. She doesn't need to be second or third; that just confuses the audience and everything." Many judges, regardless of their stance on the relationship between muscularity and femininity, did not understand how the judges could have chosen whom they did as the top two contestants at the show because they represented two extremes on the continuum of muscularity. Where did this series of decisions leave the sport?

The Aftershocks

I interviewed most judges and female bodybuilders in this study within a year of the Ms. International contest when the sport was still reeling from the fallout over that show's decision. Most judges believed that judging inconsistency—as indicated by the two different types of physiques that were rewarded at the Ms. Olympia and the Ms. International contests, as well as the internal inconsistencies at the Ms. International contest—was a problem endemic to the sport, but their explanations for these fluctuations varied. Many judges gave multiple reasons for such discrepancies. For instance, Heather explained that just as there are fluctuations in society's fashions, there are also changes in what is considered the ideal physique in female bodybuilding:

> Any sport goes through its growing process. I mean, women's bodybuilding, the first contest was only judged in 1978. So it's not really that old of a sport and you see trends. Just like in society, longer dresses come in fashion for a couple of years, then short dresses . . . we see ups and downs. You know, women didn't have a lot of muscle back in the early '80s because they had not been training that long, so it's a very dieted down, ripped look. Then as some of the girls got bigger, it was the more muscular look. Then it was back to being the more feminine look. So it has gone through the ups and downs.

However, the growing process for male bodybuilding was much different—there has been a trend toward an increase in musculature. Oscillations from more to less musculature did not occur in the early history of male bodybuilding as it has in female bodybuilding. Moreover, Heather attributed the first fluctuations in female bodybuilding to women's brief experience with weight training. However, she failed to explain the reasons for the trend back toward less muscular female bodybuilders. Her quote also reveals her underlying premise that "more muscular" indicates "less feminine."

Heather later attributed some of the fluctuations in the judging decisions to the inconsistency in the quality of athletes:

> I think part of the problem with our sport is that we're very inconsistent in judging because we can only judge what level or what type of athlete is on stage that day. . . . You know most of the judges, especially at the national level, they know what the ideal is and they know what the organization likes to see. But lots of times, it's not there so you have to try to find the degree of physique that's closest to it. . . . You see more of the inconsistency, or what is termed inconsistency at the local level because there is so much inconsistency in the athletes themselves.

First, it is her contention that judges know what the organization likes to see. Therefore, the problem stems not from the national office failing to disseminate information to its athletes or from judges' biases, but rather from the quality of the athletes' physiques.

Others provided less individual-level explanations for the inconsistencies. Many judges blamed officials for wavering on what they wanted female bodybuilders to look like on stage. For instance, Tracy revealed:

> Well, it's very confusing because they switch from one year to the next. One year they pick someone who is big, the next year they pick another woman who is not so big like Anja Schreiner, you know. They switch so much and this is the complaint from a lot of contestants. The bodybuilders don't know what the judges want, but we don't know either. Because the national office switches on us all the time so it's still confusing for all of us.

The major cause of such inconsistencies, according to Tracy and others who shared her views, was that judges were not getting consistent information from officials. Tracy also concluded that since the national office did not clearly and concisely disseminate information about the preferred look for female bodybuilders, confusion is to be expected among both contestants and judges.

Patty, a former national competitor, gave comparable structural reasons for such fluctuations:

> They don't know what they want in female bodybuilders and I think that it really stems from the national level because we went through cycles with female bodybuilding. When it first came in you had the little Rachel McLishes then they went from the Rachel McLishes to the Bev Francis type woman and then they decided they didn't want that, now they want to go back toward the Rachel McLishes.

Without hesitation, she placed the blame for judging inconsistencies on the national office. From her vantage point, the officials annually change their minds about the preferred physiques for female bodybuilders. Again, these fluctuations may be an attempt by social gatekeepers to keep the sport marketable to a wider audience in an attempt to increase profits, i.e., it is planned obsolescence.

In Your Eyes: The Variability in Salience of Muscularity and Femininity

It is the responsibility of the top officials to disseminate information about rules and regulations to their judges and contestants. They do this at judges' meetings before contests, at meetings with state chairs, through informal communication channels, by meeting people at contests, and finally through IFBB and NPC literature. Officials inform the judges, and it is up to the judges to enforce the new regulations and rules. However, the information is not always received by bodybuilders in time for their contests. Thus, bodybuilders often express confusion and frustration about the fluctuations or inconsistencies in judging standards. In fact, one of the issues heatedly debated throughout the sport of female bodybuilding is that of judging inconsistencies, as was illustrated in the last section.

Inconsistency even invades the "set" criteria for evaluation—judges disagree as to which of the three "equally important" factors is most salient. Thus, while some judges revealed that symmetry is the most important criterion by which they judge female bodybuilders, others emphasized the importance of muscularity. For instance, Tracy, a state judge, revealed:

> Well, of course, female bodybuilders have got to have muscle and I look at the shape of the muscle in each muscle group. And the one with the best overall shape, muscular shape, really is who I go for. If she's big, and she's got really good shape, and she still looks feminine, and I've got somebody else who is not so big and has equal shape, I will go for the bigger one as long as she looks feminine.

Overall, for Tracy, muscularity is the most important criterion when she evaluates a female bodybuilder. However, she also qualified this statement by saying that the female bodybuilder must also still look feminine. Perplexed by this qualifier, I asked her what she meant, and she replied: "Well, you can tell her hips from her waist. In other words, that she has a waistline. No facial hair, makeup is on, her hair is in a flattering style. The way she carries herself on stage, her posing routine." Thus the manifestations of femininity are multifaceted. Not only can a bodybuilder not exhibit signs of steroid use (as is illustrated by the comments about hip-to-waist ratio and facial hair), she must also make sure that all signifiers of femininity are enhanced, including use of makeup, hairstyle, walking style, and posing routine. While female bodybuilders engage in an activity with stereotypically masculine qualities (extreme muscularity, for instance), they must compensate with enhanced femininity. They must set themselves apart from their male counterparts.

Tracy's comments are suggestive of the feminine apologetic in which female athletes are, in essence, compensating for entering a traditionally masculine domain (sports in general) by amplifying aspects of their femininity.[15] The feminine apologetic functions to legitimate women's involvement in sport and to reduce role conflict that they might experienced in sport.[16] The apologetic may take a number of forms.[17] The one most applicable to female bodybuilders is the exaggerated use of feminine accouterments such as makeup, jewelry, breast implants, and the like. The apologetic implies that female athletes can still look feminine, are feminine, and want to be feminine,[18] thus helping to encourage the participants and others that athletic involvement does not invalidate their claim to being "real" women.[19] In other words, in female bodybuilding, such exaggerated displays of femininity by female bodybuilders may be used to counter the displays of ostensible muscularity (and thus in some people's minds, masculinity as well). This tactic serves to reinforce the femininity of the athletes.

Similarly, Michelle, a national judge, unequivocally declared that muscularity is the most important criterion for her when she evaluates female bodybuilders: "Well, I still like muscle. I still have no problem with a woman who is up there and she's really separated and she's really got excellent definition and then she's still got a lot of mass on her, that's fine with me as long as the muscle is balanced and rounded, she doesn't look drawn." Her comment about the muscles not "looking drawn" refers to the effect that diuretics have on muscles. However, in addition, Michelle also qualified her acceptance of muscularity with statements about the importance of feminine enhancers much like Tracy had done:

> But I want to see a female body there. I want to see the broader shoulders, small tapering waist. I don't want to see a blocky waist, and for women bodybuilders, I like a slimmer hip. I want her to walk on stage, her carriage has to be that of a woman, she can't come lumbering on the stage. When she does her posing, I want to see some fluidity, I don't want to see a lot of what are generally considered male power poses like a crab or just very masculine way of standing, carrying herself.

In addition to enhancing femininity on the body, Tracy emphasizes the importance of the face and hair as sites for the enhancement of femininity:

> From the neck up I want to see as much attention put in to her appearance in her face as she has on the rest of her body. I want to see a groomed woman up there. I want her to make an attempt to put on some makeup, fix her hair, and I'm not saying that she's got to look like a beauty queen when she's up there and that I'd take a beauty queen over someone who doesn't have those looks. Because it's still what I see from the neck down that is important.

Nothing on the body or face can be left unfeminized. Female bodybuilders must enhance their femininity to compensate for the fact that they have entered into what Tracy and others define as dangerous somatic territory—the muscular domain of masculinity. Thus, to ensure that they are not mistaken for a male, they wear makeup, have feminine hairstyles, and walk, pose, and stand onstage in conspicuously feminine ways. Judges who have the power to reward or penalize a physique make certain that their views of the appropriate relationship between femininity and muscularity are reinforced.

The parallels between Michelle's and Tracy's comments are noteworthy. While both think that muscularity is the most important criterion, they qualify this with an animated discussion of the importance of female bodybuilders presenting an unequivocal feminine self. In their opinion, female bodybuilders should not only adorn themselves with feminine accouterments, they should also obfuscate any indicators of steroid use. They fear that female bodybuilders, when too muscular, may lose their femininity.

However, not all judges shared Michelle's and Tracy's opinions about the positioning of the three main criteria. While Michelle and Tracy placed muscularity high on their list of criteria as long as their femininity is also enhanced or exaggerated, others believed that symmetry, not muscularity, was the most important criterion. Heather, a national judge, explained that the first criterion she looks for is symmetry, because she finds it the most esthetically pleasing of the criteria:

> Okay, first of all, we look for—and this is in any competitor whether it's male or female—you first look for the esthetics, the symmetry. First of all, are the genetics there? Is the bone structure equal? Does

> the bodybuilder have a small waist, small joints? That plays a big part in how your muscle is going to develop on your frame. Have they developed all of their muscle groups? Is the upper and lower body proportional as well as the right to left sides? There is a lot of asymmetry when you look at some physiques because some people being a dominant right-handed person, you will see the right side of the body a lot more developed than the left. So you really look for the esthetics. Is the symmetry there? And I think that plays the biggest part to go on to win a national contest.

She then described what she wants to see in terms of muscular development:

> To do it on a consistent basis you really have to have nice genetics as far as bone structure and your proportions. So I look to see that all my muscle groups are developed. I will place somebody higher when they are totally developed in the package, even though the package might be a little bit smaller than somebody who's got a couple of outstanding body parts but are real, real lacking in others. And then after you get done with symmetry, and the development of the muscle, then you look to see what their nutrition is like. Are they very . . . do their muscles look drawn, do they look nice and full, you know, where the insertion sights are; are they doing their weight lifting? Like, are the motions, the full range of motion? You see a lot of people do the movements improperly. So their muscles develop not in the symmetrical way. So you really look at each of the muscle groups to see that everything is developed.

After examining the symmetry and muscularity, Heather looks at the final, yet important, components of the total package:

> And also how they present themselves . . . especially when you get to the national level because it comes down to little things like how well they present themselves, how well their routine is choreographed. How much poise they have on stage. What are their overall features as far as how their coloring is put on. How their suit is, you know, does it fit their physique? The hair, the makeup, the whole, everything comes down to it when you get to the higher levels.

Heather's quote, when compared to Michelle's and Tracy's quotes, highlights the disparity in the judges' criteria. Symmetry is most important to Tracy. Furthermore, whereas Tracy and Michelle candidly revealed that they had "no problem with" cut, ripped, and muscular female bodybuilders, Heather mentioned that in her mind it was important for female bodybuilders to have "muscle groups that are developed." Thus, even the ways in which Heather defined and discussed muscularity varied from Tracy's and Michelle's; for these two judges, a female bodybuilder can still be big if she has not diminished her femininity in the process. Heather was more interested in the overall muscular development from a symmetrical and nutritional perspective. In addition, while Tracy and Michelle indicated that they would choose a muscular, symmetrical, and feminine bodybuilder over a smaller-sized athlete, Heather declared that she would vote for a smaller-packaged female bodybuilder over a larger one, if the smaller one had a better overall symmetrical package.

Once again, these three judges emphasized the importance that female bodybuilders must look like women and they should possess feminine attributes in the way they carry themselves onstage (no lumbering to and fro like a male bodybuilder) and how they wear their makeup and style their hair. Furthermore, by discussing the importance of small, tapered, and nonblocky waists in female bodybuilders, they implied that steroid use should be limited.

The Effects: Confusion, Frustration, Departure

The fluctuations in judging have led to confusion among both bodybuilders and judges as to what is expected of them. Diane, a professional bodybuilder sighed, "Sometimes I don't understand what they are doing," and Mark, a judge, explained that "the women who want to compete don't even know what to do anymore." The ones who ultimately pay the price for such inconsistencies in judging protocol are the bodybuilders themselves. They prepare for competitions not knowing which criteria the judges will be told to emphasize for a particular competition. This type of confusion quickly leads to frustration, as Heather revealed, "What female bodybuilders are expressing to me is basically that they still want to compete, but they have to know what they need to do. They're very confused so they're also very frustrated." Michelle stated:

> I think that you're going to find a lot of women at the higher levels of competition who have used steroids or I should say have that kind of

> muscularity that they are now frowning upon, they're the ones that are really in the Catch-22. They have spent the last, what, five, six, or whatever years developing their body with the thought that's what the judges wanted to see. They wanted to see that kind of muscularity. And sometimes, yes, they have used steroids and endangered their health to get to that point and I have to quite honestly say that if they're at that level of competition, they have that kind of muscularity, they probably have been. So, they're in a really bad situation because they have done all this to get where they are, and now the judges are turning around and telling them, "I'm sorry, but that's not what we want after all." Yeah [the rules have basically changed on them], and they're kind of stuck going, "Oh, you mean I just spent the last some odd years and some odd thousand dollars and all of this—I've lowered my voice, I've grown hair on my chin, and all this stuff—for nothing." I think it's very unfair.

Later in the interview, Michelle tied the recent changes in judging to the sponsors' desire to attract more people to competitions. Female bodybuilders are thus left in a quandary as to what is expected of them from judges. This is not a harmless situation because female bodybuilders' livelihood depends on being able to read accurately what is expected of them for competitions. However, when the criteria change from one contest to another and from one year to another, this task becomes virtually impossible. Changing one's physique cannot be done overnight, and if female bodybuilders misread the evaluative cues, they may be out of contention for the top placements in contests and any product endorsements for well over a year.

Patty, a former national competitor, echoed the sentiments of many of the bodybuilders:

> I have seen contests where a woman . . . I mean she almost looked like a man, but she was still the best one on that stage. Even if I didn't agree with what she had done to herself, she was still the best bodybuilder on that stage and the judges purposely did not give it to her. Well, where's the fairness in that? If you're going to have a drug-tested show or say "we don't want you looking like men," then write down some rules that we have to go by. Don't wait until you get onstage after you've busted your butt all these years training and then decide to give it to somebody else. So, I just think they need to get their act together and decide what they want to do with women's

> bodybuilding. There's only two national contests now because I think women are tired of not knowing what the powers-that-be want.

Patty thus believes that the central issue is fairness to those who "bust their butts" day in and day out to compete effectively at competitions. If women do not receive fair and consistent treatment by judges and officials, regardless of their passion for and dedication to the sport, some will choose not to compete. As Tracy said, "That's why we are seeing the level of women going down, because they don't know what the judges want, but we don't either." In the eyes of some bodybuilders and judges, the sport, by sending inconsistent messages to its athletes, is weeding out some of its best competitors. Therefore, the sport as a whole must agree on the criteria by which female bodybuilders will be judged and must strictly adhere to them.

Why are many of those associated with women's bodybuilding so concerned with increasing femininity and limiting muscularity? Is this concern limited to judges and officials, or do female bodybuilders themselves share some of these opinions? In the following chapter, I address the interrelated issues of femininity, muscularity, and marketability.

FIVE

Profitable Physiques, Precarious Hegemonies

The Maintenance of the Feminine Apologetic

> There's a lot of people in the general public who really think "Female bodybuilding is gross and freaky. That's not what a woman is supposed to look like." . . . I would say that they think that the whole thing, the whole sport of bodybuilding is a freak, with women being the biggest freaks in the show.
>
> —Michelle, a national judge

IN THE PREVIOUS CHAPTER, I discussed Jan Felshin's feminine apologetic, wherein female athletes may compensate for their participation in the traditionally masculine domain of sports by emphasizing their femininity.[1] As we have seen, this phenomenon is irrefutably operative in the sport of female bodybuilding. Judges and officials serve as gatekeepers to ensure that female bodybuilders actualize the feminine apologetic. In the minds of some gatekeepers, however, female bodybuilders do not fully understand the importance of embodying the feminine apologetic and the extent to which they are expected to comply. Angered by what he considers incorrigible female bodybuilders, with overly developed musculature, Kyle, a highly ranked official, asserted:

> The women are too extreme. And by them being too muscular we don't attract mainstream fans to come see the contest. They'd rather go see a fitness show or bikini show or something like that because when the women bodybuilders are so muscular they look like guys. . . . [In the beginning of female bodybuilding] these women were very

> attractive and other women wanted to look like them and the guys wanted to look at them. That's why it drew a large crowd. But now, with the women being so extreme, you don't find many women that want to go to the gym and train to look like that.

Kyle wants female bodybuilders to embody the feminine apologetic more fully chiefly because feminine female bodybuilders attract more spectators and thus more money enters the sport. In this chapter, I rely on the work of Dan C. Hilliard who, in his analysis of the portrayals of female and male tennis players in magazine articles, argued that the apologetic is particularly important when women's sports become commercial enterprises that must attract sponsors and paying spectators.[2] He maintained, "It is of great economic interest [to sponsors] that the athletes participating in the events they sponsor be perceived as feminine by the potential buyers of their products."[3] Female bodybuilders are economically motivated to pay homage to the feminine apologetic because their personal-endorsement incomes will be cut if they are not perceived as feminine. This interrelationship between the economic interests of the social gatekeepers and female bodybuilders creates a system where both, "as participants in an ongoing commercial athletic system, may enter into an unspoken complicity to present an image that emphasizes underlying femininity.[4] By excluding overly "masculine" female bodybuilders from the monetary reward system under the guise that they repel paying spectators, social gatekeepers are able to promote their own vision of what female bodybuilders should look like.

Onstage Gendered Creations

Bodybuilders enhance and display their gender in a variety of ways in bodybuilding competitions. One way is by their musical selections and posing routines during the presentation round of a competition. During this ninety-second round, both female and male bodybuilders display their musculature to the music of their choice. However, there are significant differences in the musical selections and posing styles of female and male bodybuilders. Females are more likely to perform fluid, balletic movements and poses onstage; they are also more likely to select popular dance tunes or sentimental love songs from such artists as Janet Jackson, Mariah Carey, or SNAP!. Some women incorporate seductive poses, glances, and lyrics in their routines as well. For example, at one competition, a professional female bodybuilder performed her musical presentation to a song with the following lyrics, "I know what boys want, I know what guys like . . . na . . . na . . . na . . . na . . . na. I know what boys want, boys want, boys want." Reminiscent of Marilyn Monroe's infamous "happy birthday" performance for John F. Kennedy, this bodybuilder mouthed the words to the song, as she moved and danced in suggestive poses with intermittent coquettish glances toward the audience members and judges. This dance routine, in combination with the musical selection, served to reaffirm her femininity and heterosexuality to the audience members and judges, particularly the males.[5]

Male bodybuilders are more likely to strike their muscular poses in a hard, distinct, and fast manner, and they are also more likely to incorporate poses known as "power poses" such as the crab.[6] Although they smile at the audience and judges during the presentation round of competition, they do not appear to do so with the same frequency as female bodybuilders. Also, they are more likely to grimace, growl, and at times, even yell during the presentation round. Moreover, their musical selections differ markedly from those of female bodybuilders in that they are more likely to pose to loud and thunderous rock music such as that of Guns N' Roses, Nine Inch Nails, or Metallica.

Another way bodybuilders construct their gender onstage is by their hairstyles. According to regulations, female bodybuilders must not allow their hair to cover any of their musculature during competitions. However, this rule does not translate into allowing them to cut off most of their hair for competition—in fact short-cropped hair for female bodybuilders is a rarity. In the 1992 Ms. Olympia line-up, only one bodybuilder out of nineteen had short hair. Rather, they simply pull their hair up off their shoulders and still present it in a feminine way. Male bodybuilders, on the other hand, are likely to sport very short haircuts, often even crew cuts, on the day of the competition. Susan, a regional bodybuilder, talked about the differences between female and male bodybuilders in preparing to present their gendered selves on the day of the competition:

> Women put on makeup and care a whole lot more about their hair before a show than guys do. I mean guys, in getting ready for a show, get their hair cut as short as they can. I haven't seen one yet putting on mascara. For women, its like they're getting married the day

> of the bodybuilding contest. They pay their hairdressers god-awful amounts of money to come in on Saturday morning to do their hair and do their makeup.

Furthermore, whereas only 5 percent of adult American women are blond,[7] the vast majority of white professional female bodybuilders have bleached-blond hair. At the 1992 Ms. Olympia, for instance, eight of the ten white American female bodybuilders were blondes—perhaps because of its association with youth and fun,[8] and with an All-American, California beach, healthy, fit, and playful look—an image with which bodybuilding actively attempts to associate itself because of its marketability.

In their quest to construct a feminine presentation of self,[9] many female bodybuilders, especially those who compete at the national and professional levels, go even further than the above. Many go to unhealthy extremes to appear feminine while simultaneously sporting immense musculature. For instance, because female bodybuilders undergo extensive training and dieting regimens, they have very low levels of body fat when they are in competition shape; high-level competitive female bodybuilders have body-fat levels of only about 3 to 10 percent on the day of competition, compared with body-fat levels of approximately 23 percent for the average American woman. At such low levels of bodyfat, female bodybuilders lose the majority of their breast tissue; and because breasts epitomize femininity, many get breast implants to compensate for this loss. In a recent article addressing the prevalence of cosmetic surgery among bodybuilders, it was suggested that perhaps as many as 80 percent of professional as well as a substantial percentage of national-level female bodybuilders have undergone breast augmentation despite the well-publicized potential health risks for doing so.[10] While both the IFBB and the NPC have outlawed muscle implants for male and female bodybuilders, breast implants are legal. And not only are they legal, they appear to be widely condoned and even encouraged by individuals at every level in the sport.

Female bodybuilders' reasons for going to such lengths include their perception that it improves their appearance and thus enhances their self-image.[11] In fact, Stephanie, a professional female bodybuilder, confessed that part of the reason she got breast implants and had facial reconstructive surgery was because it made her feel better about herself:

> Female bodybuilders dye their hair, get breast implants, get nose jobs, because I've been through my share of that. Part of me doing what I've done didn't totally have to do with what the judges wanted. It's just the fact that I'm on stage in front of all these people and I'm the one that has to constantly look in magazines and see pictures of myself. And when you see pictures of yourself over and over again, you start to look at the things that are wrong and you go, "Wow, look at my side view. God, that can be corrected a little bit." I mean, I look at myself in the mirror every day, but I don't have to look at a still shot and just keep looking at it. That caused me to say, "Well, you need a little work on your nose or something." Breasts are something I always wanted . . . because I never ever had any. . . . I think on a female bodybuilder, though, part of the reason a lot of us do it is because one of the questions we are commonly asked is, "Why don't women bodybuilders have breasts?" Really, it's stupid because most female athletes period don't have a lot of breast because we're athletes and we [have] low body fat [levels] and breasts are just body fat.

Notice, however, that there are other reasons Stephanie gave for having reconstructive breast and facial surgery. First, she wanted to feel better about how she looked onstage and in magazines. Second, she mentioned being partially influenced by "what the judges wanted." She was not the only bodybuilder to mention being approached or influenced by comments made by judges about getting breast implants. Others also revealed that judges approach them and talk about the positive effects that breast implants would have on their placements in shows. For instance, Vicky, a professional bodybuilder, reported that a few of her bodybuilding peers had asked judges what they would need to do to improve their placing. In one case, a judge responded, "When are you going to get breast augmentation?" Later in the interview, she said, "I think it's wrong to tell women 'you're not feminine unless you have big breasts,' and they don't look good anyway when you get lean [for a competition]." However, other judges insisted that female bodybuilders should have moderate-sized breasts even when competing.

Some judges masked their suggestions in terminology related to bodybuilding. For instance, a regional bodybuilder, Susan, recalled: "I've heard comments from judges that if a woman doesn't have a large chest, it really detracts from her symmetry scores because women are supposed to be built like that." If judges do not think a female bodybuilder is "symmetrical," they will mark her down even if this is not a fair assessment for a judge to make. Female bodybuilders know this. Thus, although some judges may not explicitly tell women to get breast enhancements because "women are supposed to have breasts," they in effect do so by implying that it will improve a bodybuilder's chances of doing well in the symmetry rounds of contests.

Thus, in addition to personal reasons for enhancing one's femininity—feeling more attractive and feeling better about oneself—there are instrumental reasons as well, which are institutionally supported by the social gatekeepers. Female bodybuilders have clearly and continuously received messages from the gatekeepers that if they want to do well in the sport competitively and economically, they need to enhance their femininity in certain accepted ways. These individual and institutional reasons seem to be mutually reinforcing. For instance, recall Susan's remark that female bodybuilders put a lot of energy into preparing their faces and hairstyles in feminine ways on the day of the competition, much like they would on their wedding days or for a beauty pageant. When I asked her why they did this, she responded: "You worry about that stuff when you go to a show. There's still some of that stuff in you. A pretty face is more important on a female bodybuilder than a male bodybuilder. You do it because you want to win. I mean, it's part of the routine. The judges notice it." Vicky and Stephanie's comments suggest that social gatekeepers have a role in affecting the ways female bodybuilders construct their femininity. These individual and institutional reasons propel many female bodybuilders down the road to enhance their femininity in many ways—through makeup, hairstyle, posing style and musical selection, walking form, and reconstructive facial and breast surgeries. But do judges and officials really emphasize the importance of attractive and feminine-looking female bodybuilders as much as female bodybuilders think, or is there some projection on the part of these women? To answer this question, I asked both judges and officials what characteristics they felt were important when they evaluate female bodybuilders and compared their statements with those of the women.

Judges and "The Overall Package"

According to judges in this study, the "overall" or "complete package" is what is important when evaluating both female and male bodybuilders. When I asked Mary, a bodybuilder, to explain her interpretation of what is meant by this term, she replied: "When they say they're looking for the 'complete package,' it means that it's easier for a nice-looking person to win than it is for an ugly person." However, "overall package" is given more weight when judging female bodybuilders than male bodybuilders. For example, Linda, a regional judge, explained:

> You have people like "Sue." I mean I've never seen anybody train, we've been in California, we've been all over. And I've never seen anybody train as hard, or for anybody to look as hard as she does. But I don't think that she will ever . . . [do well] . . . because . . . if a man goes up there and he's got this big, I mean he is totally cut and the muscularity is unreal, and if he's not handsome, I mean they don't care whether he's handsome, whether his looks are appealing or not. He can do well. But a woman, if she is not a complete total package, if she doesn't have the showmanship or this sexy and being feminine and being this and being that . . . I mean she won't do it. So that's where I sit. But it's very . . . women's bodybuilding is very controversial.

The "overall package" for female bodybuilders is more multifaceted than for male bodybuilders. Males must be muscular, symmetrical, and neat. Females, on the other hand, must be symmetrical, muscular but not too muscular, neat, feminine, and, in the minds of some judges, attractive. Thus, although there is overlap in the characteristics on which female and male competitors are evaluated, there are differences as well. Mary, a regional competitor and judge, discussed the overlap:

> I mean if you get right down to it, male and female bodybuilders are judged alike in a lot of ways. We want to make sure we have got a thin waist, there hasn't been drug abuse involved where it's noticeable, and we want the women to stay looking like women. Men, we want the mass, the thickness, the vascularity, the muscularity. And we're looking at the same things for women. So, no there's not that much of a difference, no.

Echoing many of Mary's sentiments but also highlighting the differences, Michelle, a national judge asserted:

> Both male and female, we look at structure, we look at muscular development, we look at general condition as far as vascularity and tightness and all that good stuff. Where the difference comes in is, "Are all those criteria on the female physique pleasing or not?" So

> what I'm saying is the one aspect that is not involved in male bodybuilding that is involved in female bodybuilding is that big question of femininity. A woman's physique still has to have muscularity, separation, balance, and symmetry, but it's got to be on a feminine package . . . which is very, very subjective.

Although both Mary and Michelle contended that "male and female bodybuilders are judged alike in a lot of ways," they acknowledged the existence of gender-specific differences in the criteria by which they are judged. Judges must ensure that "the women stay looking like women" and that the criteria of muscularity, separation, balance, and symmetry look pleasing on "a feminine package." These judges thus institutionally reinforce the importance of gender distinctions by limiting female bodybuilders' muscularity. They are the institutional gatekeepers of the feminine apologetic. Because, in the judges' eyes, muscularity, vascularity, and thickness are perceived as being congruent with masculinity, no similar concern exists in judging male bodybuilders.

Not surprisingly, female bodybuilders and judges mentioned the same characteristics of femininity. For instance, judges see importance of makeup use among female bodybuilders. Tod, a national judge, claimed that "wearing makeup is part of the package, but I think it's a small part. The main look is at the body, but facial qualities come in too." Mark placed more weight on the importance of makeup use: "Oh yes, it is very important that women do their makeup and hair for a show because they want to look presentable." Thus for a female bodybuilder to look "presentable" in Tod's eyes, she must wrap herself in a feminine overall package. Similarly, Tracy, a state judge, argued that "wearing makeup is important for female competitors. I mean, actually not only for bodybuilders, but it is important for everyday life. So, it's just really not any different from you going to compete in something else. You want to look as nice as possible." Again, following the feminine apologetic, Tracy felt that if women want to look their best, they must wear makeup to accentuate their femininity. For female bodybuilders to attain an acceptable overall package and thus score well at competitions, they must be concerned with "looking nice," which Tracy defined as looking feminine.

Heather, a national judge, explained that it is important for female bodybuilders to wear makeup and be feminine because it is part of American culture: "Sure it is important that female bodybuilders wear makeup. Just like if you look at the Olympics and you look at the little thirteen-year-old gymnast. They've all got makeup on. It's part of our feminine culture. Whether it's right or wrong right now, that is part of our society now."

There are two particularly interesting points about Heather's comments. First, Heather's choice of sports metaphors is interesting. Although it is true that female gymnasts wear makeup while competing, gymnasts are not as fearful about transgressing hegemonic gender boundaries. Rather, gymnasts probably wear makeup to be seen more as women than as the young teenagers they are. Drawing again on the feminine apologetic, I maintain that it is more important for female bodybuilders to wear makeup than for female gymnasts because the former are involved in a more nontraditional sport. Second, it is interesting that Heather argued that female bodybuilders wear makeup because "it's a part of our feminine culture"—few people would think of building large muscles as part of this same culture. Thus, it seems more likely that because female bodybuilders participate in a traditionally unfeminine sport, they take in other elements of that culture to reinforce their femininity—which is simply another way of stating the feminine apologetic.

Similarly, for Mary, it is important for female bodybuilders to wear makeup, have their hair done, and look neat because female bodybuilders still want to look like women:

> I really think it is important for female bodybuilders to have their hair done, wear makeup, and look neat because we have to remember this is women's bodybuilding so we want to look like women. If a woman has dieted properly and she looks terrific from the neck down, she looks horrible in the face. She looks haggard, tired, and drawn—that's why she's got to go that extra length to make up for that. Putting on extra makeup, making sure the nails look groomed and that she looks professional.

The suggestion is that in order to "look like women again," female bodybuilders owe it to themselves to completely disguise their pain, exhaustion, hunger and thirst with a veil of mascara, makeup, nail polish, and hair spray.

Michelle, a national judge, also felt that female bodybuilders can and should enhance their femininity. She explained, "From the neck up, I want see as much attention put into her appearance in her face as she has on the rest of her body." Later in the interview she described her idea of the ultimate female bodybuilder:

> I'd like to see some cleavage, not a lot, because I think at that level of low body fat it's kind of silly to see somebody with 36 C's up there, but I would like to see some fullness there. I don't want to see it flat, I don't want to see it where the bikini top is wrinkled, [that] there's nothing to fill it [the bikini top]. I'd like to see a woman who has taken the time and effort to put on a good face, arrange her hair in a nice feminine way. I hate the butch haircuts on female bodybuilders."

I asked her what she meant by "butch" and she responded:

> Well, it looks like a male haircut. . . . To me it doesn't matter if it is short hair or long hair, just as long as it is fixed nicely. . . . I just don't like to see that kind of butch in-and-out of the shower type hair. . . . The reason why I say that is because we're in such a sport that is so atypical of what people are used to seeing a woman being so the things that we can do to offset that, we should try to do the best that we can, meaning hair, face, carriage, that kind of thing. Fluidity in the way they pose.

Such compensatory displays, according to Michelle, serve to signal to viewers that these women, although participating in a nontraditional endeavor, are not gender freaks—they still adhere to key elements of traditional feminine appearance.

Closely related to the issue of femininity and the presentation of a feminine self is that of physical attractiveness which, in the stated opinions of several judges, is defined as part of the "total package" for female bodybuilders. The judges were asked the importance of the attractiveness of female bodybuilders when they were evaluating them onstage. David, a regional judge, responded that in his opinion, attractiveness was important not only for female bodybuilders but for male bodybuilders as well:

> It's sad to say, but attractiveness does come into account sometimes. It does with women and it does with men also. I find myself noticing the attractiveness of a female bodybuilder and when I find myself being aware that this woman is what I consider to be attractive . . . I stop right there and look at the rest of her appearance and judge the body instead of just judging the face. There is a tendency, I think, on some people's part to judge attractiveness more than others. In fact,

> I've heard that being the case from what judges would say to each other.

And yet, facial attractiveness still affects his judging because note that he said "and judge the body instead of just judging the face." Thus, although facial attractiveness is not the only characteristic he looks at, it is part of the package and it affects the way he evaluates female bodybuilders. In addition, from his comments it appears that it is common for judges to notice and evaluate female bodybuilders by other criteria besides their physique.

Sam, a national judge, admitted that because he was a heterosexual man who enjoyed watching beautiful women, his judging has probably been affected by pretty female bodybuilders, although he has attempted to rectify the situation. He confessed:

> Well, from a male perspective, I'm sure subliminally it must affect me. Since I'm a heterosexual, since I find beautiful women, beautiful and attractive, I think subliminally, it must. Although I do my best not to allow it to affect me. But if there are two women that look similar in body structure and one is facially more beautiful than the other, I probably will be affected. But I try not to allow that because I do know a lot of these women personally. I try to go beyond what Mother Nature gave them, what their mom and dad gave them in the "above the neck" department.

Indeed, female judges have noticed that some male judges might be prone to evaluate attractive female bodybuilders more positively than less attractive ones. Tracy recalled: "Well, sometimes we have problems with male judges looking at the contestants' face and thinking, 'Oh, well this girl is real cute and she's got large boobs, and she looks real good to me.' Of course, I'm talking about a couple of male judges, not all men do that. I know a couple of them that do. So that's where it kind of varies." Although breast size and a "girl" who is really cute are not criteria they should be judging, this female judge contended that a few male judges can be less than "objective" and are affected by such esthetics. Michelle also noticed this phenomenon:

> I think I've seen some situations where some male judges, not all male judges, . . . choose the female bodybuilders who they'd like to sleep with. . . . That's not what they say, that's just a feeling. It's kind of crude, but sometimes I get really pissed off about it. Goddamn it,

> what are they doing, this girl doesn't deserve to be up there, she may have the potential to someday be at that placing, but not now. She's just got a pretty face, they look at her and go, "Yeah, I'd like to screw her, yeah."

Perhaps the female judges, who were likely to have been competitors themselves at some point, felt empathy for the current contestants because they, too, felt that they had been judged unfairly on characteristics such as physical attractiveness and breast size by the even more male-dominated judging panels of previous generations. Only one male judge claimed at first that he did not let contestants' attractiveness cloud his judgment. However, he then explained, "Well, I won't say that, in females probably if there were two people who were even and one had a looks advantage, I would probably lean to vote that way, but overall, I try to vote who I thought was the most symmetrical and had the most amount of muscle." So in the case of a tie, attractiveness would break the tie for female bodybuilders.

Accordingly, all judges, both female and male, to some degree believed that wearing makeup and being attractive were important for female bodybuilders. Whether they agreed with "looks" being important in determining the winner of a contest was another question; some agreed that it should be important, while others argued that it may contribute to unfair outcomes at female bodybuilding meets. Some of the male judges admitted that they had allowed the looks of attractive female bodybuilders to affect their judging momentarily. Many of the judges disclosed that if there were a particularly close competitive match between two female bodybuilders, and the only thing that distinguished them from each other was their looks, they would opt for the more attractive one.

Some of the feminine accouterments mentioned by female bodybuilders and female and male officials and judges as important for female bodybuilders are institutionally enforced in the bylaws of bodybuilding organizations. I now turn to these institutional mandates.

Institutional Attempts to Create Gender Distinctions

At the institutional level, the importance placed on "feminine" appearance extends beyond hairstyle, posing routines, and breast size to attempts at limiting women's muscularity. One only has to look at the

IFBB *Official Guidebook* to understand the institutional ethos. Recall from chapter 4 that in 1991 the IFBB and NPC officials felt that female bodybuilders were getting too muscular and too masculine looking. Fearing that the sport would no longer be able to attract mainstream fans, officials reinforced the judging guidelines for female bodybuilders, which stated:

> First and foremost, the judge must bear in mind that he/she is judging a women's bodybuilding competition and is looking for an ideal feminine physique. Therefore, the most important aspect is shape, a muscular feminine shape. The other aspects are similar to those described for assessing men, but in regard to muscular development, it must not be carried to excess where it resembles the massive muscularity of the male physique.[12]

In addition to excessive muscularity, the IFBB *Officials' Handbook* stated that "judges may find other faults not seen in men, such as stretch marks, operation scars, and cellulite. The judges shall also observe whether the women competitors walk to and from their positions in a graceful manner."[13] Why would operation scars be more acceptable on a male than a female physique? Why do officials feel it necessary to inform female bodybuilders that they must walk gracefully onstage but not have a similar statement for male bodybuilders to walk in a "masculine" way? In addition to these guidelines, the guidebook explicitly stated that female bodybuilders must limit their muscularity so that they have a "muscular feminine shape" and their physique should not resemble "the massive muscularity of the male physique." But how do judges interpret the meaning of such terms, and in turn, how do they accurately, honestly, and objectively measure them? For instance, who is to say that a bodybuilder like Lenda Murray does not have a physique that resembles "the massive muscularity of the male physique," but Bev Francis does? Thus, instead of clarifying the criteria for judging female bodybuilders, the officials may have made the judges' decisions more difficult.

Furthermore, by enacting and enforcing these rules, the IFBB accomplished two goals: (1) they defined femininity and masculinity as oppositional constructs, and (2) they attempted to institutionally control female competitors' bodies in gender-specific ways—only female athletes were to be concerned with limiting their muscularity and enhancing their gender.

Reasons for the Institutional Reproduction of Gender Distinctions

Throughout this chapter, I have suggested that there is a multitude of individual as well as institutional forces at work to create feminine-looking female bodybuilders. The question still remains, however, as to why it is so important at the institutional level that female bodybuilders appear "feminine"? One reason is that gatekeepers bring with them preconceived ideas of acceptable comportment and appearance for women. To illustrate their influence on the evaluations of female bodybuilders, I have included excerpts from a few judges who felt that since the mid 1980s, female bodybuilders had gotten too muscular and "masculine-looking."[14] For instance, Sam, a professional judge, stated that "a woman can bring out the best in her body without going over this imaginary limit that takes away from her femininity, from . . . looking like a male to me." Another male official reflected, "Some of the women bodybuilders started to use steroids and became excessively developed and grotesque." It is highly unlikely that he would use such a description in describing a male bodybuilder. One national male judge, Clay, commented that he thought female bodybuilding "maybe makes them [women] a little too independent. Women are independent enough I think without making them more independent." One can see how judges' opinions about what is appropriate and inappropriate for women in general may influence their evaluations of female bodybuilders.

Besides this concern of women transgressing the gender boundaries for appropriate comportment and appearance is the issue of the marketability of the sport. These two issues are often mutually reinforcing of the hegemonic notions of femininity within the sport. For instance, listen to Kyle:

> Well, women's bodybuilding is an unnatural sport. It is not natural for a woman to have muscles, so of course there is confusion in the judging. . . . It's not like men where you're just looking for the most perfectly built guy. And we all have the concept of what that should look like. Before, you go back 15 years, there was no concept of muscular women. And if there was one in drawings or something that you would see, it would be [a] fit woman, but she would also have, she'd also look very feminine. And some of these women onstage don't look feminine and sexy, they just look like guys with bikini tops.

His beliefs describe some of the many gendered ideological constraints with which female bodybuilders have to contend. Kyle's statements that female bodybuilding is "an unnatural sport," and that "it is not natural for a woman to have muscles" indicate his bias in evaluating female bodybuilders. In fact, this quote is an excellent illustration of ideology in the Gramscian sense—in this case, it reflects patriarchal ideology. His assertion that "some of these women onstage don't look feminine and sexy, they just look like guys with bikini tops" reveals his preference for less muscular and thus more feminine competitors. Thus, according to Kyle, female bodybuilders should not only limit their muscularity but they should enhance their femininity and sexiness as well. However badly he wants female bodybuilders to be "sexy," it is not one of the stated criteria in either the NPC or IFBB and should therefore, ideally, not enter into the decision making of judges, since judges and officials are asked to evaluate female bodybuilders' physiques "objectively" and by the stated criteria. However, as we have seen, "sexiness" does become a criterion in the minds of some judges.

The emphasis on men's definitions of women's "sexiness" serves to reinforce the importance of heterosexuality (at least in appearance) as a criterion for female bodybuilders in achieving success in their sport.[15] Furthermore, in Kyle's assumption that if a female bodybuilder does not meet his own standards of femininity and sexiness, then she must look like a man, he is simplifying the range of gender possibilities for women to the dichotomy of "feminine and sexy" or "men with bikini tops."

One rather perplexing issue arises when one stops to consider why a man, who has stated that he thinks that it is unnatural for women to have muscles, is involved in a sport where the goal is for the women to build large, symmetrical, buffed muscles. Here is where the issue of marketing a sport that is also a commercial enterprise emerges. In Kyle's opinion, muscular female bodybuilders turn off fans and thus take away money from the sport. His ideological rationale that a muscular woman is "not natural" is fueled by an economic concern that ticket and magazine sales are dropping. It appears that he is attempting to mold the market for female bodybuilding according to his own vision of what type of female bodybuilders people will pay money to see.

The people in this study had a lot to say about the connection between feminine-looking female bodybuilders and the commercial aspect of the sport. Some, as we have seen, simply acknowledged this association. Tracy, a regional judge, explained the link between the two concerns,

"They usually pick the people who will increase their money flow in the magazines. They want somebody who is good looking where people are going to watch them on TV." Similarly, Linda, a regional judge, revealed that female bodybuilding has become dictated by who can sell bodybuilding products most effectively:

> I think that mainly it's . . . selling the product. I think that a lot of people feel that people would freak out with a woman with a lot of muscularity like a Bev Francis. And a lot of women would feel that it's repulsive to look like that. You know talking to a lot of people in bodybuilding, you get the opinion that they don't want female bodybuilders as hard, as muscular. And yet some are. I feel that it's mainly the people trying to sell a product. What will be acceptable in public.

Some might argue that Bev Francis poses a counterpoint to this argument, and in some ways, she in fact does. She is extremely muscular and yet has received major endorsements, has been prominently featured in Weider magazines, and is currently an IFBB judge. I believe there are a few factors that may have contributed to this anomaly. First, Bev Francis literally underwent a metamorphosis from her first bodybuilding contest at the 1983 Caesar's Palace contest represented in *Pumping Iron II: The Women* to the early 1990s. She changed her image drastically; although still muscular, she altered her appearance (hairstyle, attire, makeup) to align herself more closely to hegemonic feminine standards. Second, after the release of the *Pumping Iron II* movie, Bev has been one of the best-known bodybuilders on the circuit. Because of her popularity, her image is exceptionally profitable. Her persona and history virtually guarantee media attention—something in which gatekeepers are very interested. Third, by giving her endorsements, the IFBB could successfully quiet those critics who accused them of being opposed to large-muscled female bodybuilders. Bev should be viewed as an anomaly, and not as a sign that the bodybuilding establishment is accepting big women.

A few people in this study were critical of the extent to which social gatekeepers allow their hegemonic views of femininity and attractiveness effect the outcome of competitions and product endorsements. For example, Christy had won her weight class at a very prestigious female bodybuilding contest and found herself watching the bodybuilders who had placed behind her in the competition get interviews and product endorsements:

> This year, ESPN didn't profile me. They said that I'm not marketable. No I still haven't found out why. I was real frustrated the first couple of weeks after the show. I was getting rejections like all over the place from magazines. I was like "Jesus, I won the show, how much better can I do?" I have no idea, but they profiled all the pretty blond girls. Every single one of them was profiled . . . they didn't even interview me at the show and I was favored to win and I went up to the guy and I said, I mean, I walked upstairs with my trophy, I said, "You guys want to do something now? I'm in shape, let's set something up right away" and they didn't want to do it. I don't know what that's all about. I just felt like the reality of the sport is that you're not going to get rich being a competitive bodybuilder and the exposure is really the only reward that you get, and the magazine articles and whatever they might do with you on ESPN. I was like, "Fuck it, if they don't want to use me now, I'm not going to beat anybody's door down." I'm not that much into the promotional aspect of all this to really keep on going after people and phoning them and writing them and doing all the promotional stuff that I need to do. I do a little bit of it, and I've had some, a couple of articles have come out, but I don't know, I really don't know why they don't think I'm marketable.

Some were critical of the emphasis placed on the attractiveness of female bodybuilders simply in order to increase social gatekeepers' profits. In fact, in the following quote, Michelle, a national judge, explicitly stated that the driving force behind changing women's bodybuilding is the attempt by the heads of the bodybuilding industry to attract more fans to the sport:

> That's where I tend to disagree with the direction they say they are going in now, because right now they are definitely saying, "You get to a point where there is too much muscle, regardless of how symmetrical" and I don't think so. And I think that in that sense, they're trying to play to that audience that they're trying to bring into the sport. The couch potato that they think will, if we just tone it down might become a ticket buyer or a supplement buyer or . . . because the vitamin companies are sponsors at bodybuilding shows. The whole health industry is there in some form or another. So if the shows are successful then that means that their product is being seen and so there's a direct tie in. Right now a lot of them are saying, "We want to tone it down, let's tone it down, because maybe if we tone it

> down enough we'll get that couch potato off the couch, he'll go in the gym, he'll buy the supplements, he'll buy the tickets, he'll come to the show." I don't agree because I think that when someone is that far removed from being in a workout frame of mind, that it doesn't matter how much we tone it down, they're not going to be interested because there is too much of his own guilt and own anxieties going on in his own head is why he is not in the gym. He will never relate. I think they're [the hard core fans] getting pissed. But I don't think the hard core fans are going to stop coming to the sport.

This is particularly problematic if the reason that a female athlete "can only go so far" is in order to sell the sport and the related products as effectively as possible.

Many of the people in this study, including bodybuilders, judges, and officials, understood and advocated the gatekeepers' institutional practice of rewarding attractive, feminine-looking female bodybuilders with lucrative product endorsements because it helped to sell the sport to the general public.

Richard, a regional judge, candidly revealed that it all comes down to a pretty face because that is the look that makes money for those involved in the sport:

> A pretty face is important [in female bodybuilding] because it sells and you know the whole thing is that professional bodybuilding is making money. "Betty" has a tremendous amount of muscle for her size in the upper body and she is not blessed with really good looks so therefore she can go to contests and be in the best shape but she usually does not place in the top ten at a professional meet. She was able to win all the amateur levels all the way usually, but at the professional level, especially now, they are looking more for . . . well, you've got to have the looks as well as have the muscle.

Others, however, mentioned, in essence, the importance of a female bodybuilder's "overall package," to be able to sell the sport effectively. For instance, Becky, a regional bodybuilder, stated:

> Officials are looking for more marketable people. A woman who has a good look to her, a healthy look to her, and is aesthetically appealing to other people. You want to have a body that you can show off. Or that you can advertise to other people. If you have this huge monster woman who advertises for you, people aren't going to want

> to be like that. They're not going to buy your equipment or use your stuff because they're not going to want to look like that. It all comes down to who's promoting whom and how marketable you are. And Cory Everson (six-time Ms. Olympia) is very marketable. She's got that good looking, all American look to her. She's toned her body down to where its feminine yet still hard and toned and sculpted beautifully. She's not trying to get bigger, she's just trying to define it better—sculpt it more—to make it more ideal—more aesthetically appealing.

Comparably, Diane, a professional bodybuilder, also endorsed the link between presenting feminine and attractive female bodybuilders and increasing the popularity of the sport to others. She personalized this argument by relaying her own experiences about getting involved with the sport:

> They want somebody who is marketable who can be a good role model because if I would have opened the magazine five years ago and saw an ugly person, a real jocky-looking gross-looking girl, I would think "I don't want to look like that. Is that what I'm going to look like when I start lifting?" But I opened it and saw Rachel McLish, pretty model like and then you saw Cory and you know they promote the women who are more attractive, more model type.

She believed that having attractive female bodybuilders who are not excessively muscular is important for the sport because it gets women, as it did with her, to want to start lifting and begin to work out. Had she been confronted with a "jocky-looking, gross-looking girl" when she first flipped through a bodybuilding magazine, she would have tried her hand at another activity besides weight training. Attractive female bodybuilders like Rachel McLish and Cory Everson got her interested in lifting weights because, echoing the words of Kyle, she wanted "to look like them."

Similarly, Richard, a regional judge, argued that women in the general population do not want to look really muscular and therefore are fearful to begin lifting weights because they are afraid of becoming too muscular: "The average women being ignorant of training rules and ideas and whatever think they're going to look like that and so they say, 'Well I don't want to train. I don't want to look like that.' So if they can go back more into the Rachel McLish look well then they figure more women will get into it and be involved in the sport." He argued that the popularity of female bodybuilding will never be what it once was because the sport will not be able to go back to the Rachel McLish look, and therefore there will always be controversy. Diane, a professional female bodybuilder, contended: "We can't go walking around looking like freaks, looking like we're some apes or something because I think it's gross myself." Thus, in attempting to align herself with those outside of bodybuilding who may pick up a bodybuilding magazine for the first time and either be repulsed by overly muscular women or attracted to the look of feminine-looking, moderately muscular ones, Diane supports the marketing of more feminine bodybuilders.

In the opinion of Kyle, the IFBB official, the reason female bodybuilding has decreased in popularity is because female bodybuilders have become so muscular that men no longer want "to look at them" and women no longer want "to look like them." We see the link between marketability and attitudes about women's "proper" appearance: it is important that female bodybuilders look feminine so female fans will want to buy tickets and products so that they can look like them, and so male fans will want to buy those same bodybuilding items in order "to look at them." Thus, we have a situation in female bodybuilding where capitalism, manifested by the profit motive, and patriarchy, manifested by the desire to keep women within appropriate gender boundaries, are intertwined and reinforcing entities that contribute to the officials' push for smaller-muscled, feminine-looking female bodybuilders.

The price of treating bodybuilding solely as a business detracts from its already questionable sportslike qualities. Choosing a bodybuilder who is the most marketable rather than the best is antithetical to the sports creed, "May the best person win." In no other sport are athletes limited in their performances because of fear of offending paying spectators. One would not hear a track coach tell Jackie Joyner-Kersee or Gail Devers to slow down because the public thinks they are running too fast to be palatable or to be feminine. When the importance of selling products taints the way judges evaluate female bodybuilders, the business aspect of the sport has gone too far and severely jeopardizes the fairness on which every sport is premised. Female bodybuilding is different from most other sports for a combination of two reasons: (1) few sports have their profits related so closely to what the public thinks are appropriate displays of femininity, and (2) few sports place such a premium on making a profit that they compromise the very integrity of their goals.

SIX

Countering the Hegemony, Coopting the Resistance, and the Future of Female Bodybuilding

IN THE PROLOGUE, I included an ethnographic account of the 1992 Ms. Olympia contest in Chicago. I would like to revisit the evening show of that contest for a moment. During the ninety-second musical presentation round, in which bodybuilders present their musculature to the music of their choice, bodybuilder after bodybuilder opened her posing routines to the first part of the song "In Control" by Janet Jackson. This song begins with Janet Jackson determinedly stating: "This is a song about control. Control of what I say. Control of what I do. This is a song about control. And I have lots of it." At the end of the presentation round, after all twenty bodybuilders had climbed onstage and performed their posing routines, four of them had started their routines with this song.

These lyrics are both telling and ironic when applied to the political positioning of female bodybuilders in a sport dominated by both economic and patriarchal interests. These women are singing about control, but control of what? Perhaps they are referring to the astonishing control they have of their bodies—created and maintained by a type of focus and determination that enables them to compete or succeed in such a physically demanding activity.[1] Connected to their discipline is the perception that their bodies are objects in need of control, that the corpus is something apart from themselves—something that is untamed and not to be trusted. When most bodybuilders spoke about control, they discussed being in control of their bodies, and in particular, their weight. Much as an anorectic talks about feeling a sense of power because she can control her body through weight loss, some bodybuilders are obsessed with their weight, and to them power means ability to control their bodies and their appetites.

I will now turn to the various forms and nuances of female bodybuilders' resistance to the hegemonic standards set by the powerful social gatekeepers of the sport. In the two years I collected data, I noted some instances in which female bodybuilders, both individually and collectively, resisted the hegemonic norms of their sport. What precipitated these acts of resistance? How did the actors at the various levels interpret and respond to the resistance? Did their resistance lead to structural change in the sport?

By definition, members of a dominant group have more economic and political power than individual members of marginalized groups. With preponderant economic and political power, dominant group members also have more definitional power than others. Definitional power involves the dual ability to (1) establish successfully one's definitions of reality as the hegemonic standards to which others must consent, and (2) set boundaries that distinguish between acceptable and deviant behavior. Because hegemony is based on ideas and beliefs, it is volatile. It is continuously negotiated, defended, and modified by members of the dominant group. Thus, because this reality is constructed and must be continuously maintained, it can be challenged at any moment by members of marginalized and subordinated groups. Consequently, there is always "room for antagonistic cultural expressions to develop."[2]

These challenges to the dominant hegemonies are referred to as counter-hegemonies and can take multiple forms, ranging from overt physical resistance to more subtle symbolic forms. Furthermore, although Giroux[3] argued that resistance should be reserved for collective action that seriously challenges the status quo, I believe that individual resistance can also serve such ends. Counter-hegemonies, in the form of overt resistance to the dominant powers, are usually used as a means of last resort by members of subordinated groups because they are often harshly sanctioned by authorities. Thus, if resistance occurs, it is likely to happen at the symbolic level in everyday cultural practices. For instance, members of subordinated groups may coopt, redefine, and use symbols from the dominant culture to attempt to challenge the dominant groups' power over them and as an effort to "find dignity in an oppressive class society."[4]

As the previous chapters have suggested, female bodybuilders vary in their opinions about the current and future ideal physiques and standards of judging in their sport. When they have complaints about how a meet has been judged, or if they are concerned with the direction of the sport, they have few places to air their concerns within the organizational structure. They may talk to a number of different people, from the judges on the judging panel, the head judge of a meet, the state chair (if they are in the NPC), the NPC women's chair, to the professional director of the IFBB (if they are professional-level athletes). The information that a female bodybuilder receives from members of these groups center around how they could improve themselves in the eyes of the judges. For instance, female bodybuilders in the NPC may talk with the NPC women's chair, who acts as the mediator between various key male officials and the female bodybuilders. She informally advises female bodybuilders of the sport's rules and regulations. Michelle, a national-level amateur judge, discussed Sandy's job at contests:

> Well Sandy Ranalli . . . is the woman chairperson for the NPC and as far as a ranking administrator, she is the highest-ranking woman in the organization. Basically, it's one of her jobs to disseminate information to the women on competition rules, regulations, and she has talked to women at several shows that I have been at. She has made herself available to discuss the judging criteria, and she has made herself available at every show that I've ever been at for anyone to ask her or seek information from her.

The chairperson's job is to clarify any confusion about judging criteria on the part of the bodybuilders. However, her duties are limited to distributing information from the top down, not vice versa. It is not her job to act on behalf of bodybuilders to bring forth their concerns and complaints to the officials.

In keeping with the individualistic nature of the sport of bodybuilding, all of these institutional avenues—ranging from female bodybuilders talking to judges, the head judge, the state chair, the NPC women's chair, and the professional director of the IFBB—are set up for individual bodybuilders to meet one-on-one with specific gatekeepers. There is no organized body that enables bodybuilders as a group to give their input about the current and future status of bodybuilders or to talk about their grievances. Hence, although bodybuilders do have access to judges and officials, their ability as a group working within the system to influence policies, rules, and the direction of the sport is limited.

Consequently, the only other recourse bodybuilders have is to express their dissatisfaction in extra-institutional ways that may potentially jeopardize their careers in the bodybuilding organization. Some have attempted individually to resist the hegemony by publicly challenging those in power. Over the years, others have intermittently attempted to organize female bodybuilders so that as a group they have the power to negotiate for their rights within the extant political structures in the sport. Both types of attempts—those that have entailed working within the system and those outside—have, for the most part, proven ineffective. In fact, the 1995 IFBB Constitution states, "The IFBB forbids any and all racially, politically or religiously motivated discussions, demonstrations or acts," making any political protest or discussion by bodybuilders against the organizational status quo potentially career-ending since the term "political" is so broad.

Why have female bodybuilders, unlike their counterparts in other sports, been unable to organize successfully to protect their interests? First, the individualistic ethos of the sport combined with the dispersion of female bodybuilders in gyms across the United States make opportunities for collective action, and positive attitudes toward them, unlikely. Second, there are few organizational alternatives to the IFBB and NPC, so female bodybuilders aren't able to threaten to go elsewhere to compete. Recall from chapter 2 that in many ways, from the number of contests held to the amount of prize money awarded, the IFBB and its national amateur affiliate are unsurpassed by any other bodybuilding organization. If a person wants to make a living as a professional bodybuilder, the IFBB is the organization to which he or she wants to belong. Even when rival organizations existed, many judges and bodybuilders have insisted that "the IFBB is the only game in town."

Third, female bodybuilders compete against one another for relatively few rewards. Although female bodybuilding offers more prize money today than in the past, there is still only a limited amount of money available and it goes only to the top few athletes. Those making the money are unlikely to sacrifice their earnings to equalize the playing field. Recall from chapter 2 that female bodybuilders have fewer professional bodybuilding competitions and less prize money available to them than their male counterparts which only may serve to exacerbate the feelings of competition between female bodybuilders. Combine the fact that there are few organizational alternatives outside the IFBB and the NPC with the fact that only a few top female bodybuilders make substantial money in the sport, and one gets the picture of how much economic power the Weiders and other social gatekeepers hold over bodybuilders' heads. As Alan Klein has contended: "The bodybuilders' inability to merge common interests was compounded by the hierarchical relations fostered by Weider, who knows that he is in a position to reward and punish, in the course of which he can destroy any nascent organizing effort. In true aristocratic fashion, Joe Weider keeps his minions just hungry enough to let them know from where their next meal is coming."[5] Although Klein was referring to male bodybuilders, this statement is even more applicable to female bodybuilders who have fewer opportunities to make money in the sport of bodybuilding than their male counterparts.

Fourth, female bodybuilders lack an organizational structure through which to air their problems and concerns as a group. They have little to no voice in determining the rules, regulations, and thus the future of their own sport. This combination does not readily foster close ties among bodybuilders.[6] As of this date, female bodybuilders as a group are isolated and segmented with few means to protect their interests from those who direct the sport.

Accordingly, although bodybuilders do have access to judges and officials, their ability to influence policies, rules, and the direction of the sport is limited. As previously stated, a bodybuilder can approach the head judge and even particular judges to ask them why they placed her where they did. One male judge, Sam, talked about this process: "She [a disgruntled female bodybuilder] can ask to speak to the head judge and ask permission to speak to the individual judges and they can tell her exactly why they placed her where they did. You know sometimes in a competition like the Ms. Olympia, you can have one judge that will place someone five places higher or lower than another judge because it's so subjective." A bodybuilder can only *ask* why they were placed where they were. Though some judges contend that female bodybuilders should be more willing to discuss their placements with the judges, there are two factors that help explain why female bodybuilders may be hesitant to take this route of action. The first is that from their perspective, such action is probably futile. Once a decision has been made, nothing can change it, so why protest a decision that is not going to be overturned—and get labeled as a troublemaker in the process? No decision has ever been overturned. For instance, one female judge, Michelle, asserted: "I mean, you get what you get. You can ask why and you can talk to the head judge or any judge that sat on that panel, but as far as any kind of appeal process to change the decision, there isn't any." Second, judging is subjective; the answer of how to improve will depend on whom you ask, and their suggestions may in the end not help you at the next meet.

Female bodybuilders who are proactive and attempt to find out what "look" officials and judges want have no guarantee that they will get the guidance they seek. According to Tod:

> At the nationals, the judges don't tell the athletes what is expected of them. They kind of expect it to get around by word of mouth. I think that's a big problem for these girls. For instance, for the nationals, this girl, who was expected to win, had lost 10 pounds from last year trying to get smaller. She came in, I thought, a lot better-looking, but still looked too much. She got third and after the show, she went around to every judge that judged her, and asked what she could do, because she didn't know. Sitting there saying, "I'm ripped to shreds, I'm big, what do I do?" They're not really making it clear to the competitors.

Perhaps this confusion by high-level social gatekeepers and the concomitant fluctuations in ideal physique is a calculated strategy used to keep the sport open to a wider range of phenotypes as well as to make the sport marketable to a wider audience. Maybe, as is argued by Kathryn, this "confusion" approach also has a more sinister purpose: "There's a backlash and it's covert. If it were that obvious, then we would have something to fight against and we could deal with it better. But when it's kept in more of a covert sense—covert by constantly confusing us and keeping us in not only a state of confusion but a state of being sort of at odds with one another." "Confusion" may be a tactic that prevents female bodybuilders from effectively coming together to fight collectively for their rights against "the powers that be."

Furthermore, bodybuilders who approach judges and challenge their evaluations are likely to be labeled as troublemakers; a label, once applied, is difficult to change. This represents an additional reason that may discourage bodybuilders from approaching judges. Diane, a professional bodybuilder, stated that although she has disagreed with the judging of meets in which she was a participant, she has never voiced her displeasure to the judges because she feared being called a troublemaker and thus could never advance in the sport. When I asked her what her response was, she remarked, "I didn't say a word. Because [when] the judging scores are tallied [that's it]. . . . The more upset you get, that gives you a bad name as a 'bad attitude competitor' and you'll never get anywhere." Similarly, Denise, a national-level amateur bodybuilder from the Southwest, mentioned the negative reactions she has received from judges when she has voiced her disagreement with them: "They get pretty pissed off. I went through a couple of years of pretty hard thrashings but when they found out I was going to back up my feelings totally now . . . they respect my opinion because they know I'm not just there to bitch about it once or twice. I'm going to do something about it. I'm not going to go away." She alluded to the fact that judges know that she means what she says and that she is not there simply to complain. However, Denise is also a state-level judge, and has recently participated on the judging panel of a national-level meet, though not as an official judge. Her "dual role" may be one reason that she has gained the respect of other judges (because they saw her as "one of their own"). Even if she were not a judge, the belief that bodybuilders complain because they did not do well as opposed to having a "real complaint" is quite prevalent among the judges. A common attitude among the judges is that bodybuilders behave like spoiled children; they "bitch and moan" when things don't go well.

In fact, some judges went so far as to say that they believe bodybuilders are not to be trusted because they have their own agenda. To illustrate this sentiment among the judges, I have included an excerpt from Sam, a professional-level judge. Sam seemed very cautious about female bodybuilders in general because they "will give you extreme perspectives," yet at the same time, he was also critical of female bodybuilders who do not discuss their placings with judges:

> I can tell you that the women will give you extreme perspectives. I can guarantee you that. Because the professional women, unless they are the winner, the ones that place second, third, fourth, fifth, sixth, down the line, are all unhappy because they have not won and they feel they have been discriminated against. For example, "Adrienne," if you speak with her I can almost guarantee you that she will tell you that she has been discriminated against in the past . . . because of

> ultra-muscularity, because of poor judging. She has never spoken to me as a judge . . . yet she criticizes all the judges without asking where she was placed and for what reason.

Sam discounted the concerns and questions of female bodybuilders, and distrusted their motives for complaining in the first place.

This situation sheds light on the unequal distribution of definitional power. Judges have the power to label female bodybuilders who attempt to seek information or criticize the judging of meets as "bad-attitude competitors" who are simply "bitching and moaning." In doing so, some judges do not take bodybuilders' complaints seriously. Yet this attitude of some judges, and the corollary negative labeling that it entails, may be one reason why female bodybuilders do not come forward, as Denise illustrated in her statement. Consequently, female bodybuilders appear to be in a Catch-22 situation: if they come forward and try to get information on how to improve their placements, they may be told they need to get breast implants to enhance their symmetry. If they question a ruling, they get labeled as "troublemakers." If, on the other hand, they do not come forward, judges label them as being incessant complainers who only want to criticize judges from a distance and find flimsy and inaccurate excuses for not placing well.

Despite the limits and dangers of dissent, there are instances of such resistance by female bodybuilders. One incident that was mentioned repeatedly by both bodybuilders and judges occurred at the 1992 Ms. International Competition. This show was supposed to set the tone for a more feminine future in female bodybuilding. In so doing, the judges chose one of the least muscular but most traditionally attractive female bodybuilders as the winner: she had blue eyes, long blond hair, good symmetry—and she was not very muscular. In fact, she used to be a fitness-show competitor, but switched to bodybuilding. She was perfect for supporting the officials' belief that female bodybuilders who are attractive and not very muscular should win the meets and appear on the covers of their magazines, so that more women will want to join gyms, go to contests, and buy bodybuilding products and magazines.

Paula Bircumshaw, a bodybuilder who was not only extremely muscular but sported this muscularity on a truly symmetrical physique, did not place in the top six at the 1992 Ms. International competition. This meant that she would be unable to compete in the fourth and final stage, the posedown. In response to getting "shut out" of the top six places, she yelled obscenities at the judges and Joe Weider. Mark, a state judge, who was at the competition, described what he saw:

> I was at this year's Arnold Classic and Ms. International contest in Columbus and that was probably the most unpopular decision I've ever witnessed because this girl from England, Paula Bircumshaw, should have won the contest and she wasn't even in the top six. And she came out onstage after the top six were announced; she had on her warm-ups and she made obscene gestures to the judges and said a lot of things to them, then she jumped off the stage and ran up and down the aisles, and she stopped right next to Joe Weider and she was holding her arms up and she got a standing ovation from the crowd of about four thousand people. It's just not popular to pick somebody that doesn't have muscle to win a bodybuilding contest, I don't care what you think.

Diane, a professional bodybuilder, explained that Paula "got a two-year suspension and I'm sure she'll never do any good because they're mad at her." Noteworthy about Diane's response is that even after Paula's punishment has been completed, she will still not do well in the IFBB "because they're mad at her."

The implication of this incident is that female bodybuilders should not overtly resist the hegemonic standards set by the officials in the sport—they must not offend or upset IFBB judges and officials, particularly in public—or they will pay the price of ending their bodybuilding careers. Thus, female bodybuilders, women who are physically strong and powerful people, have little voice in directing their sport. Not only must they look like they are playing the game by the officials' hegemonic rules, but they must also look like they are enjoying it. This example brings to mind the extraordinary definitional power these social gatekeepers wield—if they label a bodybuilder a "troublemaker," the label for all intents and purposes will do irreparable damage to a bodybuilder's career. As Alan Klein has maintained, "being ostracized from this organization is tantamount to being drummed out of the sport. Those who have experienced suspension from the IFBB are quick to point out that continuing to succeed—economically or in competition—is difficult."[7] Because "just as one needs to attract the beneficence of the Weider machine, one must steer clear of their animosity, for being shunned by the Weiders can irreversibly damage one's career. Ostracism can take the form of economic retribution, as in pulling ads from his magazine or political repudiation by the IFBB."[8] For example, bodybuilders who in the early 1990s went to the McMahon's ill-fated World Bodybuilding Federation, and then returned to the IFBB after the WBF folded, had to pay a fine of 10 percent of each individual's annual WBF salary, which was deducted from their IFBB contest winnings and guest appearances. There were six former WBF bodybuilders who competed in IFBB contests in May 1993, and none of them qualified for the Mr. Olympia.[9] Similarly, since the 1992 Ms. International competition outburst, Paula Bircumshaw has failed to compete effectively in the United States, even after her suspension was shortened by IFBB officials.

In their attempts to explain such power dynamics, some female bodybuilders pointed to the patriarchal structure of the sport. They felt that the sport would be fairer and would have a different image if it were run and maintained by women. For instance, Patty, a former national competitor, exclaimed: "Well, my problem with that is we have men up there dictating what women bodybuilding is all about and needs to be put in the hands of women. Well, some women have tried to do that and once they tried you never heard from them again. Okay, the Weiders of the world just ban them." Again, as Klein contended, "being ostracized from this organization is tantamount to being drummed out of the sport."[10] Patty alluded to previous attempts made by female bodybuilders to take control of their own sport. She pointed to 1985, when a successful female bodybuilder attempted to form a female bodybuilding union, failed, and was unofficially persona non grata in bodybuilding from that point onward. Patty asserted:

> I think women should set the criteria for what they want and I think it should be all women judges. They should set down the rules. They tried to form a woman's union and the woman who headed it was "Sarah" and she was absolutely going for everything, she was taking Ms. International, she was doing everything. She tried to start this women's union, you have never heard her name since. She has never had her picture in a magazine, she has never won a contest, she just disappeared from the bodybuilding scene and she was the absolute up-and-coming female bodybuilder but she tried to form a women's union to take over women's bodybuilding and that's it. Unless you're a Joe Weider cutie pie, adhere to everything. I think Cory Everson is an absolutely beautiful woman, I think she has a phenomenal physique, but there's no way she would lose because she was in Joe Weider's right pocket.

In addition to these individual forms of resistance by female bodybuilders, there were two collective acts to gain power within the organization. One occurred at the 1992 Ms. Olympia competitors' meeting (this was the next Ms. Olympia after the 1991 Ms. International contest). Nineteen top professional female bodybuilders were together in the same room, and they wanted to voice their opinions and attitudes about the current state of female bodybuilding. However, the officials said that the purpose of the meeting was to talk about the upcoming Ms. Olympia show; if the bodybuilders wanted to talk about other issues, they had to do it on their own time. The female bodybuilders did not convene after the meeting, and had not yet met to discuss any issues about their status in the organization as of 1994. A few female bodybuilders attempted to get a female representative who is outside the reach of the Weiders and the IFBB to be their representative and to take a more active role in voicing the bodybuilders' concerns to those in power. This position was to be quite different from that of the current NPC women's spokesperson, who mainly disseminates information from the officials to bodybuilders. Although there was talk among female bodybuilders in the early 1990s to get someone to fill such a position, it has yet to materialize.

Looking Forward

What does the future hold for female bodybuilding according to those who currently participate in the sport? Most argued that female bodybuilding will continue to embrace the "middle-of-the-road look" between the large, muscular women of the late 1980s and the smaller female bodybuilders of the late 1970s and early 1980s. In addition, they believed that this pattern will continue because female bodybuilding will still be motivated by the same factors that propel it today. The images that the social gatekeepers think will sell the most products, tickets, and magazines will dominate the future of the sport. Thus, future competitive female bodybuilders will likely still be cloaked in a veil of hegemonic femininity that includes feminine hairstyles, makeup use, and moderate-sized breasts. Onstage, they will need to display their femininity by the way they walk and pose. Although they will still be more muscular than the average female athlete, they will continue to be directed by gatekeepers to temper their muscularity.

Many judges and bodybuilders felt that the rise of fitness shows would have an impact on the sport of female bodybuilding. Fitness competitions are now sponsored by various organizations, including the NPC and IFBB. At fitness contests, which fall between a female bodybuilding competition and a beauty pageant, contestants are judged on their athletic fitness and attractiveness. There are usually swimsuit and dance/aerobics rounds in which contestants are evaluated by a panel of judges. Some organizations that sponsor fitness contests have evening-gown rounds in which contestants give a 30-second brief biography as well as share their philosophy on fitness. One fitness show sponsor pressures its contestants not to flex their muscles or emphasize muscle size.

There was no consensus among the participants in this study about the impact of these contests on female bodybuilding. Those who voiced an opinion felt that such competitions could have one of a couple of possible effects on judging the contests. On the one hand, they may lessen the pressure on female bodybuilders to limit their muscularity since fitness contestants will fill the need to comply with the hegemonic displays of femininity. However, the existence of these contests may also serve to place further limits on female bodybuilders' muscular displays because fitness show contestants will be considered as the hegemonic embodiment of femininity and female bodybuilders may be judged according to this standard. A number of judges and female bodybuilders thought these newer competitions would indeed put limits on the muscularity that female bodybuilders are allowed to display. For instance, Linda, a state-level female judge, explained, "Well, if it's called bodybuilding, and I think it should be, it should be judged accordingly. But I think it's going to be more, like I say, like a Ms. Fitness contest. Where it's not going to be as much looking for the muscularity." Tracy, a regional judge, agreed with Linda's forecast and included her reasons for her prediction:

> I don't know where it's headed. There are a lot of people that want it to still be the hardcore sport that they've known all these years as muscle. And there are some people who want to switch it and try to get it more fitness-oriented. The people who benefit from it, the people who sell the magazines, the people who sell the sponsorships, want to bring it into mainstream America, which it's never going to be.

Because the people who want bodybuilding to be a hardcore sport are not those in power, they have little say about the future direction of the sport except perhaps in editorials in bodybuilding magazines.

Others also felt that the social gatekeepers would advocate limited muscularity because this look is more profitable. However, they were more adamantly critical of the gatekeepers' reasons for doing so. For instance, Michelle voiced her frustration this way:

> I think that you are still going to see a lot of indecision on the part of the organization and the powers that be to decide which direction, the judging criteria is going to go. I think sometimes they totally miss the mark in that they're trying to appease a portion of the population who doesn't care about bodybuilding, will never be interested in bodybuilding, who couldn't give a shit less about bodybuilding. I think that everybody wants to open new markets, but I think they are just off the mark. You're never going to get the couch potato to a contest. But you got to get him into a gym and then maybe you can get him to a contest. Even then, you either love this sport or you don't. You just love it and go and it becomes part of your life, or you just don't even care that it exists. It's not a thing like football or basketball or any of these sports where you never have to have been a player and still be a fanatic about it. Most of the people who are fanatics about bodybuilding are people that bodybuild themselves, people that train on a serious basis. Now they may or may not have ever competed but they can relate to it, and so I just don't think the general public is ever going to deal with it and I get really resentful sometimes when I think that the powers that be are catering to people who aren't even involved with the sport that are compromising the sport for the sake of the extra buck from some guy who's got a tire around his midriff.

It is clear that Michelle felt that the future of female bodybuilding would be greatly influenced by the profit motive of those in power. Social gatekeepers will always support attractive female bodybuilders because they have the look that they think the public wants to see. Michelle sighed and explained:

> You're always going to have that kind of cover girl look in the sport. Somebody once explained it to me. He said, "As far as what you see on the Olympia line-up, there's a recipe there, the faces may change, but the recipe or the makeup is still there. And it's going to have the people that actually really deserve to be there, the real, real competitors who have the muscle, have the symmetry, and all that should be there, then you're going to have one or two that are just really photo-

> genic because it's a visual event and if they still want to get some sponsors or get some television time, you're going to have your Tanya Knights, you're going to have people there who really are marginal pros but they have a cute face. So, their recipe is always going to be there, the faces may change to sell it depending on where they belong in the total scheme of things." I think that Olympia will always be won by the most deserving. We are going to go through a lot of growing pains, because the problem is you still have these competitors who haven't gotten the word on what the judges want to see. And they have not at this point had a chance or know better to let some of that muscle atrophy a little bit and tone it down. Once you get to that point where everybody is aware of it, then I think you'll see more and more feminine women up there because the harder, the hard core big muscular, will fade out of the sport.

Such an emphasis on profitability, according to Michelle, leads to indecision on the part of the gatekeepers. The ones who suffer the most from such indecisiveness are the female bodybuilders. Michelle felt that the attempts to increase profits are, ironically, in vain because the average American will never find the image of any female bodybuilders attractive enough to spend money trying to emulate them.

Mark, a state judge, also argued vehemently against the officials' attempts to impose the less muscular look on female bodybuilders, but he emphasized slightly different reasons for his disapproval:

> If they don't change back to their original direction, because I know what they are trying to do, they're trying to get the women to quit using the drugs, but it's not going to work because it's already happening. It's like the men; they tried to get them to quit, and of course now, they don't test anymore. Once you get started competing it's kind of like in football or anything else, you want to have the edge and you don't want to have anybody else win, so you do whatever it takes to win.[11] Ben Weider is trying to get bodybuilding into the Olympics, but it will never happen. It's just not that big of an interest and there probably will never be. I don't think it's ever going to be anything bigger than a minor sport, a small fish in a big pond. . . . And they are kind of going in the wrong direction trying to please the wrong people and they are going to end up having fewer people show up to contests and they will lose interest in women's contests, and it's already started to happen. I think bodybuilding in general would be more popular if they would take the restraints off the women. It's

> caused the women's numbers to decrease . . . this year's expected to be real low. And especially with the women who want to compete, they don't even know what to do. They don't know what direction to go in.

Mark argued that by emphasizing smaller-muscled female bodybuilders, gatekeepers are turning away not only fans, but bodybuilders as well. Again, much like Michelle, Mark believed that attempting to market bodybuilding to the general public is futile because of a lack of interest. Thus marketing the sport to a larger audience is not only damaging to the integrity of the sport, it is also misguided.

Not everyone saw the move to a less muscular and more attractive female bodybuilding look in a negative light. Some judges and bodybuilders felt that the recent trend is warranted, should be continued, and in fact, occurred in the nick of time to save the sport. For instance, one state-level female judge, Jan, discussed how the proliferation of steroid use among female bodybuilders has led to the popularity of bodybuilding's sister sport, the fitness shows:

> The changes they are trying to make, as far as having the muscular female bodybuilders, but still heading toward a more feminine look. I think that would be beautiful. Because I think a muscular body is absolutely something to admire. I think it's going to take a long time to go back to the feminine muscular. Because sometimes people don't put those together. Either you're muscular or you're feminine. And that's why the fitness shows are becoming so popular. A lot of the women are getting so frustrated with thinking they have to take the steroids or whatever to compete with the bigger women. They go for the fitness shows because they can look fit. They can look muscular without having to be overboard. I don't want to see it go to that either. I'd like to see the bodybuilding shows continue. But again, still look like a girl. If the steroids can get cleaned up, God that would be so wonderful.

Jan acknowledged the frustration felt by female bodybuilders, but she attributed this discontent not to the inconsistencies in judging, as previous judges and bodybuilders had argued, but to the pressure of feeling they had to use steroids to compete effectively in the sport; therefore many of them turned to fitness shows instead. She hoped the future would bring the feminine, athletic nonsteroid look to female bodybuilding, which would bring more women back to the sport.

Most male judges and officials were also positive about the change toward less muscular female bodybuilders, because they felt the public is turned off by larger-muscled women and smaller-muscled women would attract more people to the sport. One high-ranking official stated:

> I see it, it will continuously improve. I think the popularity will expand because it's expanding right now all over the world. I think when the women were a little too masculine, it turned a lot of people off. Not only the women who wanted to go into bodybuilding, but also the public because nobody thought that a real muscular massive looking woman was feminine. See a bodybuilder could still be feminine but not when they turn into males almost because some of the bodybuilders, if you look at them, look like men. When they flex a bicep, it's a real bicep.

We can infer from his words "when they flex a bicep, it's a real bicep" that he believes that women do not naturally have "real biceps," only men do. Thus, when women flex a "real bicep," it must not only be drug-enhanced, but it also is offensive to the general public.

Some felt that the public would be more accepting of female bodybuilding if it found a middle area between the two extremes. For instance, David, a state judge, stated:

> I think there is going to be a middle ground. There's got to be a middle ground where the general public is going to accept it a little bit more. There are still going to be those women like the muscular women . . . the Lenda Murrays, the Tanya Knights, the Laura Creavalles . . . Debbie Muggli, Shelley Beattie, Diana Dennis. . . . In fact, between Anja Schreiner and Laura Creavalle, I think is where it's going to end up somehow. So it went from "this is too masculine" to "this is a little bit too feminine." We need some ground that is in-between.

Brooke, a professional bodybuilder, also thought that female bodybuilding would begin to embody a more moderate look. However, she was not concerned, as other bodybuilders have been, that interest in the sport might fade:

> First of all, I don't think that female bodybuilders have anything to worry about. There have been various people who have said they feel it is going back toward Miss Fitness type competition. And I don't

> see that. At least not from the contests I've seen in the past year. I think female bodybuilding will continue in its own way to advance. What that means, I don't know. I don't think, like I said, that they are going to go really backwards. But I think it's going to temper itself to the point where it will allow the general public to catch up to it. It always seems to be a little ahead of the general opinion of what women should look like.

Seeing female bodybuilders as a type of vanguard of femininity—pushing the boundaries of acceptable appearances for women— Brooke believed that in the immediate future the sport would experience a moderating "cooling-off period" so the general public could "catch up" with the muscular images of female bodybuilders. When the general public finds the muscular look more palatable, the muscularity of female bodybuilders could be increased. Here again we see that participants must consciously limit their "athletic" displays in order not to risk offending the fans.

A sentiment expressed by bodybuilders and judges alike was that bodybuilding should at least return to portraying a healthy image to the public,[12] so that female bodybuilding would remain a popular and economically viable sport. For instance, Clay, who is adamantly opposed to women taking steroids, stated, "I see female bodybuilding heading more towards not so much the fitness look, but basically, the athletic attractive active female-look—with the women being healthy, they look better." As we saw in chapter 3, some people are more critical of women who take steroids than men, and Clay fits this camp. However, not everyone applied the no-steroids rule in a gender-specific way. Applying the importance of portraying a healthy look more generally to all bodybuilders, Christy, a national amateur competitor, explained:

> I'd like to see it stay intact. This is the biggest thing that's unfortunate about bodybuilding is that it started out as the key to be healthy and it turned into one of the most unhealthy sports that there is. One of the guys just died and I think that women take themselves down to a pretty unhealthy state and take the drugs and take diet aids, and do whatever is necessary to maintain that. I would like to see bodybuilding in general kind of be cleaned up a little bit and get back to being a symbol of health rather than freakiness.

The various opinions expressed by the participants in this study show that the future of female bodybuilding remains unpredictable. One thing is certain: the rise of fitness shows will continue to have a significant impact on female bodybuilding. As of fall 1996, not only do the NPC and IFBB hold fitness competitions, but so do other organizations such as the National Amateur Bodybuilders Association (NABBA), the National Fitness Sanctioning Body (NFSB), and the International Fitness Sanctioning Body (IFSB). Fitness competitions are receiving publicity from all of the major bodybuilding magazines and a couple of other magazines, *Ms. Fitness Magazine* and *Women's Fitness and Bodybuilding*, devote a substantial amount of coverage to these competitions. The look that is rewarded at fitness contests—athletic, feminine, fit, and trim—is closer to the appearance norms associated with hegemonic femininity,[13] a look that is more marketable. For instance, recall Kyle's descriptions of female bodybuilders in chapter 6 (see p. xxx). Not only is the fitness look seen as a more "appropriate" look, it is also touted as a more profitable image, making an unbeatable combination in the eyes of the social gatekeepers.

It appears that female bodybuilding is at a crossroads: the existence of fitness competitions may act to free female bodybuilders from the muscular restrictions placed on them by social gatekeepers because fitness shows will fill a niche for the less muscular but fit and athletic woman who is not muscular enough to compete in bodybuilding. On the other hand, the existence of such competitions may operate to tighten the social gatekeepers' restraints on muscular female bodybuilders because many of them believe that the fitness look is the more appropriate and marketable of the two. Most of the participants in this study saw fitness shows as working to limit female bodybuilders' muscularity. Some judges and bodybuilders preferred the smaller-muscled, more feminine look for female bodybuilders touted by social gatekeepers, but others disagreed, giving an economic-political rationale for their views. They resented the fact that their sport has to change in order to appeal to "couch potatoes" who will never care about bodybuilding anyway. Although some are annoyed with the role that marketability plays, they have little power to stop it.

Social gatekeepers will probably continue to focus more and more attention to what they consider the more profitable endeavor: fitness competitions. Fitness contestants are not perceived as crossing the gender order, as some contend female bodybuilders do. In fact, their looks put them somewhere along the continuum between a sexy, in-shape, toned, all-American *Playboy* centerfold and an athletic, feminine, toned, and sexy beauty pageant contestant who has abundant energy, can do the splits onstage, wears a thong while competing (as long as a the contest is not being filmed for television), and smiles incessantly. In other words, these women are not "monsters to behold" because they can still "be taken home to mother," as Harry Crews quipped in his novel, *Body.*[14] There is no confusing these women with men. Consequently, social gatekeepers think there is enormous profit to be made.

Female bodybuilders will more than likely be left to fight among themselves for increasingly smaller amounts of money and publicity. If this scenario plays out, gatekeepers may have found an area that efficiently and effectively solidifies their dual economic and patriarchal interests. Even if social gatekeepers do not fully turn their backs on female bodybuilding, they can always use fitness competitions as a kind of trump card to get female bodybuilders to continue to enhance their femininity and limit their muscularity. In other words, social gatekeepers will be able to use the threat that if female bodybuilders do not cooperate, they will withdraw their economic resources from the sport. Hence, it appears that the once potentially radicalizing image of the strong, powerful female bodybuilder may be almost completely coopted to fit back within the dominant hegemonic norms of femininity.

I began this research with a relatively simple question: How does the sport of female bodybuilding deal with the strong and muscular image of female bodybuilders? Through my ethnographic research, which includes both participant observation and in-depth interviews, I conclude that although, at first glance, female bodybuilders appear to embody an empowering image of women—one that exudes physical strength and emphasizes impressive musculature—when placed in the patriarchal and capitalist context of the IFBB and NPC bodybuilding organizations, their strength and power are tempered significantly. Albeit over the years female bodybuilders have gotten decidedly more muscular, they have also been institutionally constrained by social gatekeepers who continually reinforce the importance that female bodybuilders must not only enhance their femininity, they must limit their muscularity to a certain extent as well. For instance, recall that the judging guidelines for female bodybuilders, in the IFBB *Official Guidebook,* clearly states:

> The most important aspect is shape, a muscular feminine shape. The other aspects are similar to those described for assessing men, but in regard to muscular development, it must not be carried to excess where it resembles the massive muscularity of the male physique.[15]

In addition to scoring down excessive muscularity,

> Judges may find other faults not seen in men, such as stretch marks, operation scars, and cellulite. The judges shall also observe whether the women competitors walk to and from their positions in a graceful manner.[16]

By having different standards for female and male bodybuilders, gatekeepers institutionally reinforce the importance of gender distinctions between women and men in their sport. By doing so, they institutionally reinforce the feminine apologetic for female bodybuilders.

The feminine apologetic—a tactic some female athletes take to "apologize" for their participation in the male domain of athletic competition by exaggerating their femininity—has a vibrant history in the arena of female bodybuilding. If we look back at the history of this muscular domain, we see that as female bodybuilders have developed larger musculature, their displays of femininity have also become more enhanced and exaggerated. Currently, female bodybuilders go to unhealthy lengths to "prove" their femininity to others both inside and outside their sport. For instance, it is estimated that approximately 80 percent of professional female bodybuilders get breast implants so that they can still show some cleavage when competing.[17] The feminine apologetic does not simply stem from the female bodybuilders' individual wishes to exaggerate their femininity, but this tactic is institutionally promulgated and reinforced by upper- and lower-level gatekeepers.

Gatekeepers play a significant role in the emphasis on femininity displayed by female bodybuilders. Not only do they have tremendous political and economic power, but they also wield an enormous definitional power that allows them to set the boundaries in the appearance and comportment for female bodybuilders. In their zealous attempts to popularize bodybuilding, gatekeepers leave little room for dissenting opinions. Those who disagree with them are not given the opportunity to rise in the organizations to positions of power, and they are not given a fair chance to air their opinions and concerns. If female bodybuilders voice their displeasure with the direction of the sport, they do so with the risk of being labeled "a troublemaker," and thus may irreparably damage their careers. With more fitness competitions now on the horizon, female bodybuilders also have to watch what they do so the social gatekeepers will not withdraw their financial support, which would be a devastating blow to female bodybuilding. Female bodybuilders have few options. They can (1) agree with the current gendered power structures; (2) comply while quietly disagreeing; (3) covertly organize into a cohesive group and hope there is power in numbers; and (4) overtly protest. The latter two options could meet with harsh and swift action from officials and would probably lead to suspensions from the sport.

As Michael Messner argued, organized sport, as a cultural sphere defined largely by patriarchal and capitalist interests, represents "an important arena in which emerging images of active, fit and muscular women are forged, interpreted, contested, and incorporated."[18] We see these same dynamics being played out in the domain of female bodybuilding. Female bodybuilders have earnestly tried to take control of their own bodies, but the social gatekeepers have diminished this control by enforcing rules and regulations that make them enhance their femininity and limit their muscularity. These female contestants have also tried to have more political control, but these attempts are constrained by the unequal gendered power arrangement and the profit motives of officials and sponsors within the sport. Also playing against them are the historical and cultural forces outside the sport that continue to exclude, for the most part, muscular, strong, and powerful women from the ideal of femininity. Kathryn, a journalist, lamented:

> Ironically, all the people in charge of the sport are very old world men. There's not one powerful woman in the sport of bodybuilding today who has a hand in making any of the judging standards, who has a hand in controlling where the money goes. It's all controlled by men and they're extremely old world. They're extremely patriarchal. At this point, the best way to describe it is, it's like the fox guarding the hen house. I think they are holding women back. It could be much bigger.

Thus, in an arena that does not give female bodybuilders much voice, the goals of successful contestation and control is still elusive even for these incredibly strong and muscular women.

Although female bodybuilders in many ways have enormous control in shaping their bodies, they neither have institutional control over their own destinies nor do they have much political voice in the future of their sport. In fact, even their corporal control is mitigated by social gatekeepers. Hence, the words to Janet Jackson's song that opened this chapter ring painfully hollow when placed in the political and economic milieu of female bodybuilding.

APPENDIX A

Profiles of the Competitors, Judges, and Officials

Note: Some of the demographic information has been changed slightly and/or omitted to protect the privacy of the participants in the study.

Female Competitors

Lois—early thirties at the time of the interview. She is a high school graduate and is currently working in the fitness industry. She is married and competes at the state amateur level.

Susan—mid-twenties at the time of the interview. She has some college experience and is currently working at a job outside the fitness industry. She is divorced and has not remarried. She competes at the state amateur level.

Mary—mid-thirties at the time of the interview. She has some college experience and is currently working two jobs: one outside and the other inside the fitness industry. She is divorced. She competes at the state-level. She is also a bodybuilding judge.

Patty—mid-forties at the time of the interview. She is a high school graduate and is currently involved in the fitness industry. She is divorced and competes at the national level.

Ellen—mid-thirties at the time of the interview. She is a college graduate. She is single and has never married. She works in the fitness industry and has competed at the national amateur level.

Vicky—late thirties at the time of the interview. She is a college graduate, is engaged to be married, and works outside the fitness industry. She competes at the professional level.

Denise—early thirties at the time of the interview. She is a high school graduate beginning college, is currently married, and works within the fitness industry. She competes at the state amateur level. She is a state-level judge.

Christy—early thirties at the time of the interview. She is a high school graduate, is single, and works in the fitness industry. She competes at the national amateur level.

Diane—late twenties at the time of the interview. She is a college graduate, is single, and works outside the fitness industry. She competes at the professional level.

Jill—mid-thirties at the time of the interview. She is a high school graduate and is married. She competes at the professional level.

Stephanie—early thirties at the time of the interview. She is a college graduate and engaged to be married. She works outside the fitness industry. She competes at the professional level.

Pam—mid-thirties at the time of the interview. She is a college graduate and is currently married. She works inside the fitness industry and competes at the professional level.

Brooke—late thirties at the time of the interview. She is a college graduate and is currently married. She works inside the fitness industry and competes at the professional level.

Kim—early thirties at the time of the interview. She is a high school graduate and is currently single. She works outside the fitness industry and competes at the state amateur level.

Female Judges and Officials

Tracy—early thirties at the time of the interview. She is currently enrolled in college and is single. She participated as a female bodybuilder before becoming a judge. She holds jobs both in and out of the fitness industry and is also a bodybuilding official.

Rachel—early thirties at the time of the interview. She has a graduate degree. She works outside the fitness industry and is currently married. She participated as a female bodybuilder before becoming a judge.

Heather—early forties at the time of the interview. She is in college and currently separated. She participated as a female bodybuilder before becoming a judge. She is also a bodybuilding official.

Michelle—late thirties at the time of the interview. She has a high school degree and is currently married. She works outside the fitness industry and participated as a female bodybuilder before becoming a judge.

Jan—late thirties at the time of the interview. She has a high school degree. She is currently married and works outside the fitness industry. She participated as a female bodybuilder before becoming a judge.

Lynn—early thirties at the time of the interview. She works outside the fitness industry and is attending college. She participated as a female bodybuilder before becoming a judge.

Linda—mid-forties at the time of the interview. She is a high school graduate and works inside the fitness industry. She is married and has not competed as a female bodybuilder.

Karen—early forties at the time of the interview. She has a college degree and works both inside and outside the fitness industry. She is married and participated as a female bodybuilder before becoming a judge.

Renee—mid-forties at the time of the interview. She works inside the fitness industry and is married. She participated as a female bodybuilder before becoming a judge. She is also a bodybuilding official.

Male Judges and Officials

Mark—mid-forties at the time of the interview. He works inside the fitness industry and is currently separated from his spouse. He has a college degree. He still participates as a competitive bodybuilder.

David—early forties at the time of the interview. He is married and works outside the fitness industry. He participated as a bodybuilder and powerlifter before becoming a judge. He attended college but did not graduate.

Sam—mid-forties at the time of the interview. He works outside the fitness industry and is married. He has some college experience. He never participated as a competitive bodybuilder.

Kyle—mid-forties at the time of the interview. He works inside the fitness industry and is single. He is a high school graduate. He never participated as a competitive bodybuilder. He is also a bodybuilding official and he has promoted bodybuilding shows.

Richard—late forties at the time of the interview. He works inside the fitness industry. He is married and is a high school graduate. He competed as a powerlifter but not as a bodybuilder before becoming a judge.

Tod—early forties at the time of the interview. He works both inside and outside of the fitness industry. He is married and is a college graduate. He participated as a competitive bodybuilder before becoming a judge and is a bodybuilding official.

Steve—late forties at the time of the interview. He works inside the fitness industry. He is married and is a high school graduate. He participated as a competitive bodybuilder before becoming a judge and has promoted bodybuilding shows.

Clay—late forties at the time of the interview. He works inside the fitness industry. He is married and has attended graduate school. He participated as a competitive bodybuilder before becoming a judge. He has promoted bodybuilding shows and is a bodybuilding official.

Stan—early forties at the time of the interview. He works inside the fitness industry. He has a graduate degree and is married. He participated as a competitive bodybuilder before becoming a judge. He has promoted bodybuilding shows and is a bodybuilding official.

Mike—late thirties at the time of the interview. He works both in and out of the fitness industry. He has a college degree. He never participated as a competitive bodybuilder. He has promoted bodybuilding contests and is a bodybuilding official.

Ralph—late sixties at the time of the interview. He works inside the fitness industry. He has at least a high school degree. He never participated as a competitive bodybuilder and is a bodybuilding official.

Journalists

(To protect the confidentiality of these journalists, I will not provide any demographic information)

Shelley

Kathryn

Bob

APPENDIX B

Data, Methodologies, Theory

It is up to the sociologist to confer meaning to meaningless data—a rewarding responsibility indeed! It puts sociologists, and sociology as a whole, into the position of conferring meaning to the meaningless chaos of appearances—a task that historically has been that of the natural sciences.[1]

Methodological Tools and Theoretical Perspectives

My methodologies are participant observation and in-depth semistructured interviews. These two methods are often used in tandem and are integral components of ethnography. Historically, ethnographic work, sometimes called fieldwork, was developed to undertake the problems of studying other cultures,[2] and was thus closely associated with anthropology. Since the 1920s, however, ethnographic research has been undertaken by sociologists, and more recently by scholars in Cultural Studies, to study groups within the researcher's own culture.[3]

Regardless of the group being studied, ethnography offers an intimate view of various types of cultural forms. John Van Maanen contended that ethnography "rests on the peculiar practice of representing the social reality of others through the analysis of one's own experience in the world of these others."[4] The compelling nature of ethnographic work rests in its ability to offer rich and detailed knowledge of a groups's distinctive way of life.

Participant observation emerged as a sociological method as part of the "Chicago school" in the 1920s and 1930s.[5] The sociological qualitative tradition continued in the 1940s with W. F. Whyte's work, and endured in the 1950s and 1960s with the work of Howard Becker and other subcultural theorists.[6] According to Stuart Hall, scholars in the "Chicago school" and the subcultural theorists "were sensitive to the differences in 'lived' values and meanings that differentiated subcultures from the dominant culture." They "stressed the importance of the ways in which social actors define for themselves the conditions in which they live—their 'definitions of situation.' And they deployed a qualitative methodology."[7]

Since the 1970s, ethnography has experienced a revival that some scholars attribute to the emergence of Cultural Studies and the prevalent use of ethnographic research by scholars in that field.[8] The main purposes of ethnography are to document the lived experiences of the actors being studied, ascertain their definitions of the situation, and determine how these definitions are affected by cultural and historical conditions.

According to Hall, Cultural Studies scholars have "stressed the importance of the ways in which social actors define for themselves the conditions in which they live—their definitions of situation."[9]

The Research

I combine participant observation at regional and professional bodybuilding meets as well as interviews with female bodybuilders, NPC and IFBB officials and judges, and journalists at bodybuilding magazines. For the participant observations, I took extensive notes while observing how bodybuilding meets are run and organized. In all, I observed five different bodybuilding shows: three regional shows—the 1991 Texas Cup, the 1992 Texas Championships, and the 1992 Lackland Classic; two professional shows—the 1992 Ms. Olympia and the 1993 Ms. International. The observations that I conducted allowed me to see what the protocol is for bodybuilding shows, what types of people go to these events, what bodybuilders look like when they are onstage, what types of poses they are asked to do, the role the audience plays, the role of vendors who sell bodybuilding products at shows, and to see for myself what types of bodybuilders win at these different levels of competition.

At the bodybuilding contests, I met numerous people, many of whom I formally interviewed for this research. I also casually talked to others (not recorded) about both female and male bodybuilding, why they were there, and why they enjoy bodybuilding. Most of the interviews I conducted with those I had met at the bodybuilding contests were completed within weeks following the meet. This was done because they were either competing and needed a few days to recover from the meet experience or were judging and did not have time to talk with me at the contest.

In addition to observing bodybuilding contests, I had the opportunity to watch individuals working out with free weights, since some of my interviews were conducted in regional gyms. This aspect of the research is important because, as the respondents have said, the gym environment is an integral part of a bodybuilder's life. Thus, by watching people work out and interact with one another and by looking at the gym environment, I became more cognizant of the role of the gym, its ambiance, the interaction of its members, and the role it plays in the lives of bodybuilders, especially when they are getting ready for a bodybuilding competition. Furthermore, I had access to a few bodybuilders in the local area and watched them train; I also had the chance to ask them various questions about the whys, whens, and hows of training for bodybuilding shows, which gave me an appreciation of what is involved in a bodybuilder's workout routine.

The majority of my data come from thirty-seven in-depth, semistructured interviews with competitive female bodybuilders, judges, officials, and journalists. There were a total of twenty-five women and twelve men. They were asked a list of preset questions (not always asked in the same order), and follow-up questions were asked to probe their answers. The follow-up questions differed for each respondent because the content depended on their initial responses. However, for the most part, every respondent answered the same series of questions. This study consists of a total of eleven face-to-face interviews and twenty-six phone interviews.

Although phone interviews may not have elicited responses as thorough as the more intimate face-to-face interviews, they proved to be quite useful in researching the subject matter. A number of the respondents did not have time to talk with me at meets, and others I interviewed lived outside of Texas; therefore, the most efficient way to interview them was by telephone. Telephone interviews followed the same format as in-person interviews. I informed all respondents that the interviews were going to be taped, that their responses would remain confidential, and that they could refuse to answer any question.

There were benefits and drawbacks to using telephone interviews. One benefit was that I was able to include people outside the state of Texas who would otherwise have been excluded. By including a national sampling of female bodybuilders and judges, I have a more accurate picture not only of Texas bodybuilding, but of national and professional bodybuilding as well. A second benefit had to do with the steroid controversy. Many of the national and professional-level judges and officials were willing to discuss their feelings about the steroid issue openly because the only characteristic about me they could ascertain was that I had a relatively high voice; thus I probably did not take steroids and perhaps was anti-steroid as well.

Drawbacks of conducting interviews by phone include not being able to connect as well with the respondent because the interview is experienced as more impersonal, and the inability to read facial expressions and body language.

The Sample

I relied on nonprobability sampling for this study. According to Earl Babbie and Russell Bernard, the disadvantage of using nonprobability sampling techniques is that one's study has very low external validity, which makes generalizing beyond the sample quite difficult.[10] However, the advantage is that it often yields highly credible and reliable data about the group. The nonprobability sampling technique that I used is snowball sampling, which is useful in studies of small, bounded, or difficult-to-find populations[11] such as people connected with competitive bodybuilding. Snowball sampling refers to the technique in which the researcher locates one or more key individuals and asks them to name others who would be likely candidates for the research. Each, in turn, gives the name of one or two people they think will be a good interviewee.

Most of the respondents I interviewed gave me the name and phone number of someone they knew who was also involved in female bodybuilding as a competitor or as a judge. I then got in touch with these people, interviewed them, and then asked them for the name of someone else involved in bodybuilding. I had a total of four key informants who helped me in my research endeavors by putting me in touch with some of my respondents, and by giving me informal yet integral information about the sport and subculture of female bodybuilding. Once I had access to them and could use their names to get in contact with other respondents, the bodybuilding network opened up more easily for me.

Face-to-face interviews were conducted in Austin, San Antonio, Chicago, and Columbus. The two Texas locations were chosen because Texas is considered one of the "hotbeds" of female bodybuilding and also because they were convenient; the other two locations were chosen because they were the sites of the professional female bodybuilding shows. In-person interviews were conducted mostly in gyms, but some were conducted in people's homes, in restaurants, or in my office. Twenty-nine interviews were taped and fully transcribed; eight were either taped and partially transcribed, or I took copious notes during the interview.

The interview for the female bodybuilders (see appendix C) consisted of numerous open-ended questions on five general areas: sports socialization, the process of getting ready for a meet and the meet experience, attitudes about judging, attitudes about the importance of attractiveness for female bodybuilders and what constitutes the ideal female bodybuilder, and attitudes about their own experiences in the sport and the future of the sport.

The interview for the female and male judges (see below) consisted of open-ended questions on four general areas: sports socialization, judging experiences, attitudes about the importance of attractiveness of female bodybuilders, and their vision of the future of female bodybuilding.

These groupings of questions represent the major categories that I was interested in exploring at the outset of the project. The groupings of questions on the respondents' previous sports experiences address the level of activity in sports before their involvement in female bodybuilding and also the process of getting involved in such a nontraditional sport. To personalize their experiences and to illustrate the rigor of the sport, I asked a series of questions about what it takes to get ready for a meet and what the day of the meet is like for them. The heart of the research lies in the middle set of questions that relate to the importance of attractiveness, attitudes about judging, and responses to the system by female bodybuilders. They served to focus my interest on the importance of the construction and negotiation of femininity, as well as studying the feasibility of female bodybuilders having a voice in their sport. Since the journalists and officials have media available to tell their side of the story, it is important that female bodybuilders' experiences are heard and acknowledged as well.

For the data analysis of my research, I was influenced by John McPhee's style of organizing data into conceptual categories.[12] Thus, I read each transcribed interview several times. Then I made a hard copy of the transcribed interview and placed notes beside responses to indicate into which conceptual category each excerpt fell. I then cut out each response and placed it into a labeled folder. Each folder represented a chapter, and within each folder were numerous subgroupings representing conceptual categories. Clusters of subgroupings were arranged in order, fastened together by paper clips, and kept within the appropriate file folder. Once the transcribed interviews were cut, organized, and placed in their groupings, I reexamined each file folder individually to ensure that the data were in their proper place. I then entered each excerpt from the first file folder into the computer and then I rearranged the excerpts, analyzed their content in greater detail, and attempted to comment on each one. After all of the excerpts that fit into chapter 1 were cut out, arranged, typed up, and analyzed, I moved to chapter 2 and the process started again.

Limitations

One of the major problems with this research was that information about the highest-level social gatekeepers is very scanty and some data were obtained only secondhand. Since most officials serve as judges as well, it was difficult to find people who were officials. In fact, I think the president of the IFBB is the only person who does not hold the dual positions of judge and official. If I were to continue this research, I would interview more social gatekeepers, concentrating on promoters and endorsers to better understand their influence on the current and future direction of the sport.

Some interrelated limitations of this research project deserve mention. Some are directly linked to my lack of available funds to do the research. Every aspect of the research cost money, including but not limited to long-distance telephone calls, all of which lasted a minimum of forty minutes; four of the five trips to bodybuilding meets that were held out of Austin; and the transcription of the interviews. Because of these expenses, the number of interviews I was able to transcribe was limited. Therefore, the questions arise: "What more would have been gained with greater access to funds? Would I really have learned that much more about the world of female bodybuilding or would I simply have had further confirmation of the experiences I had already recorded?"

To answer these questions, I would like to draw attention to Daniel Bertaux's 1981 research on the bakers' trade in France. In his study, Bertaux went through a process of what he called a "saturation of knowledge."[13] He stated:

> In our study of the bakers' trade, we were confronted with a population of about 160,000 people (90,000 bakers and bakers' wives, 70,000 bakery workers). No "representative sample" was ever drawn. We gathered life stories following what is pompously called "a snowball strategy." For instance, we gathered about thirty-five stories from bakery workers. The first life story taught us a great deal; so did the second and third. By the fifteenth we had begun to understand the pattern of sociostructural relations which makes up the life of a bakery worker. By the twenty-fifth, adding the knowledge we had from life stories of bakers, we knew we had it: a clear picture of this structural pattern and of its recent transformations. New life stories only confirmed what we had understood, adding slight individual variations. We stopped at thirty: there was no point going further. We knew already what we wanted to know.[14]

When one begins to hear the same stories with slight variations, one has hit the "saturation of knowledge" which, according to Bertaux, gave the idea of "representativity" a totally different meaning.[15] This is the point I reached in my interviews with female bodybuilders, judges, and officials. The backgrounds, experiences, and attitudes began to overlap, and the inclusion of more interviews led only to slight variations on established patterns. I thus thought it was acceptable, but not necessarily preferable, to end the interviewing aspect of the research process.

In his discussion of "representativity," Berteaux[16] argued that his sample of workers in the bakers' trade is representative, not "at the morphological level" (at the level of superficial description), but at the sociological level, at the level of sociostructural relations (*rapports sociaux*). In my case, the collected data gave enough information to determine the characteristics of the basic patterns involved in the sport of female bodybuilding. Although this study cannot be taken as a representative survey of the socio-demographic characteristics of the individuals involved, their experiences together speak for a large group of people involved in female bodybuilding, as evidenced by the repetition of the stories and experiences the respondents shared with me.

My research is helpful to those who want to understand the sport of female bodybuilding, how it is shaped by both internal and external factors, and how it is experienced by those who participate in it.

Furthermore, this research sheds light on the ways in which gender is constructed and negotiated, and how patriarchal and capitalistic influences shape these processes. It suggests that the relationship between gatekeepers, gender-norm enforcement, the labeling process, and gender boundaries are important in the construction and negotiation of femininity, particularly when norms of femininity are being contested. Issues related to the various forms of resistance by women to hegemonic norms of femininity are also explored. Although the numbers are limited, I am confident that this sample of individuals associated with female bodybuilding captures a wide variety of experiences that are common to the judges, bodybuilders, and officials.

Theoretical Lens: The Cultural Studies Paradigm

To shed light on the construction and negotiation of female bodybuilders' femininity, I incorporate a Cultural Studies perspective, in which I take as a starting point the notion that gender is not biologically determined, but rather is socially constructed.[17] In this section, I briefly describe how these two interrelated perspectives inform my research. It is my hope that the theoretical framework I use serves to guide my analysis, not determine it.

Cultural Studies is a critical, interdisciplinary approach to the analysis of culture and cultural forms that provides "a sophisticated theory of the relations of dominance and subordination structured along class lines."[18]

Feminist Cultural Studies seeks to expand orthodox Cultural Studies further by theorizing about the complex connections of relations of dominance and subordination structured along gender, ethnic, and class divisions.[19] Since the

1970s, the scholars at the University of Birmingham Centre for Cultural Studies have been, and continue to be, essential in expanding the work of Antonio Gramsci,[20] who coined and used the terms cultural hegemony, counter-hegemony, relations of dominance and subordination, and resistance to provide a more thorough analysis of the power dynamics found in modern capitalist societies. Gramsci and Cultural Studies scholars have attempted to show how relations of dominance and subordination are maintained in the spheres of culture and ideology by the dominant groups, and how these same relations are often challenged by oppressed or marginalized groups.

In the arena of culture, oppression of subordinated groups in capitalist societies is predominantly maintained by consent to dominant ideas. Gramsci called this "cultural hegemony," which consists of the values, norms, beliefs, prejudices, and lived experiences that support and legitimize the existing power relations.[21] Hegemony is based on compliance to certain dominant ideas by marginalized and subordinated groups which in fact express the needs of the dominant group.[22] Inequality is therefore seen as natural and legitimate by those who are oppressed.

However, because hegemony is based on ideas and beliefs, it has to be re-created, defended, and modified by members of the dominant group as time goes on. It can be challenged at any moment. In fact, hegemony is "a process of continuous creation, which, given its massive scale, is bound to be uneven in the degree of legitimacy it commands, [however, we must] leave some room for antagonistic cultural expression's to develop."[23]

Thus, society, or what Gramsci called "civil society,"[24] is in constant process, where the creation by subordinate groups of alternatives to hegemony, known as counter-hegemonies, is always a possibility, to some extent.

Counter-hegemonies, attempts to resist dominant ideology, occur when members of subordinate groups overtly resist the dominant ideology that legitimates their oppression through strikes, factory takeovers, or mass movements.[25] The civil rights and feminist movements of the 1960s as well as the Polish Solidarity movement were counter-hegemonies. However, overt resistance of the dominant powers is usually used by members of the subordinate group as a last resort because they are often harshly sanctioned by authorities through physical coercion, or what Gramsci called domination.[26] In addition to the responses of those in power, people in the subordinated groups are not likely to directly challenge the hegemonic relations of power because, as Gramsci argued, "normally most people find it difficult, if not impossible, to translate the outlook implicit in their experience into a conception of the world that will directly challenge the hegemonic culture."[27]

Therefore, resistance, if it does occur, may often take place in everyday cultural practices, which, as Doug Foley argued, members of subordinate groups "invent to find dignity in an oppressive class society."[28]

Often resistance occurs on the symbolic level. People may coopt, redefine, and use symbols from the dominant culture to attempt to challenge the dominant groups' power over them. For instance, when African Americans in the 1990s wore caps with an "X" on the front representing their support of Malcolm

X and his teachings, they were exhibiting a symbolic act of African American resistance to white dominance. Postwar British youth, such as "punks," voiced their despondency over their perceived hopeless future in British society through the use and cooptation of clothing and hairstyles that served to offend members of the dominant group.[29] Thus, given their lack of power, marginalized and subordinated groups have usually covertly and symbolically attempted to resist the unequal power structures that oppress them.

One of the central issues in Gramsci's vision of society is the issue of power—not physical power, but power to determine reality, power to set boundaries. For that reason, Gramsci's work is extremely important when examining the relations of dominance in American society because, as T. J. Jackson Lears argued,

> it points us toward cultural definitions of race, ethnicity, and gender and toward an exploration of the ways those definitions justify or challenge existing power relations. To resort to the concept of cultural hegemony is to take a banal question—"who has power?"—and deepen it at both ends.
>
> The "who" includes parents, preachers, teachers, journalists, literati, "experts" of all sorts, as well as advertising executives, entertainment promoters, popular musicians, sports figures, and "celebrities"—all of whom are involved (albeit often unwittingly) in shaping the values and attitudes of a society. The "power" includes cultural as well as economic and political power—the power to help define the boundaries of common-sense "reality" either by ignoring views outside those boundaries or by labeling deviant opinions "tasteless" or "irresponsible."[30]

The struggle, then, is multifaceted on a variety of fronts including cultural, economic, and political. These issues are central to this research. Particularly critical are the questions of who has the power to set and maintain the norms of gendered behavior and appearance—the boundaries of what is acceptable, what is unacceptable, what is deviant, what is normal.

The ability to define reality is integrally intertwined with the economic and political power of a group. Those in power have the upper hand in the negotiation of gendered norms.

APPENDIX C

Interview Schedules: Female Bodybuilders and Judges

Bodybuilders

Sports Socialization

- Tell me a bit about your sports background. Did you play any sports when you were a kid? High school? College? Professional?
- How did your family respond to your interest in sports?
- Tell me how you first got interested in bodybuilding. What was going on in your life at the time?
- When did you first compete? What was it like? Was it what you expected? How old were you?
- How has your family responded to you being a bodybuilder?
- What has been the response of your significant others and friends?
- Does your boyfriend or significant other attend the meet? Does your family? Do you like that?
- Have you had to deal with negative reactions from people? How do you respond?
- I have heard that being a competitive bodybuilder can be very expensive. How have you financed your bodybuilding?

Getting Ready for the Meet and the Meet Experience

- When you're getting ready for a meet, how do the people in the gym treat you?
- Are other competitive female bodybuilders supportive when you are getting ready for a show? What about male bodybuilders?
- What's the hardest thing about getting ready for a meet? Why?
- Tell me about the day of the competition. What's it like for you?

Judging

- Are you happy with the judging at meets?
- In your experience, is there consistency in the judging from meet to meet?
- How do you feel about male vs. female judges? Does it matter to you if you have more male or more female judges? Why?
- In your opinion, can any improvements be made in the judging of meets?
- Have you ever disagreed with the judging at a bodybuilding meet in which you were competing? What did you do?
- What course of action can female bodybuilders take if they disagree with their placing?

Importance of Attractiveness/Ideal Female Bodybuilders

- How important is smiling while posing? Is it important for male bodybuilders as well?
- Do you put on makeup and style your hair for the meets? Why? How do you feel about that?
- Do you think prettiness and sexiness are important attributes for female bodybuilders? How do you feel about that? Do you think the same is true for male bodybuilders?
- Do you think men find your type of physique attractive and sexy? Is that important to you?
- Describe the ideal female bodybuilder. Who has come the closest to that ideal? Why is that the ideal for you? What qualities does she have that make her the ideal?
- Can a female bodybuilder be too muscular even if she has good symmetry? Why or why not?

Attitudes about Their Own Experience in Bodybuilding and the Future of Female Bodybuilding

- In your own experience, what's the thing you like the most about female bodybuilding? The thing you like the least?
- What have you learned about female bodybuilding that you didn't know when you first started competing?
- How would you describe your overall experience in bodybuilding?
- How has being a competitive female bodybuilder affected how you see yourself? Has becoming muscular affected your self-image?

- What are your reflections on how you see female bodybuilding changing?
- What words of wisdom would you tell a woman who was interested in becoming a competitive bodybuilder?

Background

Age:
Educational level:
Marital status:
Occupation:
Length of competing:
  national level:
  state level:
As a bodybuilder: your best placing at your most prestigious meet:

Judges/Officials

- What is your previous sports background?
- Were you ever competitive in bodybuilding? If so, what is your previous bodybuilding background?
- How long have you been a judge for female bodybuilding meets?
- Why did you decide to become a judge? Do you like it?
- What do you like the most about being a judge?
- What do you like the least?
- In your experience, is there a difference between how female and male judges evaluate female bodybuilders?
- In your opinion, is there consistency in judging from meet to meet?
- What are the criteria you look for in a female bodybuilder?
- Is there a difference in the way you judge male and female bodybuilders?
- Is attractiveness (a pretty face) important to you when you judge female bodybuilders? Is it important when you judge male bodybuilders?
- Do you think it is important for female bodybuilders to wear makeup and do their hair?
- Given that a female bodybuilder has good symmetry, can she be too muscular? Why or why not?
- In your experience, are the female bodybuilders happy with the judging of meets?

- Let's say there is a female bodybuilder who disagrees with the way a meet was called that she was in. Is there any recourse she can take if she disagrees with the judging of a meet?
- In your experience, what have most bodybuilders done who disagree with the judging?
- In your own words, describe the ultimate female bodybuilder. Who comes the closest to that ideal?
- Since you have been involved in female bodybuilding, have you seen any changes in the way female bodybuilders are judged? What do you think about that?
- What's the biggest change in female bodybuilding that you've seen since you've been associated with the sport?
- Where do you see the direction of female bodybuilding heading? How do you feel about that?

Background

Age:
Educational level:
Marital status:
Occupation:
Length of judging:
 national level:
 state level:
As a bodybuilder, your best placing at your most prestigious meet:

APPENDIX D

Glossary of Terms

Bitch Tits: A condition known medically as gynecomastia. It occurs among male bodybuilders who take steroids, making the area around the nipples become puffy. This condition is due to an increase in the production of estrogen and a concomitant growth of mammary glands.

Buffed: A term used to describe a bodybuilder with big, lean quality muscles. The bodybuilder also has good muscle lines. E.g., "Sheila is really buffed."

Cross-striations: Muscle fibers are visible. One can see ridges or "shreds" in the muscle groups. Occurs when the bodybuilder has quality muscle and minimal fat and water retention.

Cut: The bodybuilder has good separation between muscle groups. This term is similar to the term "defined." The bodybuilder has reduced bodyfat levels and maintained muscularity. E.g., "David is cut."

Definition: Muscular groups are separate and distinct from one another; e.g., the biceps are clearly distinct from one another and from the triceps. E.g., "Marc's muscles are well defined. He has good definition."

Flat: This condition occurs when the bodybuilder does not achieve the healthy maximum muscularity displayed when the muscles are hard and cut. Perhaps the person peaked too early or overtrained for the competition. The muscles are not full.

Grunt out: A term used by bodybuilders to indicate what they do to get through a particularly arduous workout. They "grunt out" the workout or "grind it out." The bodybuilders know beforehand that the workout is going to be especially painful but they just "suck it up and grunt out."

Hard: A term used to describe a bodybuilder who has good quality muscles with little subcutaneous water and fat retention. E.g., "Lisa looks hard."

Invisible line: A subjective demarcation that connotes that a female bodybuilder has gotten too muscular. A sign of unacceptable muscularity. This line varies for different people. If a judge thinks that a female bodybuilder has crossed this line, he or she will mark the bodybuilder down. Some female bodybuilders who are said to have crossed the line are described as "masculine-looking."

IFBB: The International Federation of Bodybuilders, the premier professional bodybuilding organization founded by Ben and Joe Weider in 1946. The IFBB is also the predominant international amateur organization.

Lean: Used to describe a bodybuilder who has dieted properly and has little subcutaneous water and fat between the muscle and skin.

NPC: The National Physique Committee, the American amateur bodybuilding organization. It is the American national affiliate of the IFBB.

Overall package: A term used by bodybuilding judges and officials to describe the overall appearance of bodybuilders on stage. For a female bodybuilder, the overall package revolves around the enhancement of femininity. Thus, it includes such feminine accouterments as makeup, hairstyle, fit and color of posing suit, posing style, the manner in which she carries herself on stage, and, for some judges, breast size. For a male bodybuilder, the term means presenting a neat appearance.

Reps: The contraction of the word "repetitions." The number of times in a set that a bodybuilder lifts a particular set of weights. There is no rest period in between reps. Reps are subsumed under the broader term, "set." For instance, a bodybuilder may do three sets of dumbbell curls, and for each set he or she may do twelve reps.

Ripped: This term refers to a person who has more separation in the muscles than someone who is merely "cut." The separation of muscles is more defined in that some cross-striations are visible. This condition occurs when a bodybuilder has low levels of body fat and excellent muscle separation. Sometimes referred to as "sliced."

Roids: Short for steroids.

Set: A grouping of reps with a rest period in between each grouping. Oftentimes, a bodybuilder will do three or four sets of ten to fifteen reps for each type of lift.

Shredded: The highest level of muscle separation. There is no subcutaneous water or fat between the skin and the muscles, to the extent that muscle fibers (cross-striations) can be seen easily (there are ridges in the muscles). A male bodybuilder who is shredded is the ultimate because he has quality muscle and has effectively purged his body of excess water and fat. However, female bodybuilders are judged down for getting "shredded" because it is assumed they can get this way only through the use of illegal substances and diuretics.

Smooth: A term that describes nice, full-bodied muscles, though the bodybuilder is not lean enough for any type of muscular definition. There is still too much subcutaneous water or fat between the muscles and the skin. There are no muscular cuts or definition. E.g., "Jim looks smooth." Not an optimal condition for bodybuilders on competition day, but better than being labeled "soft."

Soft: This terms means that the muscles are not good quality, i.e., they are not etched or defined because there is too much subcutaneous water and fat. This condition is worse than being smooth because not only did the bodybuilder not diet and dehydrate herself properly, she also did not train well. Her muscles are not full, big, and healthy-looking.

Symmetry: One of the criteria by which bodybuilders are evaluated. For the symmetry round, bodybuilders stand in groups of two or three on stage in the semi-relaxed position. Judges evaluate how symmetrical/proportional their various muscular groups are to one another. For instance, are the size and shape of a bodybuilder's quadriceps proportional to that of the biceps or calf muscles? Is the upper and lower body proportional, as well as the right and left sides? In this round, judges determine if bodybuilders have ignored any part of their physique during training; if they have, judges will deduct points.

Vascularity: A condition in which the blood vessels in the body are prominent. This condition is considered to be related to low bodyfat levels.

APPENDIX E

A Muscularity Continuum

Less Muscular Bodybuilders:
Sharon Bruneau
Rachel McLish
Anja Schreiner

Muscular Bodybuilders:
Shelley Beattie
Laura Creavalle
Cory Everson
Tanya Knight
Lenda Murray

More Muscular Bodybuilders:
Paula Bircumshaw
Bev Francis

NOTES

Notes to the Introduction

1. The following are the names and products of the twenty-three vendors. Powerhouse Gym: clothes; Platinum Everywear: clothes; Totally Tanna: tanning liquid; Sampson and Delilah: clothes; Great Earth: vitamins and nutritional supplements; Universal Nutritional Supplements: vitamins; ICOPRO Integrated Conditioning Programs: vitamins and supplements; Hotskins: clothes; OTOMIX: athletic clothes; Carbofire: carbo powder and other supplements; artist selling 1992 Ms. Olympia prints; Megamass: vitamins; Teddy B. Sportswear: clothes; Health Care U.S.A.; IFBB Apparel; Mr. Olympia souvenirs: clothes; VALEO: workout belts; Powerhouse Bar: carbo sportsbar; HammerStrength: workout equipment; Weider Gear: clothes; California Body Wear: clothes; Ironman: clothes; Ms. Olympia: clothes and the official 1992 Ms. Olympia program.

2. Similarly, Hughes and Coakley (1991: 313) talk about the creation of special bonds between male athletes, particularly in the sports "wherein athletes are perceived to be unique because they endure extreme challenges and risks. These special feelings separate athletes form other people when it comes to what athletes see as a true understanding of the sport experience." Those within the sport are seen as brothers and superior to those outside the group, who are usually viewed with disdain and contempt. Hughes and Coakley also refer to Tom Wolfe's (1979) work, *The Right Stuff,* in which similar in- and out-group patterns exist among test pilots and astronauts.

3. IFBB *Guidebook,* 1987: 10.

4. IFBB *Guidebook,* 1987: 10.

5. IFBB *Guidebook,* 1987: 10.

6. IFBB *Guidebook,* 1987: 10.

7. IFBB *Guidebook,* 1987: 10.

8. Actually, Klein (1993) argued that one of female bodybuilders' goals is to be attractive to men. One way they achieve this is through their posing styles. He maintained, "There is no repudiation of wanting to be desirable to men: posing is a 'turn-on'" (p. 190).

9. IFBB *Guidebook,* 1987: 7.

10. For simplicity's sake, I will refer to the activity of bodybuilding as a sport throughout this research, keeping in mind the scholarly controversy surrounding this issue. For instance, Alan Klein (1986: 116) applied Coakley's (1982) three criteria necessary for an activity to be called a sport: physical exertion, competition, and organization, and concluded that bodybuilding lies "precipitously between sport and spectacle."

11. Schur, 1984; Chafetz, 1990.
12. Adamson, 1980.
13. Schur, 1984.
14. Cahn, 1990: 196.
15. For more strategies, see Boutilier and SanGiovanni, 1983; Twin, 1979; Lenskyj, 1986.
16. Jan Todd, 1992b.
17. Jan Todd, 1992a.
18. Twin, 1979.
19. See Hilliard, 1984; Cahn, 1990; Birrell, 1990; Hargreaves and Tomlinson, 1992; Messner, 1992; Crossett, 1995.
20. Hargreaves and Tomlinson, 1992: 217.
21. Messner, 1988.
22. Messner, 1988: 197.
23. Messner, 1988: 208.
24. Until the mid-1980s, there was a paucity of scholarly work on either female or male bodybuilding. Since that time, however, there has been a virtual plethora of interest in male bodybuilding (Ewald and Jiobu, 1985; Klein, 1985a, b, 1986, 1989, 1990, 1992, 1993; Page, 1989; Gillett and White, 1992) and female bodybuilding (Duff and Hong, 1984; Schulze, 1990; Miller and Penz, 1991; Aycock, 1992; Bolin, 1992; Daniels, 1992; Guthrie and Castelnuovo, 1992). The issues addressed by these scholars include the increased feelings of attractiveness by women participating in competitive female bodybuilding (Duff and Hong, 1984); efforts by female bodybuilders to renegotiate the dominant masculine meanings of bodybuilding (Miller and Penz, 1991); the role of the media in shaping the images of female bodybuilders (Schulze, 1990); issues of the body and diet in bodybuilding (Bolin, 1992); the practice of "femininity control" of female bodybuilders (Daniels, 1992); and the compliance and resistance of female bodybuilders to the dominant discourses of feminine body beauty (Guthrie and Castelnuovo, 1992).
25. Weber, 1993.
26. Attendance for the 1992 Ms. Olympia was not nearly as high as it was for the 1985 Ms. Olympia, when there were five thousand in attendance (interview with bodybuilding official). The 1985 Ms. Olympia is considered by some officials to have represented the peak of interest in female bodybuilding.
27. Lee Haney (eight-time Mr. Olympia), Mike Matarazzo, Sean Ray, Cory Everson (six-time Ms. Olympia), Jeff Everson, and Flex Wheeler are selling bodybuilding products and their own autographed pictures, which go for ten dollars each. When bodybuilders sell products at a company's booth, they are usually sponsored by that company.

Selling their own pictures is a way for bodybuilders to promote themselves to their fans as well as help defray costs. In the pictures, the bodybuilders are usually either in a bodybuilding pose or in revealing clothes with a sexy pose.
28. IFBB *Guidebook*, 1987: 8.
29. IFBB *Guidebook*, 1987: 8.
30. IFBB material.

31. The total prize money for the 1992 Ms. Olympia was $100,000, with first place worth $35,000, and a gold medal.

32. Tenth place went to Debbie Muggli; ninth place: Nikki Fuller; eighth place: Yolanda Hughes; seventh place: Claudia Montemaggi; sixth place: Anja Schreiner; fifth place: Diana Dennis; fourth place: Sandy Riddell; third place: Shelley Beattie; second place: Laura Creavalle; first place: Lenda Murray.

Notes to Chapter 1

1. The names used in this book are not the real names of the participants. I have used pseudonyms to protect their identity.

2. Greendorfer and Lewko, 1978; Landers, 1979; Portz, 1973; Ziegler, 1973.

3. This finding supports earlier research conducted by Snyder and Spreitzer (1973), who found that same-sex parents had a greater influence on female sport involvement than opposite-sex parents.

4. Langloise and Downs (1980) discovered that boys and girls both received negative reactions from their mothers and fathers when the children played with "cross-sex toys." However, fathers, more than mothers, dispense more vigorous differential treatment of their sons and daughters. Thus, the researchers suggest that "socialization pressure for sex-typed behaviors may come most consistently from fathers" (Langloise and Downs, 1980: 1245).

The findings of Roopnarine (1986) also support the conclusion of greater sex-typing by fathers. In their study on parental interaction with toddlers, they found that while both parents were less likely to pay attention to the block play of their daughters than their sons, this behavior was even more true for fathers than mothers.

5. Alan Klein (1993) argued that those who get involved in bodybuilding do so in order to compensate for perceived weaknesses, limitations, insecurities, or self-doubts. He maintained, "It becomes apparent that the formidable bodies are responses to a shaky psyche, that the powerful arms and chests are a bodybuilder's way of working out a range of personal issues . . . because to me physique and psyche were different words for overdevelopment and underdevelopment. What bound them was compensation; the bodily fortress protected the vulnerability inside" (Klein, 1993: 3).

6. Todd Crossett's (1995) study on the women's professional golf tour revealed similar dynamics among professional golfers.

7. Klein, 1985.

Notes to Chapter 2

1. McGough, 1993.

2. Weider, 1983: vii.

3. Wayne, 1985.

4. Today the official IFBB journal is *Flex* magazine, which is still published by Joe Weider.

5. Weider, 1983; Wayne, 1985.
6. Hoxha, 1995.
7. Thomas and Wennerstrom, 1983.
8. Gaines and Butler, 1981; Jan Todd, 1987.
9. Jan Todd, 1992a.
10. Wennerstrom, 1984a.
11. Wennerstrom, 1984a: 76.
12. Wayne, 1985: 30.
13. Wennerstrom, 1984a.
14. Wayne, 1985.
15. Wennerstrom, 1984b: 65.
16. Wennerstrom, 1984b.
17. Wennerstrom, 1984b.
18. Wennerstrom, 1984b.
19. Wennerstrom, 1984b.
20. Wennerstrom, 1984b: 66.
21. Wennerstrom, 1984b.
22. Wennerstrom, 1984a: 77.
23. Wennerstrom, 1984a: 77.
24. Wennerstrom, 1984b.
25. Gaines and Butler, 1984.
26. Gaines and Butler, 1984: 35.
27. Wennerstrom, 1984c: 28.
28. Gaines and Butler, 1984: 35.
29. This early history parallels the process Crossett (1995) describes in his book on the history of women's professional golf, in which he discusses the development of women's professional golf. In 1944, the Women's Professional Golf Association (WPGA) was chartered by three professional women golfers. According to Crossett (1995: 40), "The primary goal of the organization was to organize and promote professional tournaments for women." Promoting golf products was not its main goal. In 1950, the organization was revised and renamed the LPGA. The LPGA was different from the WPGA in a few ways, one of the most important being that it "relied heavily on outside, non-golfer, male management professionals, while the WPGA was player managed" (Crossett, 1995: 45). The LPGA had player representatives that were backed by golf-equipment manufacturers.
30. Gaines and Butler, 1984.
31. Wennerstrom, 1984b.
32. Wennerstrom, 1984b.
33. Klein, 1993: 97.
34. There are some parallels between the rise of the LPGA and that of the IFBB. See Crossett (1995) for a discussion on the rise of the LPGA. There is overlap particularly in the rise of corporate sponsorships and how they served to influence the nature of the game and the control athletes in both sports are able to wield in relation to the social gatekeepers.
35. Klein, 1993: 97.

36. Wayne, 1985.

37. For instance, he was a judge at the 1992 Ms. Olympia contest as well as the 1993 Ms. International contest.

38. JMP Management homepage: http://www.getbig.com/jmp/jmpwho.htm.

39. JMP Management homepage.

40. Klein, 1985a: 13.

41. Wolff, 1996: 158.

42. Wolff, 1996: 159.

43. Wolff, 1996: 159.

44. Wolff, 1996.

45. IFBB material.

46. IFBB material.

47. Terry Todd, 1987.

48. Joe Weider has met the criteria of "special conditions" because he is able to use the IFBB symbol and logo to advertise his products as well as Joe Weider's Mr. and Ms. Olympia contests. IFBB material.

49. There is a tremendous discrepancy between the men's and women's bodybuilding money prizes. For instance, the first place winner at the Mr. Olympia received $100,000, but the first place winner at the Ms. Olympia took home only $35,000. Another example is the Arnold Schwarzenegger Classic and the Ms. International Competition, which are held annually in tandem at Columbus, Ohio. The first place male winner received $80,000 in 1993, but his female counterpart only received $20,000. For these two shows, the top male bodybuilders have the potential to make approximately three times more than the top females. Furthermore, if one considers that male bodybuilders have more opportunities in which to make more money because there are more professional shows, the difference in earnings between the two is even greater. If we take into account all of the prize money for the male bodybuilding shows in the 1992–93 season ($808,000 total prize money for eighteen shows) and compare it to that of the female bodybuilding shows ($160,000 total prize money for three shows), then male bodybuilders will make more than four times that of female bodybuilders.

The following prize money awards were given to the top female and male bodybuilders at the 1993 Ms. International Contest:

	Women	*Men*
1st place	$20,000.00	$80,000.00
2nd place	9,000.00	35,000.00
3rd place	4,500.00	20,000.00
4th place	3,000.00	13,000.00
5th place	2,000.00	10,000.00
6th place	1,500.00	5,000.00

50. Ravo, 1992: B1.
51. Ravo, 1992.
52. When promoters for shows need a popular guest poser, the Weider office can, for a fee, offer the top bodybuilders to guest pose at the contest.
53. Joe Weider is the sponsor for the Mr. and Ms. Olympia Contests. In fact, the contests have been renamed, "Joe Weider's Mr. and Ms. Olympia." His brother, Ben, is the president of the organization (IFBB) that hosts the shows.
54. Stone, 1988, as quoted in Leigh, 1990.
55. Klein, 1985a: 6.
56. Stone, 1988, as quoted in Leigh, 1990.
57. This has not always been the case for the Weiders. In the 1950s, the Weiders' distribution company was dismantled in a buy-out, which left Joe Weider with no distribution for his products as well as a $2.3 million debt.
58. Klein, 1993.
59. Klein, 1993: 87.
60. Hoxha, 1995.
61. Hoxha, 1995.
62. Wayne, 1985.
63. Hoxha, 1995.
64. Wayne, 1985: 97.
65. Klein, 1993: 99.

Notes to Chapter 3

1. Solotaroff, 1992.
2. As Terry Todd (1987: 101) stated: "Professional bodybuilding, a sport nearly synonymous with steroid use."
3. The drugs include Dianabol (the first U.S. anabolic steroid), testosterone (both Dianabol and testosterone cause extreme aggressiveness and mood swings), Anavar, Equipoise (a veterinary steroid), methandrostenalone, methandriol, aqueous testosterone, and human growth hormone (no test now exists that can effectively discover its presence in the body), to name only a few. These drugs can physically, and sometimes permanently, alter an athlete. Some of the side effects for female athletes may be a dramatic increase in facial and chest hair, male-pattern baldness, clitoral enlargement, and a significantly lowered voice (Terry Todd, 1987).
4. The IOC established a medical commission in 1967 and banned certain drugs. However, anabolic steroids and testosterone were not among the banned substances. The IOC subsequently banned anabolic steroids in 1975 and testosterone in 1982.
5. IFBB material, p. 5.
6. IFBB material, p. 15.
7. IFBB material.
8. Wayne, 1985: 231.

9. Wayne, 1985.

10. This condition, due to steroid use, enlarges the breast tissue of men. It is referred to as "bitch tits." See glossary of terms for definition.

11. Wayne, 1985: 230.

12. In fact, the IFBB began testing its female bodybuilders a couple of years before it tested its male bodybuilders even though it has been known that male bodybuilders have been taking steroids since the 1960s and steroid use has always been more prevalent among male bodybuilders.

13. Some drugs, such as human growth hormones, enlarge the soft bone tissue such as the cartilage in the nose, feet, hands, joints, and ears.

14. Nelson, 1991.

15. Wayne, 1985.

16. For example, in November 1992, one professional male bodybuilder died of severe dehydration due to diuretic abuse after a European Grand Prix competition, and in March 1993, a professional male bodybuilder was taken to the emergency room after a competition for the same condition.

17. Davis and Delano (1992: 1) discuss the gender assumptions embedded in over forty anti-drug campaigns. They argue that those campaigns dealing with steroids are particularly troubling "because they encourage readers to assume that . . . steroids are artificial substances that disrupt this natural gender dichotomization."

18. However, even members of this group acknowledge that certain steroids and the amount one takes do have the potential of having masculinizing effects on women such as a lowered voice, male-pattern baldness, and facial hair. What separates this group from the previous group is the fact that members of this group object only to the extremes. They do not object to muscular women.

19. The bodybuilder to whom this respondent is referring died of heart arrhythmia approximately two months after this interview due to overuse of diuretics. He died a few hours after one of the last 1992 European Grand Prix events.

Notes to Chapter 4

1. Wennerstrom, 1992.

2. Crews, 1990: 74–5.

3. The IFBB is the premiere professional bodybuilding organization, and the NPC is the national amateur association officially recognized by the IFBB. Because the IFBB is a closed federation, everyone within the organization must accept and abide by its rules and regulations or face being barred.

4. In the IFBB, the five mandatory poses for women are: front double bicep, back double bicep, side chest with bicep, side tricep, and an abdominal pose in which the bodybuilder also displays her quad muscles.

5. How balanced are the muscle groups to one another and how balanced is the upper torso as compared to the lower torso?

6. In the IFBB, this round lasts approximately 90 seconds, and the bodybuilder displays her muscles to music in a series of poses and movements she has choreographed.
7. IFBB material.
8. IFBB material.
9. "How to Become a Judge."
10. "How to Become a Judge."
11. IFBB *Guidebook,* 1987.
12. Chodorow, 1978, and Rubin, 1983.
13. See Asch 1952.
14. Ptacek (1981: 25) as quoted in Klein, 1993: 99.
15. Felshin, 1974.
16. Felshin, 1974, as discussed by Greendorfer, 1983.
17. Greendorfer, 1983.
18. Felshin, 1974: 204.
19. Greendorfer, 1983.

Notes to Chapter 5

1. Felshin, 1974, 1976.
2. Hilliard, 1984.
3. Hilliard, 1984: 261.
4. Hilliard, 1984: 261.
5. See Duncan (1990) for analogous photographic representations of female athletes.
6. Made famous by Hans and Franz on the television sitcom "Saturday Night Live," this pose allows bodybuilders to show off their trapezius, pectorals, and other muscle groups in their upper bodies. It is considered one of the most muscular and vascular poses and may be performed either with teeth clenched or with an accompanying growl.
7. Freedman, 1986.
8. Freedman, 1986.
9. Goffman, 1959.
10. Weber, 1993.
11. Lowe, 1993; Weber, 1993.
12. IFBB *Guidebook,* 1987: 20.
13. IFBB *Guidebook,* 1987: 20.
14. Although the following excerpts are exclusively from male judges and officials, female judges and officials also expressed similar views.
15. See Rich, 1980, for a discussion of compulsory heterosexuality. As Klein (1986) argued, male bodybuilders' sexuality, and thus their masculinity, are also regulated by male gatekeepers. However, the regulation of women's sexuality and gender in the context of female bodybuilding is accomplished through a male gaze.

Notes to Chapter 6

1. This type of determination, inner strength, and drive based on the Protestant work ethic which female bodybuilders talk about is related to the "prowess ethic" that Crossett (1995) found among women golfers. According to Crossett (1995: 106), "the prowess ethic is the way LPGA players make sense of this world. It informs the way they administer justice and bestow awards. It is at the ideological root of the players' understanding of success and failure, and their frustration with people's overt concern with their sexuality. It is an ideology that arises from the individualistic, meritocratic, and uncertain world of the tour." Crossett argued that this precluded them from taking a more critical feminist perspective on their endeavor.

2. Adamson, 1980: 174.

3. Giroux, 1983.

4. Foley, 1990: 166.

5. Klein, 1981: 31.

6. This, too, is true of women on the LPGA tour. Being intense competitors in an individual sport, they cannot afford to "get too close," which undercuts any sense of group solidarity among the players. Crossett (1995: 147) argued, "The players share an understanding of the difficulties of tour life and thus view each other as risky investments for emotional energy. Because they lack the necessary trust, players are not likely to rely on fellow golfers for emotional support. . . . Given the uncertain, competitive, individualistic structure of the LPGA, the subworld's lack of community between players is understandable."

7. Klein, 1993: 97–98.

8. Klein, 1993: 99.

9. McGough, 1993.

10. Klein, 1993: 97.

11. This illustrates Hughes and Coakley's (1991: 307) concept of "positive deviance," wherein athletes excessively overconform to the norms and values embodied in sport, such as "sacrificing for the game, seeking distinction, taking risks, and challenging limits."

12. In fact, Klein (1986) argued that competitive bodybuilding is extremely unhealthy and merely presents a facade of good health.

13. One can look at the criteria by which the contestants are judged in fitness contests to see that judges are emphasizing qualities more in line with hegemonic femininity. Keep in mind that these criteria hold across organizations. For instance, at NPC-sponsored contests, there are three judged rounds: two swimsuit rounds in which the contestants' degree of firmness and overall appearance are evaluated, among other criteria; and a musical fitness round in which contestants perform their best dance or aerobics routine. In this round, judges look for style, personality, athletic coordination, and overall performance, which includes their apparel. If contests are being filmed for television, contestants may not wear thong or T-back swimsuits; otherwise they may. Another fitness organization, the National Fitness Sanctioning Body (NFSB), sponsors the Ms. National Fitness contests in which contestants are informed,

"Please do not flex or try to emphasize muscle size. This is not a bodybuilding contest." Competitors are evaluated on beauty, poise, and projection during the evening gown round; physical beauty and muscle tone during the swimsuit round; and strength, flexibility, and endurance during the fitness outfit round, in which contestants "are encouraged to perform a high energy routine which includes movements to show their strength and flexibility" (Getbig WWW homepage).

14. Crews, 1990: 75.
15. IFBB *Guidebook,* 1987: 20.
16. IFBB *Guidebook,* 1987: 20.
17. Weber, 1993.
18. Messner, 1988: 208.

Notes to Appendix B

1. Bertaux, 1981: 38.
2. Grimshaw, Hobson, and Willis, 1980.
3. Grimshaw, Hobson, and Willis, 1980; Willis, 1980; Van Maanen, 1988.
4. Van Maanen, 1988: ix.
5. Van Maanen, 1988.
6. Willis, 1980.
7. Hall, 1980: 24.
8. For example, Willis's (1981) study of the cultures of school and work among working-class lads, McRobbie and Garber's (1976) work on girls' gender and sexuality negotiations in youth subcultures, and Hebdige's (1979) work with post–World War II British youth subcultures, to name a few.
9. Hall, 1980: 23–4.
10. Bernard, 1988; Babbie, 1992.
11. Bernard, 1988; Babbie, 1992.
12. McPhee, 1976.
13. Bertaux, 1981: 36.
14. Bertaux, 1981: 37.
15. Bertaux, 1981.
16. Bertaux, 1981: 37.
17. See Kessler and McKenna, 1978; Gerson and Peiss, 1985; Connell, 1987; West and Zimmerman, 1987; Messner, 1988, 1992; Williams, 1989; Reed and Whitehead, 1992.
18. Birrell, 1990: 295.
19. Birrell, 1990.
20. Antonio Gramsci was an Italian communist who was imprisoned by Mussolini for his communist sympathies and writings. He died in 1937. During his ten-year prison sentence, Gramsci wrote thirty-two notebooks that are today available as *Selections from the Prison Notebooks,* in which he discusses the aforementioned concepts (Adamson, 1980). Not until 1972 was an extensive English translation of Gramsci's *Prison Notebooks* available (Boggs, 1976).

The work from the Centre for Contemporary Cultural Studies at Birmingham University in England provides insight into how people interpret the dominant culture and appropriate its symbols to create cultures of resistance. According to Cahn (1990: 12–13), in particular, "the works of Dick Hebdidge and Paul Willis on youth subcultures, and Stuart Hall's ideas on the negotiated meanings in popular media supply clues about how women use sport as a resource to expand the parameters of womanhood beyond prescriptive femininity. Feminists have begun to use poststructuralist theories of subjectivity to suggest ways that women can call upon the multiple concepts and ideals of womanhood circulating within a society to negotiate the contradictions and difficulties inherent in their subordinate status. Women do not simply accept a set of imposed definitions and prescribed roles. Instead they select, reject, and creatively combine different conceptions of womanhood—pure virgin, lustful whore, loving mother, strong but overburdened wage worker, sensitive listener, tender spouse—to name just a few."

21. Lears, 1985.

22. Lears, 1985.

23. Adamson, 1980: 174.

24. Civil society, which consists of all of the social relations including, among other social institutions, sports and the mass media, is the sphere in which a dominant social group organizes hegemony (Simon, 1991). Civil society, however, is also "the sphere where the subordinate social groups may organize their opposition and construct an alternative hegemony" (Simon, 1991: 87).

25. Lears, 1985.

26. Lears, 1985.

27. Lears, 1985: 569.

28. Foley, 1990: 166.

29. Hebdige, 1979.

30. Lears, 1985: 572.

BIBLIOGRAPHY

Adamson, Walter. 1980. *Hegemony and Revolution: A Study of Antonio Gramsci's Political and Cultural Theory.* Berkeley: University of California Press.

Asch, Solomon E. 1952. *Social Psychology.* Englewood Cliffs, NJ: Prentice Hall.

Aycock, Alan. 1992. "The Confession of the Flesh: Disciplinary Gaze in Casual Bodybuilding." *Play and Culture* 5: 459–462.

Babbie, Earl. 1992. *The Practice of Social Research.* 6th ed. Belmont, Ca.: Wadsworth Publishing.

Bernard, H. Russell. 1988. *Research Methods in Cultural Anthropology.* Newbury Park, CA: Sage.

Bertaux, Daniel. 1981. "From the Life-History Approach to the Transformation of Sociological Practice." In Daniel Bertaux, ed., *Biography and Society: The Life History Approach in the Social Sciences,* pp. 29–46. Beverly Hills, CA.: Sage.

Birrell, Susan. 1990. "Teaching 'Women in Sport' from a Feminist Perspective." In David L. Vanderwerken, ed., *Sport in the Classroom: Teaching Sport-related Courses in the Humanities.* London and Toronto: Associated University Presses.

Boggs, Carl. 1976. *Gramsci's Marxism.* London: Pluto Press.

Bolin, Anne. 1992. "Flex Appeal, Food, and Fat: Competitive Bodybuilding, Gender, and Diet." *Play and Culture.* 5: 378–400.

Boutilier, Mary A., and Lucinda SanGiovanni, eds. 1983. *The Sporting Woman.* Champaign, IL: Human Kinetics.

Cahn, Susan Kathleen. 1990. "Coming On Strong: Gender and Sexuality in Women's Sport, 1900–1960." 2 vols. Ph.D. diss., University of Minnesota.

Chafetz, Janet. 1990. *Gender Equity: An Integrated Theory of Stability and Change.* Newbury Park, CA: Sage.

Chodorow, Nancy. 1978. *The Reproduction of Mothering: Psychoanalysis and the Sociology of Gender.* Berkeley: University of California Press.

Coakley, Jay. 1982. *Sport in Society.* St. Louis, MO: C. V. Mosby.

Connell, R. W. 1987. *Gender and Power.* Stanford, CA: Stanford University Press.

Crews, Harry. 1990. *Body.* New York: Poseidon Press.

Crossett, Todd. 1995. *Outsiders in the Clubhouse: The World of Women's Professional Golf.* Albany, NY: SUNY Press.

Daniels, Dayna B. 1992. "Gender (Body) Verification (Building)." *Play and Culture* 5: 370–377.

Davis, Laurel R., and Linda C. Delano. 1992. "Fixing the Boundaries of Physical Gender: Side Effects of Anti-Drug Campaigns in Athletics." *Sociology of Sport Journal* 9: 1–19.

Duff, Robert W., and Lawrence K. Hong. 1984. *Sociology of Sport Journal* 1: 374–380.

Duncan, Margaret Carlisle. 1990. "Sports Photographs and Sexual Difference: Images of Women and Men in the 1984 and 1988 Olympic Games." *Sociology of Sport Journal* 7: 22–43.

Ewald, Keith, and Robert Jiobu. 1985. "Explaining Positive Deviance: Becker's Model and the Case of Runners and Bodybuilders." *Sociology of Sport Journal* 2: 144–156.

Felshin, J. 1974. "The Social View." In E. R. Gerber et al., eds., *The American Woman In Sport.* Reading, MA: Addison-Wesley.

———. 1976. "The Triple Option—for Women in Sport." In M. Hart, ed., *Sport in the Socio-Cultural Process.* 2d ed. Dubuque: Wm. C. Brown.

Flex, May 1983, vol 1, #2; June 1983, vol. 1, #3; July, 1983, vol. 1, #4.

Foley, Douglas, E. 1990. *Learning Capitalist Culture Deep in the Heart of Tejas.* Philadelphia: University of Pennsylvania Press.

Freedman, Rita. 1986. *Beauty Bound.* Lexington, KY: D. C. Heath.

Gaines, Charles, and George Butler. 1981. *Pumping Iron: The Art and Sport of Bodybuilding.* New York: Simon and Schuster.

———. 1984. *Pumping Iron II: The Unprecedented Woman.* New York: Simon and Schuster.

Gerber, Ellen W., Jan Felshin, Pearl Berlin, and Waneen Wrick. 1974. *The American Woman in Sport.* Reading, MA: Addison-Wesley.

Gerson, Judith, and Kathy Peiss. 1985. "Boundaries, Negotiation, Consciousness: Reconceptualizing Gender Relations." *Social Problems* 32 (4): 317–331.

Getbig WWW homepage: http://www.getbig.com.

Gillett, James, and Philip G. White. 1992. "Male Bodybuilding and the Reassertion of Hegemonic Masculinity. A Critical Perspective." *Play and Culture* 5: 358–369.

Giroux, H. A. 1983. *Theory and Resistance in Education: A Pedagogy of the Opposition.* South Hadley, MA: Bergin and Garvey.

Goffman, Erving. 1959. *The Presentation of Self in Everyday Life.* Garden City, NY: Doubleday.

———. 1976. *Gender Advertisements.* New York: Harper Colophon Books.

Goldman, Bob. n. d. "The Battle against Steroids Goes On: Position Paper of the IFBB." Weider Health and Fitness Co. Ltd.

Greendorfer, Susan. 1983. "The Social Context of Women in Sport." In *The Sporting Woman,* ed. Mary A. Boutilier and Lucinda SanGiovanni, pp. 93–130. Champaign, IL.: Human Kinetics.

Greendorfer, Susan, and J. H. Lewko. 1978. "Role of Family Members in Sport Socialization of Children." *Research Quarterly* 49: 146–152.

Grimshaw, Roger, Dorothy Hobson, and Paul Willis. 1980. "Introduction to Ethnography at the Centre." In Stuart Hall, Hobson, Lowe, and Willis, eds.,

Culture, Media, Language: Working Papers in Cultural Studies, 1972–1979, pp. 73–77. London: Hutchinson; Centre for Contemporary Cultural Studies, University of Birmingham.

Guthrie, Sharon R., and Shirley Castelnuovo. 1992. "Elite Women Bodybuilders: Models of Resistance or Compliance?" *Play and Culture* 5: 401–408.

Hall, M. Ann. 1988. "The Discourse of Gender and Sport: From Femininity to Feminism." *Sociology of Sport Journal* 5: 330–340.

Hall, Stuart. 1980. "Cultural Studies and the Centre: Some Problematics and Problems." In Hall, Hobson, Lowe, and Willis, eds., *Culture, Media, Language: Working Papers in Cultural Studies, 1972–1979*, pp. 15–47. London: Hutchinson; Centre for Contemporary Cultural Studies, University of Birmingham.

Hargreaves, John, and Alan Tomlinson. 1992."Getting There: Cultural Theory and the Sociological Analysis of Sport in Britain." *Sociology of Sports Journal* 9: 207–219.

Hebdige, Dick. 1979. *Subculture: The Meaning of Style.* London: Routledge.

Hilliard, Dan C. 1984. "Media Images of Male and Female Professional Athletes: An Interpretive Analysis of Magazine Articles." *Sociology of Sport Journal* 1: 251–262.

"How to Become a NPC Judge." 1996. *Muscle and Fitness.* September.

Hoxha, Tim. 1995. "How Joe and Ben Weider Became the Founding Fathers of Bodybuilding." *Flex.* September.

Hughes, Robert, and Jay Coakley. 1991. "Positive Deviance among Athletes: The Implications of Overconformity to the Sport Ethic." *Sociology of Sport Journal* 8: 307–325.

IFBB *Official Guidebook.* 1987.

JMP Management homepage: http://www.getbig.com/jmp/jmpwho.htm.

Kessler, S. J., and W. McKenna. 1978. *Gender: An Ethnomethodological Approach.* Chicago: University of Chicago Press.

Klein, Alan M. 1981. "The Master Blaster: Empire Building and Body Building." *Arena Review: The Institute for Sport and Social Analysis.* 5 (3): 29–32.

———. 1985a. "Muscle Manor: The Use of Sport Metaphor and History in Sport Sociology." *Journal of Sport and Social Issues* 9 (1): 4–19.

———. 1985b. "Pumping Iron." *Society* 22 (6): 68–75.

———. 1986. "Pumping Irony: Crisis and Contradiction in Bodybuilding." *Sociology of Sport Journal* 3: 112–133.

———. 1989. "Managing Deviance: Hustling, Homophobia, and the Bodybuilding Subculture." *Deviant Behavior* 10: 11–27.

———. 1990. "Hustling, Gender Narcissism, and Bodybuilding Subculture." In D. Sabo and M. Messner, eds., *Sport, Men, and the Gender Order: Critical Feminist Perspectives.* Champaign, IL: Human Kinetics.

———. 1992. "Man Makes Himself: Alienation and Self-Objectification in Bodybuilding." *Play and Culture* 5: 326–337.

———. 1993. *Little Big Men: Bodybuilding Subculture and Gender Construction.* Albany, NY: SUNY Press.

Landers, D. M. 1979. "Birth Order in the Family and Sport Participation." In M. L. Drotee, ed., *The Dimensions of Sport Sociology.* West Point, NY: Leisure Press.

Langloise, Judith H., and A. Chris Downs. 1980. "Mothers, Fathers, and Peers as Socialization Agents of Sex-typed Play Behaviors in Young Children." *Child Development* 51: 1237–1247.

Lears, T. J. Jackson. 1985. "The Concept of Cultural Hegemony." *American Historical Review* 90 (June 1985): 567–593.

Leigh, Wendy. 1990. *An Unauthorized Biography: Arnold.* Chicago: Congdon and Weed.

Lenskyj, Helen. 1986. *Out of Bounds: Women, Sport, and Sexuality.* Toronto: Women's Press.

Lowe, Maria R. 1993. "Beauty, Strength, and Grace: A Sociological Analysis of Female Bodybuilding." Ph.D. diss., University of Texas, Austin.

McGough, Peter. 1993. "Rise and Fall of the World Bodybuilding Federation." *Flex.* October.

McPhee, John A. 1976. *The John McPhee Reader.* Ed. William L. Howarth. New York: Farrar, Straus, and Giroux.

McRobbie, Angela, and Jenny Garber. 1976. "Girls and Subcultures: An Exploration." In Stuart Hall and Tony Jefferson, eds., *Resistance through Rituals: Youth Subcultures in Post–War Britain.* London: Harper-Collins.

Messner, Michael A. 1988. "Sports and Male Domination: The Female Athlete as Contested Ideological Terrain." *Sociology of Sport Journal* 5: 197–211.

———. 1992. *Power at Play: Sports and the Problem of Masculinity.* Boston: Beacon Press.

Miller, Leslie, and Otto Penz. 1991. "Talking Bodies: Women Bodybuilders Colonize a Male Preserve." Unpublished manuscript presented at the 1991 Popular Cultural Association Meetings, March, San Antonio, Texas.

Muchnick, Irvin. 1991. "Pumping Iron." *Spy.* June, pp. 54–56.

Nelson, Mariah Burton. 1991. *Are We Winning Yet? How Women Are Changing Sports and Sports Are Changing Women.* New York: Random House.

Page, Pamela, J. 1989. "Bodybuilding: The Ultimate Presentation of Self." Paper presented at Southwestern University, Brown Symposium.

Portz, E. 1973. "Influence of Birth Order, Sibling Sex on Sports Participation." In D. Harris, ed., *Women and Sport: A National Research Conference.* Penn State HPER Series No. 2, Pennsylvania State University.

Ptacek, Greg. 1981. "The Big Muscle behind Body Building." Part Two, *City Sports* 7 (11) (November): 25, as quoted in Alan Klein, *Little Big Men: Bodybuilding Subculture and Gender Construction* (Albany, NY: SUNY Press, 1993), p. 99.

Ravo, Nick. 1992. "Ms. Olympia Pumps Up an Image of Fit Women." *New York Times,* December 2, 1992, p. B1.

Reed, Barbara, and Tony Whitehead. 1992. "Introduction." In T. Whitehead and B. Reed, eds., *Gender Constructs and Social Issues.* Urbana: University of Illinois Press.

Rich, Adrienne. 1980. "Compulsory Heterosexuality and Lesbian Existence." *Signs* 5 (Summer): 631–660.

Roopnarine, Jaipual L. 1986. "Mothers' and Fathers' Behaviors toward the Toy Play of Their Infant Sons and Daughters." *Sex Roles* 14: 59–68.

Rubin, Lillian. 1983. *Intimate Strangers: Men and Women Together.* New York: Harper and Row.

Schulze, Laurie. 1990. "On the Muscle." In *Fabrications,* ed. Jane Gaines and Charlotte Herzog. London: Routledge.

Schur, Edwin M. 1984. *Labeling Women Deviant: Gender, Stigma, and Social Control.* New York: McGraw-Hill.

Simon, Roger. 1991. *Gramsci's Political Thought: An Introduction.* London: Lawrence and Wishart.

Snyder, E. E., and E. Spreitzer. 1973. "Family Influences and Involvement in Sports." *Research Quarterly.* 44: 249–255.

Solotaroff, Paul. 1992. "The Power and the Gory." In Thomas McGuane, ed., *The Best American Sports Writing.* Boston: Houghton Mifflin.

Stone, Gene. 1988. "The Money in Muscle." In W. Leigh, *An Unauthorized Biography: Arnold* (Chicago: Congdon and Weed, 1990).

Todd, Jan. 1987. "Bernarr Macfadden: Reformer of Feminine Form." *Journal of Sport History* 14 (1).

———. 1992a. "The Legacy of Pudgy Stockton." *Iron Game History* 2 (1): 4–7.

———. 1992b. "The Origins of Weight Training for Female Athletes in North America." *Iron Game History* 2 (2): 4–14.

Todd, Terry. 1987. "Anabolic Steroids: The Gremlins of Sport." *Journal of Sport History* 14 (1).

———. 1992. "Peary Rader (1909–1991): Our Best Man Gone." *Iron Game History* 2 (1): 1–4.

Thomas, Al, and Steve Wennerstrom. 1983. *The Female Physique Athlete: A History to Date—1977 through 1983.* Midland Park, NJ: The Women's Physique Publication.

Twin, Stephanie, L. 1979. *Out of the Bleachers: Writings on Women and Sport.* New York: McGraw-Hill.

Van Maanen, John. 1988. *Tales of the Field: On Writing Ethnography.* Chicago: University of Chicago Press.

Wayne, Rick. 1985. *Muscle Wars: The Behind the Scenes Story of Competitive Bodybuilding.* New York: St. Martin's Press.

Weber, Carol Ann. 1993. "Plastic Surgery and Bodybuilding." *Muscular Development,* March, pp. 98–102, 154.

Weider, Joe. 1983. *Mr. Olympia: The History of Bodybuilding's Greatest Contest.* New York: St. Martin's Press.

Wennerstrom, Steve. 1984a. "Women's Bodybuilding: The Beginning, Part 1." *Flex* 1 (10): 25–27, 74–77.

———. 1984b. "History of Women's Bodybuilding: Part 2, The Early Contests." *Flex* 1 (12): 64–66.

———. 1984c. "History of Women's Bodybuilding: Muscle Mania Begins." *Flex* 2 (4): 26–28.

———. 1992. "Arguments against Female Muscularity." *Women's Physique World.*

West, Candice, and Don Zimmerman. 1987. "Doing Gender." *Gender and Society* 1 (2): 125–151.

Williams, Christine. 1989. *Gender Differences at Work.* Berkeley: University of California Press.

Willis, Paul. 1980. "Notes on Method." In Stuart Hall, Hobson, Lowe, and Willis, eds., *Culture, Media, Language: Working Papers in Cultural Studies, 1972–1979,* pp. 88–95. London: Hutchinson; Centre for Contemporary Cultural Studies, University of Birmingham.

———. 1981. *Learning to Labor: How Working Class Kids Get Working Class Jobs.* New York: Teachers College Press.

Wolfe, Tom. 1979. *The Right Stuff.* New York: Farrar, Straus, Giroux.

Wolff, Bob. 1996. "History of the NPC." *Muscle and Fitness,* September.

Ziegler S. 1973. "Self-Perception of Athletes and Coaches." In D. Harris, ed., *Women and Sport: A National Research Conference.* Penn State HPER Series No. 2, Pennsylvania State University.

INDEX

About the Author

Maria R. Lowe was born in San Antonio, Texas, where in 1985 she received her B.A. in sociology from Trinity University. In 1988 she completed her master's degree at the University of Texas at Austin, and in 1993 she completed her Ph.D. in sociology there. She began her professional academic career in 1993 at Southwestern University in Georgetown, Texas, where she is currently an assistant professor in the department of sociology and anthropology.

Her research continues to focus on women's experiences in sports as well as on the construction of gender in nontraditional arenas. She is currently working on research concerning the socialization processes of elite women athletes. She lives in the Austin area with her three dogs.